S0-AZW-232

# CONTEMPORARY SOCIAL THEORY

## General Editor: ANTHONY GIDDENS

This series aims to create a forum for debate between different theoretical and philosophical traditions in the social sciences. As well as covering broad schools of thought, the series will also concentrate upon the work of particular thinkers whose ideas have had a major impact on social science (these books appear under the sub-series title of 'Theoretical Traditions in the Social Sciences'). The series is not limited to abstract theoretical discussion – it will also include more substantive works on contemporary capitalism, the state, politics and other subject areas.

# CONTEMPORARY SOCIAL THEORY
## General Editor: ANTHONY GIDDENS

## Theoretical Traditions in the Social Sciences

# A Contemporary Critique of Historical Materialism

## Vol. 1   Power, property and the state

**Anthony Giddens**
*Fellow of King's College, Cambridge*

*First published 1981 by*
THE MACMILLAN PRESS LTD
*London and Basingstoke*
*Companies and representatives throughout the world*

ISBN 0 333 30971 5   (hard cover)
ISBN 0 333 30972 3   (paper cover)

*Typeset in 10/12pt Times by*
ILLUSTRATED ARTS

*Reproduced from copy supplied and*
*printed and bound in Great Britain*
*by Billing and Sons Limited*
*Guildford, London, Oxford, Worcester*

Viewed pathetically, a single second has infinite value; viewed comically, ten thousand years are but a trifle, like yesterday when it is gone. If one were to say simply and directly that ten thousand years are but a trifle, many a fool would give his assent, and find it wisdom; but he forgets the other, that a second has infinite value.

Kierkegaard

# Contents

# Acknowledgements

I should like to thank a number of people who have helped with the writing of this book. Among others, Michael Mann and Theda Skocpol commented usefully upon an earlier version of the manuscript. I have tried to meet some of their objections, though I fear they will not be fully satisfied with the result. I owe a particular debt to David Held, who read through the whole book in the most minute detail, suggesting numerous valuable improvements. John Winckler has been an indispensable source of editorial support. The book was written mostly in Cambridge, but partly in New York. I owe a special indebtedness to the facilities of apartment 17M in 4 Washington Square Village, and to the kindness of Eliot Freidson. Finally, I want to thank Sam Hollick for her constant help and encouragement.

Anthony Giddens

# Introduction

This study is the first part of a projected two-volume critical appraisal of some of the main themes of Marx's historical materialism. In the volume to follow – as yet unwritten – I shall be concerned with Marx's conceptions of the transition from capitalism to socialism, and of the nature of socialist society itself. In the present book my objectives are concentrated upon phenomena relevant to the rise of capitalism, in conjunction with prior phases of world history. My intention is not to produce a critique of historical materialism written in hostile mien, declaring Marxism to be redundant or exhausted. There has been an abundance of attempts of that sort, written either by implacable opponents of Marx or by disillusioned ex-believers.[1] I belong in neither of these categories, though nor do I accept the label 'Marxist'. Marx's analysis of the mechanisms of capitalist production, I believe, remains the necessary core of any attempt to come to terms with the massive transformations that have swept through the world since the eighteenth century. But there is much in Marx that is mistaken, ambiguous or inconsistent; and in many respects Marx's writings exemplify features of nineteenth-century thought which are plainly defective when looked at from the perspective of our century.[2]

Let me try to put the facts of the matter as bluntly as possible. If by 'historical materialism' we mean the conception that the history of human societies can be understood in terms of the progressive augmentation of the forces of production, then it is based on false premises, and the time has come finally to abandon it. If historical materialism means that 'the history of all hitherto existing society is the history of class struggles', it is so patently erroneous that it is difficult to see why so many have felt obliged to take it seriously. If, finally, historical materialism means that Marx's scheme of the evolution of societies (from tribal society, Ancient society, feudalism, to capitalism; and thence to socialism, together with the 'stagnant' offshoot of the 'Asiatic Mode of Production' in the East) provides a defensible basis for analysing world history, then it is also to be rejected. Only if historical materialism is regarded as embodying the more abstract elements of a theory of human *Praxis*, snippets of which can be gleaned from the diversity of Marx's writings, does it remain an indispensable contribution to social theory today. [3]

These are my arguments in the book, and they imply that Marx's more general pronouncements upon human history, especially in those most famous of all passages, in the 'Preface' to *A Contribution to the Critique of Political Economy*, have to be treated with great caution and, in some major respects, simply discarded. Of course, this is not to say that Marx's comments upon pre-capitalist, or what I shall prefer to call 'non-capitalist', societies are wholly without value. One of the most frustrating and compelling things about Marx's writings is that, having found in one section a sweepingly implausible series of assertions, the reader turns to other parts of Marx's work only to discover apparently contrary views developed with the most subtle insight. Thus, as many commentators have discovered, Marx can be used against himself. This is essentially my way of proceeding in Chapter 3, in analysing those celebrated few pages in what has come to be known as the *Grundrisse*, in which Marx discusses the 'Forms of Society that Precede Capitalist Production' (the *Formen*). [4] In these pages Marx develops views that are arguably inconsistent with some of his general formulae about the course of human history. The ideas offered by Marx in the *Formen* are very important for what I have to say in this book, since one of my main aims is to follow through what he suggests there: to pick out just what is most distinctive about the social world that capitalism has created, as contrasted to other forms of societal organisation.

Marx's comments on non-capitalist societies, in the *Formen* and elsewhere, are relatively scrappy and often unoriginal. Some of them, in my view, are just as erroneous as are certain of his more general statements. It is not their unsatisfactory character but rather the tenacity with which many Marxists have sought to cling to whatever gems they claim to find there which is astonishing. We have today a much wider range of comparative evidence about the range and diversity of human societies than was ever available to Marx. Although it is not my purpose to formulate a detailed classification of types of society, I have drawn upon a considerable span of contemporary disciplines in developing my arguments: particularly work from anthropology, archaeology and geography. In formulating the conclusions I have reached, I have given special attention to those societies that Marx barely mentioned, or could not have studied in any case since little or nothing of them was known in his time: such as the ancient civilisations of Mesopotamia, or those of Meso-America. Not only in respect of 'Europocentric' interpretations of 'Oriental Despotism' do we need to escape from the deeply entrenched tendency to read history from the vantage-point of the West.

This book stands in the closest possible connection with an earlier study, *Central Problems in Social Theory*. It invokes the theoretical notions developed in the work as a whole; at the same time it is in large part a direct expansion of a few pages in *Central Problems*.[5] In that study, influenced abstractly by the philosophy of Heidegger, and more substantively by the writings of modern geographers, I argued that time-space relations have to be brought into the very core of social theory. In *Central Problems* and the present book I continually revert to the issues that this concern brings to the fore: issues that are epistemological, methodological and empirical. Let me attempt to summarise here some of the main empirical themes of this book, before coming to the more abstract suppositions which it involves – reversing the actual organisation of the book itself. I have called it *A Contemporary Critique of Historical Materialism*, but my concerns are by no means wholly critical or destructive; in diverging from Marx I want to propose the elements of an alternative interpretation of history.

A fundamental component of my arguments is the supposition that the articulation of time-space relations in social systems has to be examined in conjunction with the generation of *power*. A preoccupation with power forms a leading thread of this book. I maintain that power was never satisfactorily theorised by Marx, and that this failure is at origin of some of the chief limitations of his scheme of historical analysis. But in analysing power and domination, I do not seek to replace Marx by Nietzsche – a tendency that can readily be discerned in the writings of Max Weber, but which has recently become fashionable in a new guise in the writings of the so-called 'new philosophers' and others in France. It is useless merely to supplant Marx's reductionist emphasis upon the primacy of the forces of production in the organisation of societies, and their process of change, with a comparable reductionism of power. Rather, power has to be analysed as one element among others in the constitution of social systems. In the *theory of structuration* elaborated in *Central Problems* I sought to provide a general conceptualisation of power that is affirmed and further developed in the present book. Power and freedom in human society are not opposites; on the contrary, power is rooted in the very nature of human agency, and thus in the 'freedom to act otherwise'.[6] The notions of 'power' and 'exploitation' similarly have to be carefully separated from one another.

In the theory of structuration, power is regarded as generated in and through the reproduction of structures of domination. I distinguish two major types of resources that enter into structures of domination: those that are involved in the dominion of human beings over the material world (allocative resources) and those involved in dominion over the social world itself (authoritative resources). My thesis, as outlined abstractly in Chapters 1 and 2, and in a detailed way in Chapter 4 onwards, is that these two types of resource interlace differently in different types of society. Whereas Marx gave primacy to allocative resources in his materialist conception of history, I argue that in non-capitalist societies co-ordination of authoritative resources forms the determining axis of societal integration and change. In capitalism, by contrast, allocative resources take on a very particular significance – one which I seek to analyse in some considerable detail in the concluding chapters of the book.

In order to connect the time-space constitution of social systems with structures of domination, I introduce the notion of 'time-space distanciation' – one of several neologisms for which I ask the reader's indulgence. The structuration of all social systems occurs in time-space, but also 'brackets' time-space relations; every social system in some way 'stretches' across time and space. Time-space distanciation refers to the modes in which such 'stretching' takes place or, to shift the metaphor slightly, how social systems are 'embedded' in time and space. In the smaller societies, hunters and gatherers or settled independent agricultural communities, time-space distanciation occurs primarily as a result of two connected features of societal organisation: the grounding of legitimation in tradition, and the role played by kinship in the structuration of social relations, each of which is in turn normally anchored in religion. But these societies above all involve *presence*, or what I term 'high presence-availability'. There are relatively few social transactions with others who are physically absent. In these societies, the human memory (expressed in knowledge of tradition, as a series of continuing practices, and in story-telling and myth) is the principal 'storage container' which 'brackets' time-space.

Throughout the book I emphasise the significance of *storage capacity* to the state, in both non-capitalist and capitalist societies. Storage capacity is a fundamental element in the generation of power through the extension of time-space distanciation. Many accounts of the nature of the state in non-capitalist societies give primacy of place to the storage of 'material' or allocative resources in their analyses, as part of the thesis that the production of a 'surplus' is the key to examining how states come into being. My claim, however, is that storage of authoritative resources is normally of more decisive importance. Storage of authoritative resources is the basis of the *surveillance* activities of the state, always an under-girding medium of state power. 'Surveillance' involves two things: the collation of information relevant to state control of the conduct of its subject population, and the direct supervision of that conduct. The formation of agrarian states is almost everywhere associated with the invention of writing and notation. Writing seems to have originated in most cases as a direct mode of information storage: as a means of recording and analysing information involved with the administration of societies of increasing scale. In non-capitalist societies both aspects of surveillance are developed in a fragmentary way, when contrasted to the formidable apparatus of the capitalist state. Lack of analysis of the phenomenon of surveillance, I claim, is one of the major limitations of Marx's interpretation of the state. The concentration of the surveillance activities of the state in modern times is the chief basis of the looming threat of *totalitarianism*, a phenomenon that has to be distinguished from the 'despotism' of non-capitalist states. Although it is not my intention in this book to offer a discussion of totalitarianism, I consider that the concept of surveillance provides the means of elaborating such a discussion – which it will be one of my aims to develop in the volume to follow this one.

The theory of the city is integrally involved with these issues – or so I wish to claim. As a religious, ceremonial and commercial centre, the city is a distinctive feature of all societies characterised by extensive time-space distanciation; and it is the main locus of the state. Following Mumford, I regard the city in non-capitalist societies as a special form of 'storage container', a crucible for the generation of power upon a scale unknown to non-urbanised communities. I do not want this thesis to be misunderstood. The city is the 'power-container' of the state in non-capitalist societies – but only via its relations with the countryside. These relations may be considerably different in different contexts, and upon these variations depends the over-all nature of the society in question. In analysing the city–state relationship, I do not give much attention to the question that has been of overriding interest to many anthropologists and archaeologists – the question of the 'origin' of the state. Accepting Clastres's view that what he calls the 'political break' (the formation of the state), not the accumulation of 'surplus production', is the central feature of the emergence of 'civilisations', I place most emphasis upon discovering the consequences rather than the causes of state formation. This is not because I think the problem of 'origins' unimportant, but because the main weight of my analysis is concerned with contrasting agrarian states with the world ushered in by industrial capitalism.

Marx recognised the existence of two main forms of 'class society' other than capitalism: the Classical world and European feudalism. The so-called 'Asiatic Mode of Production' he saw as a social order in which the coexistence of 'self-contained' village communities with centralised state institutions prevented the emergence of classes. The notion of the Asiatic Mode of Production has been the subject of numerous discussions in the literature of the social sciences over the past two decades. Estimates of the validity of Marx's own comments have been very divergent, as have assessments of the usefulness of the concept of the Asiatic Mode of Production itself. I make no attempt to survey the various contributions to this debate. My own views are that the relevance of Marx's writings on the non-European civilisations is strictly limited, for various reasons, and that the term 'Asiatic Mode of Production' should be dropped. First of all, much of this book is an attack upon the idea of 'mode of production' as a useful analytical concept anyway. More specifically, there are three pronounced difficulties with Marx's analysis. He does not explain how it is that a state can come to be in a society without classes; at the very least this seems to run counter to the thesis that the state only exists as the organising medium of class domination. In addition, even if looked at only from the point of view of the development of the 'forces of production', the Asiatic societies were far from being the 'stagnant' systems portrayed by Marx. Finally, Marx seems simply to have been wrong in laying so much emphasis upon the 'self-contained' character of the local village communities in India and China, which he linked to the absence of private property. Private property seems to have been important (in varying ways and at varying levels) not only in the Asiatic civilisations, but in virtually all agrarian states (including probably even Peru, which has commonly been regarded as involving a rather extraordinary form of 'agrarian socialism').

In the light of these considerations I use the term *class-divided society* to refer generically to agrarian states. Marx was right, I think, to entertain reservations about the significance of class within the Asiatic societies, on grounds that apply also to the ancient Near Eastern civilisations as well as to Meso-America and Peru. But it was an error to suppose that Greece or Rome, or European feudalism, were distinctly different in this respect. That is, that they were 'class societies' whereas the others were not. In none of these societies was class, as founded on control of private property, unimportant; but in none of them was class domination in any direct sense the basis of state power. I define a class-divided society as 'a society in which there are classes, but where class analysis does not serve as a basis for identifying the basic structural principle of organisation of that society' (p. 108). By contrast, capitalism, I argue, is in certain very definite respects specifically a *class society*.

Spelling out the implications of the contrasts between class-divided societies and capitalism does not mean repudiating Marx's views, but again is in some degree to use Marx against himself. For in characterising 'capitalism', both as a mode of economic enterprise, and as an over-all type of society, Marx's writings are indispensable. I think it especially important to relate what Marx has to say about the mechanics of capitalist production to the unifying theme of the time-space constitution of society. Chapters 5 and 6 provide the crux of the book, in seeking to show how transformations in the organisation of social relations in time-space are integral to the very nature of capitalist societies. My arguments here depend very directly upon the theorisation of time-space set out abstractly in Chapter 1. In this book, as in *Central Problems*, I have been strongly influenced by certain views expressed by Heidegger in his various attempts to formulate an interpretation of time and Being. Neither time nor space can be properly regarded, as they have been in so many forms of modern philosophy and social theory, following Kant, as 'frameworks' of objects or activities. In social theory time-space can be understood as 'presencing', the continual intermingling of presence and absence that constitutes social conduct. I believe the implications of this standpoint, which does not pretend to resolve the enigmatic character of time, to be profound. In the book I try to demonstrate an affinity between Heidegger's conception of time-space as presencing, and Marx's analysis of *labour-time*, as focal to the nature of capitalism. The formation and maturation of capitalism is made possible by the prevalence of two processes of commodification: that of products, via the expansion of the use of money, and that of labour, via the translation of labour into labour-power. Goods and labour-power thence themselves become interchangeable commodities. The underlying element that permits this interchangeability, Marx makes clear, is the commodification of *time* itself. 'Commodities' exist only as exchange-values, which in turn presuppose the temporal equation of units of labour.

The commodification of time (and its separation from commodified space) supplies the clue not only to the transformations in social institutions brought about by capitalism, but also to the manner in which 'production' or 'the economy' assumes an importance in capitalist society quite foreign to all class-divided societies. In class-divided societies processes of class exploitation rarely intrude in a significant way into the nature of the labour process. The majority of workers in such societies are peasants, and without underestimating the diverse modes in which the peasant's work may be integrated within broader economic systems, as where irrigation schemes are involved, it is broadly true to say that the character of peasant labour is not determined by the exploiting class. In Marx's terms the peasant retains a high degree of control over the labour process (labour also being closely interrelated with the autonomous customs of the local community). The expropriation of workers from control of their means of production, creating a mass of saleable labour-power, involves the intrusion of class relations into the production process itself: labour-power, the medium of the creation of surplus value, becomes capable of being 'programmed' into the over-all organisation of the labour process, as co-ordinated by the dominant class.

In Chapter 5 I try to document the transmutations in social life brought about by the twin processes of the commodification of time and space, and by their interpolation in the labour process as mentioned above. In class-divided societies, as in non-class societies of all sorts, the experience of time is not separated from the substance of social activities. The development of 'clock time', as the organising measure of activities in day-to-day life, is a specific feature of the rise of capitalism. Mumford's writings are again of particular importance here. Power-machines, he points out (as does Gimpel), existed in Europe well before the arrival of capitalism. The harnessing of machinery to the formation of a novel system of production was made possible by the clock. The public, objectified time of the clock, I propose, is the very expression of the commodification of time; time as 'measured duration' *is* commodified time, separated from the contents of existence.

In class-divided societies there were a variety of examples of the large-scale, disciplined co-ordination of human beings in production processes: in plantations, or the construction of temples, city walls, roads or other such projects. But these were never more than ancillary to the economic order of those societies. The advent of capitalism, in which labour-power is co-ordinated within a broader production process, brings about the separation of home and work-place. In the capitalistic work-place the mass of workers experience demands for labour discipline previously only approached in isolated sectors of class-divided societies. Workers have to be 'managed'. The labour discipline sought through modern management, however, is not immediately backed by the threat of the use of force, as was most often the case in the examples alluded to above. This is a very important element in my discussion of capitalism, and connects to the theory of the capitalist state. In capitalism, employers are not the immediate possessors of the means of violence, these being centralised in the hands of the state. The main form of sanction which employers hold over workers is that the latter are propertyless: they have to sell their labour-power in the market in order to obtain a living. The capitalist labour contract is the key to analysing both the emergence of 'management' on the one hand, and the development of labour movements on the other. Workers have to be 'managed' without either religious or moral props to obeisance: the labour contract is both 'free', and concerns only economic relations. By the same token, workers acquire sanctions of the threat of withdrawal of labour that since the nineteenth century have become the cornerstone of 'industrial relations' in the capitalistic economies. The 'management' of labour is achieved primarily through the extension of surveillance into the work-place. The main phenomenon, in fact, that promotes the separation of home and work-place is the recognition of employers that labour discipline is more satisfactorily sustained if workers are under one roof.

The correlate of the commodification of time in capitalist production is the commodification of space. This returns us to the theory of the city. It is a serious error, I claim, to regard the expansion of urbanism in industrial capitalism as the universalisation of features of 'urban life' that existed in germ in cities in class-divided societies. Neither in class-divided nor in capitalist societies can the city be properly understood in separation from the societal totality. In class-divided societies the city was the 'power-container' of the state, and city–countryside relations gave basic form to the character of those societies. Capitalist urbanism is not merely the spread of the city at the expense of rural social life: it is embroiled in the structural transformations introduced by capitalism as a new type of societal totality. Capitalist urbanism eats away the differentations between city and countryside that are the structural basis of class-divided civilisations. In their stead develops the 'created space' of contemporary urban living. The 'created space' of capitalist urbanism is the milieu of what I try to analyse, in some part following Lefebvre, as the emergence of distinctive forms of everyday life. 'Everyday life' here has something of a technical sense. In all societies, of course, human beings live day-to-day lives, in which there is a strong element of continuity in the things they do one day after another. But in non-capitalist societies daily life is geared to tradition, and time is experienced as part of the re-enactment of traditional practices. Tradition is the basis of routinisation. In the capitalistic urban milieu, however, the routinisation of day-to-day activities is stripped away from tradition. In the 'everyday life' of capitalist urbanism large tracts of activity are denuded of moral meaning; they become matters of habit or of 'dull economic compulsion'. In such circumstances the level of what Laing calls 'ontological security' in the routines of daily life is low. This is a phenomenon of some significance, which later in the book I relate directly to the theory of nationalism.

Even the most orthodox of Marxists are today prepared to concede that there is little to be found in Marx's writings relevant to the interpretation of the rise of nationalism; and it is commonly admitted that Marx supplied no more than the rudiments of a theory of the capitalist state. Indeed, a considerable amount of recent work by Marxist authors has been directed towards remedying the second of these deficiencies. In my analysis in this book I offer a critical evaluation of some of this recent work. But my discussion follows closely lines of thought opened up by the ideas I have sketched in previously. The capitalist labour contract is an integral element of the separation of 'economy' and 'polity' that is a basic institutional feature of the capitalist state. I take some pains to make it clear that the separation from, or 'insulation' of, economy from polity should not be equated with competitiveness in product or labour markets. But I also want to insist that this insulation of economy and polity involves the phenomenon I have mentioned previously: the extrusion of control of the means of violence from the principal axis of class exploitation, the capital/wage-labour relation. Commitment to freedom of contract, part of a wider set of claims to human liberty fought for by the bourgeoisie, became institutionally distinguished from 'public' authority, bolstered by monopoly of the means of violence.

In this book I do not claim to examine the historical conditions giving rise to these phenomena in anything like the detail they merit. I do wish to say that there was more continuity between the period of European absolutism and the formation of the capitalist state – or, more accurately, states – than is often acknowledged (Chapter 8). Absolutism shaped the map of the European state system, which was the nexus out of which nation-states became formed. I argue that capitalist states emerged as nation-states: the association between capitalism and the nation-state was not the 'accident of history' that it has appeared to be to many Marxist and non-Marxist historians alike. In seeking to substantiate this, I make a threefold distinction: between the *absolutist state*, the *nation-state* and *nationalism*. The absolutist state coincided only with the very early formation of capitalism. The 'nation-state', as I use the term, only came to maturity in the nineteenth century. Both the absolutist and nation-state are specifically European in origin, though today the nation-state system has become a world-wide one. What is distinctive about my analysis, I think, is the claim that the emergence of the nation-state was integrally bound up with the expansion of capitalism. The absolutist state was part of a class-divided society in which, as elsewhere – although in quite different form from agrarian empires – the city–countryside relation was the foundation of the social order. My argument, in essence, is that the nation-state replaces the city as the 'power-container' shaping the development of the capitalist societies, as the old city–countryside symbiosis becomes dissolved. The precision with which the boundaries of the nation-state are drawn is the modern analogue to the circumscribing of the city by its walls. From the late eighteenth century the state has played a far more significant role in the development of capitalism as a form of economic enterprise (nationally and internationally) than was ever conceived of either in Marxist theory, or in that of its opponent, classical political economy. As I try to indicate in the text, one of the main reasons for this analytical deficiency is the prevalence in nineteenth-century social thought of the notion that capitalistic economic enterprise is essentially non-violent in nature. Such a view ignores the processes that led to the internal pacification of states, a phenomenon everywhere associated with a massive expansion of the surveillance activities of the state and with radical alterations in modes of handling crime and 'deviance'. And it ignores the fact that the capitalist state has been the purveyor of violence externally, in the context of the European state system and in the expansion of Western power across the rest of the world.

In many studies of modern history the terms 'nation-state' and 'nationalism' are used more or less synonymously. But I think it important to distinguish between these, since they may be associated in various diverse ways. What makes the 'nation' a necessary element of the 'nation-state' in my definition is not the existence of sentiments of nationalism (however strong these may be) but the unification of an administrative apparatus whose power stretches over precisely defined territorial bounds. 'Nationalism', by contrast, may be understood as symbols or beliefs which attribute a communality of experience to the members of a particular regional, ethnic or linguistic category – which may or may not be convergent with the demarcation of a nation-state. While there is a very large literature on nationalism, theoretical interpretations of the phenomenon have been notoriously lacking. Within the confines of this book I do not pretend to develop a theory of nationalism in any depth; but I do offer a discussion of some of the features that such a theory might involve. Nationalism is a specifically modern phenomenon and as such, I believe, expresses psychological sentiments that feed upon the rootlessness of an everyday life in which what Geertz calls the 'primordial sentiments' of social reproduction, grounded in tradition, have become substantially disintegrated. Virtually all writers on nationalism have commented on its 'Janus-faced' character. Nationalism may seemingly be associated with images of enlightenment and justice, but it also conjures up brutal forms of cultural imperialism. We can explain the 'Janus-faced' nature of nationalism, I argue, in terms of the fragility of ontological security in the wasteland of everyday life. A prominent component of the more active forms of nationalism has been affiliation to leaders who are felt to embody the unity of the group. The theory of identification with authority-figures worked out by Le Bon and Freud, I try to show, helps explain why such identification is both a powerful motivating force, and why it is 'Janus-faced'. Identification involves ambivalence that can fuel sentiments of either a benign or a virulently aggressive sort.

In Chapter 9 I pose the question: what is the specific nature of the capitalist state? Such a question can be perhaps best approached through a critical analysis of contemporary Marxist writings on the issue. My discussion in this chapter draws heavily upon some of the theorems of the earlier part of the book. While the recent Marxist literature has mostly approached the problem of the capitalist state in the context of comparisons with socialism, 'actually existing'[7] or hypothetical, I am mainly concerned to contrast the capitalist state with the state in class-divided societies. The key to analysing the internal dynamics of the capitalist state, I suggest, in some part following ideas of Claus Offe, is that the state's revenue is dependent upon processes of valorisation and accumulation of capital which it itself does not directly control. The structural basis of this circumstance is the insulation of economy and polity noted earlier, a phenomenon immediately relevant to the debate over what has been (mis)represented as the 'relative' autonomy of the state. I propose a framework for analysing the autonomy of the state, in relation both to the activities of the dominant class and to the struggles of subordinate classes. So far as such struggles are concerned, I argue strongly against the view that the consolidation of what T. H. Marshall calls 'citizenship rights' can be validly interpreted either as merely the beneficent gifts of a liberal state, or as some kind of 'functional response' of capitalism to the need to protect its source of labour-power. 'Citizenship rights' have been achieved in some substantial degree through the active intervention of labour movements in the political arena. At this juncture I return to the significance of the capitalist labour contract. The primary sanctions that employers have in order to control the labour force are that workers must have some form of paid employment to survive, and the imposition of labour discipline in the work-place through surveillance. These constitute the two major sites of chronic class struggle within capitalist societies: over the conditions of the labour contract, and over the control of the labour process.

Marx expected class conflict to be the medium of the transformation of capitalism by socialism. It is not my purpose to discuss this in the present work, since it is a matter I propose to examine in some detail in the next volume. In the concluding chapter, however, I attempt to set the stage for this second phase of a 'contemporary critique of historical materialism'. My particular concern is with the concept of 'contradiction', and its relation to the explanation of social change; but in the final sections of the chapter I introduce some of the themes of the volume to follow, which will have as its title *Between Capitalism and Socialism*. In the contemporary world we are 'between capitalism and socialism' in two senses. Socialism is an 'actually existing' reality, one side of a power-bloc sandwich with the capitalist states. But socialism also represents a set of ideals, the radicalisation of the promise of equality and freedom generated within the capitalist West. Can we still hope to be 'between capitalism and socialism' in this second sense? No question of political theory today poses itself more acutely.

I have said earlier that this book is based closely upon the abstract theoretical considerations raised in *Central Problems in Social Theory*. In working out the theory of structuration contained therein, I had two main general objectives. First, to acknowledge the essential importance of a concept of action in the social sciences, the corollary of this being that social science must elaborate a satisfactory account of the competent and knowledgeable human agent.[8] Second, to formulate such an account without relapsing into a subjectivist view, and without failing to grasp the structural components of the social institutions which outlive us, as individuals who are born and who die. In the opening chapter I sketch a brief outline of the theory of structuration. It will be useful here, however, to mention some of the methodological considerations that are associated with the standpoint it represents, so far as these concern the present book. My position in this book is *anti-functionalist* and *anti-evolutionary*. I have developed a critique of functionalism in *Central Problems* and other publications;[9] and my objections to evolutionism are stated in the body of this book.

The relation between Marxism and functionalism is a somewhat opaque one. There are probably very few of those sympathetic to Marx who would accept the label 'functionalist'. But functionalist notions appear, and with some considerable prominence, in the writings of many Marxists as well as in those of other social scientists nominally hostile to functionalist thought. Many passages in Marx are directly functionalist in tone, or can be construed in a functionalist way. So the repudiation of functionalism is certainly not irrelevant to a 'contemporary critique of historical materialism'.

Now, to raise the question of functionalism is almost enough to put everyone immediately to sleep. For has not functionalism been the subject of one of the most protracted and boring debates known to sociology? Might not the same be said of systems theory, sometimes thought to be closely allied to functionalism? To a certain degree I am prepared to grant these things – especially the somnambulant qualities of the functionalism debate of some fifteen to twenty years ago. What I cannot accept is that the problems raised by functionalist authors can be quietly forgotten. For one thing, functionalist notions still flourish in a variety of contexts. For another, the functionalism debate to my mind resolved few of the issues basic to the question of the relevance of functionalism to the social sciences. Nor are they resolved by appeals to systems theory – even if Luhmann's 'functional-structuralism' is undeniably more sophisticated than earlier versions of 'structural-functionalism'.

My argument is as follows. The term 'function', I want to claim, is of no use to the social sciences or history; indeed it would do no harm at all to ban it altogether as any sort of technical term. Now most of those who have attacked functionalism, in any interesting way, have tended to fall back upon subjectivist views. Those influenced by ordinary language philosophy, for example, or by some varieties of phenomenology, have seen functionalism as a deterministic type of thought, and have attempted to replace it with one that gives primacy to the intending, reasoning agent. In so doing, however, they have moved away from that area where functionalism is strongest: the analysis of institutions, of large-scale social processes. In diverging from functionalism (as is indicated in my summary of the theory of structuration at the beginning of Chapter 1) we need to be able to recognise *both* what might be called the theorem of 'knowledgeability' – that we are all purposeful, knowledgeable agents who have reasons for what we do – *and* that social processes at the same time work 'behind our backs', affecting what we do in ways of which we are unaware. Marx summed this up in the famous aphorism, 'Men make history, but not in circumstances of their own choosing.' However, working out the implications of this unobjectionable statement is difficult.

'Functionalism' means many things, but I shall regard it here as that type of doctrine which holds, first, that societies or social systems have 'needs', and second, that identifying the ways in which they meet these needs constitutes an explanation of why particular, given social processes are as they are. This characterisation thus includes the core of both 'normative functionalism' (Parsons) and 'conflict functionalism' (Merton), as well as the more covert functionalisms of many Marxist authors.

I object to functionalism, thus defined, on several grounds: that (like structuralism) it rests upon a false division between statics and dynamics, or between the synchronic and the diachronic; that, in stressing system needs, functionalist authors have been unable to see human beings as reasoning agents who know a great deal about what they are doing in their social conduct; that systems *have no needs*, save in a sense that is quite different from that which functionalist authors have in mind – that, therefore, to identify 'system needs' is not to explain anything at all: there is *nothing* which can count as 'functionalist explanation'. I shall analyse each of these points fairly rapidly, but they all could be elaborated in greater detail.

The question of the division of the synchronic and the diachronic once more returns us to the theme of time, and the thesis that time-space relations have to be brought into the very heart of social theory. I shall assert rather dogmatically that the synchronic/diachronic differentiation is *logically*, rather than contingently, associated with functionalism (although not confined to it; cf. structuralism). I wish to say that it is a division which should be abandoned once and for all. The characteristic view of the synchronic/diachronic distinction is that to study a social system synchronically is to take a sort of 'timeless snapshot' of it. Abstracting from time, we can identify functional relations, how the various contributing elements of a social system are connected with one another. When we study systems diachronically, on the other hand, we analyse how they change over time. But the result of this is an elementary, though very consequential, error: *time becomes identified with social change*. One should notice that the synchronic/diachronic division presumes the Kantian dualism of space and time, the first being available for synchronic analysis in abstraction from the second. However, it is more important in this context to stress the point that time (time-space) is obviously as necessary a component of social stability as it is of change. A stable social order is one in which there is close similarity between how things are, and how they used to be. This indicates how misleading it is to suppose that one can take a 'timeless snapshot' of a social system as one can, say, take a real snapshot of the architecture of a building. For social systems exist *as* systems only in and through their 'functioning' (reproduction) over time.

My second objection harks back to problems raised a few

paragraphs earlier. Functionalist theories have lacked adequate accounts of human *action*, in the sense in which much recent philosophy has been preoccupied with that term. I think that this judgement applies to Parsons's work as much as that of anyone else, in spite of the fact that he labelled his approach 'the action frame of reference'. This is a complicated issue, but basically I consider it true to say that human agents appear in Parsons's scheme, as in that of Althusser, as 'cultural dopes', not as actors who are highly knowledgeable (discursively and tacitly) about the institutions they produce and reproduce in and through their actions. Compare the writings of functionalists with those of Erving Goffman. Goffman treats human beings as skilled and knowledgeable actors who employ their knowledgeability routinely in the production and reproduction of social encounters. Goffman shows us many of the things we 'know' about social conventions or institutions, and which we must know for their reproduction, but which we know in the tacit sense of practical consciousness. Functionalists, by contrast, discount agents' reasons in favour of 'society's reasons'.

My third objection is the most decisive. Social systems, I say, have no 'needs' – or 'functional exigencies', or whatever equivalent term may be employed. Let me offer by way of illustration Marx's discussion of the reserve army in a capitalist economy. Marx's analysis can be interpreted, and often has been so interpreted, in a functionalist vein. Capitalism has its own 'needs', which the system functions to fulfil. Since capitalism needs a 'reserve army', one comes into being. The proposition is sometimes stated in reverse. Since the operation of capitalism leads to the formation of a reserve army, this must be because it needs one. But neither version explains anything about why a reserve army of unemployed workers exists. Not even the most deeply sedimented institutional features of societies come about, persist, or disappear, because those societies need them to do so. They come about *historically*, as a result of concrete conditions that have in every case to be directly analysed; the same holds for their persistence or their dissolution.

There is only *one* logical format in which talk of 'system needs' is defensible, but it does not involve attributing empirical needs to social systems. This format is one of *counterfactual argument*. We can quite legitimately pose conjectural questions such as: 'What would have be to be case for social system *x* to come about, persist, or be transformed?' But we have to be very careful with such propositions, because they readily lend themselves to interpretation in a functionalist mode. Take as an example the statement 'In order to persist in a relatively stable form, the capitalist economy has to maintain a certain over-all level of profit.' The force of 'has to' here is counterfactual: it involves identifying conditions that must be met if certain consequences are to obtain. The 'has to' is not a property or 'need' of the system.

The theory of structuration, I wish to propose, dispenses with the notion of 'function' without sacrificing an interest in long-term, large-scale social processes. It may help if I unpack a little at this point the summary exposition with which this book opens. According to the theory of structuration, all social action consists of social practices, situated in time-space, and organised in a skilled and knowledgeable fashion by human agents. But such knowledgeability is always 'bounded' by unacknowledged conditions of action on the one side, and unintended consequences of action on the other. A crucial move in this theory is an attempt to transcend the opposition between 'action' theories and 'institutional' theories mentioned above. This move is accomplished by the concept of what I call the *duality of structure*. By the duality of structure I mean that the structured properties of social systems are simultaneously the *medium and outcome of social acts*. One way to illustrate this idea is by taking an example from language. The structural properties of language, as qualities of a community of language speakers (e.g. syntactical rules) are drawn upon by a speaker in the production of a sentence. But the very act of speaking that sentence contributes to the reproduction of those syntactical rules as enduring properties of the language. The concept of the duality of structure, I believe, is basic to any account of social reproduction, and has no functionalist overtones at all.

We are once more drawn back to the theme of time. According to the theory of structuration, there are three intersecting planes of temporality involved in every moment of social reproduction. There is the temporality of immediate experience, the continuous flow of day-to-day life: what Schutz, following Bergson, calls the *durée* of activity. Second, there is the temporality of *Dasein*, the life-cycle of the organism. Third, there is what Braudel calls the *longue durée* of institutional time: the long-term sedimentation or development of social institutions. It is essential to see that these interpenetrate and that, according to the theorem of the duality of structure, every moment of social interaction, implicated in the 'passing away' of the human organism, is likewise involved with the *longue durée* of institutions. The most trivial exchange of words implicates the speakers in the long-term history of the language in which those words are formed, and at the same time in the continuing reproduction of that language. This is very important. For most theories in the social sciences which have focused on the knowledgeability of social actors have had at best a truncated time-sense. They have recognised the Schutzean *durée*, but not that of Braudel. In the theory of structuration I am explicitly concerned to reject the idea that either form of *durée* has logical primacy over the other.

Evolutionary theory, of course, is about time – the elapsing of time in the *longue durée*, and writing about time in the sense of the interpretation of history. Evolutionary theories, though they have quite often stood in close association with functionalist ideas, have not acquired the level of opprobrium now conventionally attached to functionalism. Such theories dominate archaeology, though opinion about them is more divided within anthropology; and they continue to exert a strong influence among sociological writers. Marxist authors are virtually everywhere committed to evolutionism, in some guise or another. For Marx's 'historical materialism' is predicated upon an evolutionary scheme that both interprets history analytically, and at the same time contains more than a trace of that 'universal history' of humankind which Hegel sought to formulate.

There are those sympathetic to Marx who would 'reconstruct historical materialism' on the basis of a reworked theory of evolution.[10] Such attempts, interesting and suggestive as they may be in their details, do not seem to me in the end to be defensible. One has to take a more radical scalpel to Marxism, in full recognition of the consequences which such surgery may have for claims long regarded as indissolubly connected with Marxist views. There are many kinds of evolutionary theory, Marxist and otherwise, and I do not devote any part of this book to attempting to survey them. Virtually all theories of evolution I have examined, however, whether 'universal', 'unilinear' or 'multilinear' in form, hinge upon some notion of *adaptation*, in which the adaptation of societies to the material conditions of the environment is given pride of place. 'Adaptation' may be understood in a more or less mechanical way in different theories. In Marx's own writings, where the term itself has no particular significance, the dominant theme is the idea that the active mastery by human beings of their environment is the medium of the progressive expansion of the forces of production in successive types of society. Of course, Marx's evolutionary scheme, which proceeds through stages of revolutionary transformation, is quite different from those forms of evolutionism which treat social change as more gradual in character.

I want to erase the notion of 'adaptation' (or any synonyms) from the vocabulary of the social sciences just as thoroughly as that of 'function', on a combination of theoretical and empirical grounds. So far as the former of these is concerned, if offered as an explanatory principle of social change, the idea of adaptation falls in the same category as the functional 'needs' to which I have already objected. Societies have no need to 'adapt' to (master, conquer) their material environments. We can pose as a counterfactual the supposition that every society which has survived over a period of time 'must' have acquired enough food, shelter, etc., for its members to have survived. But this is not an explanatory principle; it merely calls for one. Marx's views on this, to say the best, are only weakly elaborated: 'The first premise of all human existence and, therefore, of all history,' he writes [is] the premise . . . that men must be in a position to live in order to "make history".'[11] Well, of course this is so; but one cannot proceed to infer from such a 'premise' explanatory principles relevant to human society. Adaptation to, or mastery of, the material environment is a functional exigency of human society; therefore understanding how such adaptation occurs is the key to analysing the institutions of that society. This is what Marx might mean. But the 'therefore' simply does not follow.

Now we might seek to disavow the seemingly functionalist cast of such statements that appear in Marx's writings. We could propose that it is not societies as such which 'adapt' to their environment, it is precisely their members that do so, in knowledge of what they are doing and with the desire to become as 'materially productive' as they can. It is here that we have to move to the more empirical side of my arguments, which are set out in Chapters 3 and 4. Recent archaeological and anthropological evidence has placed a serious question-mark against the thesis that the drive to mastery of the material environment (and the creation of material 'surplus') governs major phases of societal transformation. It has proved suspect to presume, as Diamond has put it, that there is an 'immanent logic' in surplus production: that is to say, that if 'primitive' societies do not produce a surplus, it is because they cannot – because the forces of production are inadequately developed.[12] A good case can be made for Sahlins's view that, at least in many of what are misappropriately called 'subsistence economies', no principle of material scarcity operates. 'Scarcity,' he says, 'is a creation of modern economics – and the driving principle of the market-industrial system.'[13] Hunting and gathering societies are not necessarily impoverished; even in relatively harsh environments hunters and gatherers do not typically 'work hard' as compared with a modern industrial labourer. A similar viewpoint is advocated forcibly by Clastres: in 'primitive societies' the expansion of material production is not experienced as an impelling demand.[14] New pressures for the augmentation of production may be set up in class-divided societies. But these normally consist in the 'milking' of available resources by an exploiting class. Only with the advent of capitalism is there established a constant emphasis upon, and capacity for, the chronic expansion of the forces of production.

All of this, I think, compromises the very core of most evolutionary theories, including the scheme outlined by Marx in the 'Preface' to *A Contribution to the Critique of Political Economy*. And it does so not just by questioning old dogmas about 'adaptation' or the 'development of the forces of production'. There are implications that relate back to my discussion of structuration. Most theories of evolution, not excluding that of Marx, and notwithstanding his emphasis upon the active character of *Praxis*, underestimate the knowledgeability of human subjects – in this case, those living in relatively 'primitive' societies. Transitions from hunting and gathering to agriculture, or to class-divided 'civilisations', have no inevitability about them, and cannot be analysed as the outcome of superior material 'adaptation'. There is plenty of evidence, for instance, that those in 'primitive' societies have often known a good deal about supposedly superior 'civilisations', and have actively resisted incorporation within them.

If the central mechanism of evolutionary theories – 'adaptation' – is removed, much of the distinctiveness of evolutionary theory is lost anyway. I have some sympathy, given this reservation, with what is sometimes called 'limited multilinear evolution', but in this instance there is really no need to use the term 'evolution' at all, with its strong resonance of evolutionary theory in biology. Rather than using such terminology, I want to suggest an approach to the *longue durée* of institutional organisation and change that involves what I shall call *episodic characterisations* and *time-space edges*. 'Episodes' refer to processes of social change that have a definite direction and form, and in which definite structural transform-ations occur. Episodes include such transitions as those transform-ing tribal communities into class-divided societies – or the reverse process. In talking of time-space edges I want to emphasise the significance of the *simultaneous* existence of types of society in episodic transitions. If we take an evolutionary view of history, we tend to think of societal change in terms of 'stages', in which one type of society is supplanted by another, and so forth. But the emergence of class-divided societies, for example, did not elim-inate tribal societies from the world. Industrial capitalism has existed, and still exists, in conjunction with various other types of society (including, now, socialism), however strong its tendency to corrode or to absorb them. Time-space edges refer to the forms of contact – and often of interdependence – between different structural types of society. These are edges of potential or actual social transformation, the often unstable intersections between different modes of societal organisation.

Two further notions are particularly important in my discussion throughout this book. One is that of *inter-societal systems*. In using this term I mean to react against what can be called 'unfolding' models of social change.[15] By 'unfolding models' I refer to those conceptions which regard a society as an isolated unit, and as containing within itself the mechanisms that bring about its transformation. Until recently the social sciences have been dominated by unfolding models, in Marxist as well as in other schools of thought. In the work of Wallerstein, Emmanuel and Amin, however much it may be criticised in some respects, we find an alternative view. Their writings have thus far been mainly focused on the 'world system' initiated by the spread of capitalism. They provide ample material for criticising evolutionary theories which mistake the political/economic/military triumph of Western industrial capitalism over the rest of the world for the high point on an evolutionary scheme. But although the complexity of the contemporary world system is far greater than anything that went before, I want to emphasise the generic shortcomings of treating *any* type of society as an isolated entity. Tribal societies, for example, have usually been involved in a multiplicity of overlapping inter-societal relations, just as have other types.

It is not enough to leave matters there in seeking to break away from evolutionary theories. A further notion is called for: that of what Eberhard calls 'world time'.[16] To acknowledge 'world time' is to recognise the influence of changing forms of inter-societal system upon episodic transitions. An episodic transition that occurs in one historical conjuncture may have quite a different form, and quite different consequences, to an apparently similar episode in another conjuncture. To appreciate the importance of this is to understand the meaning of taking seriously the proposition that the social sciences are irremediably historical. The choice is not one of evolutionism on the one hand, or some kind of abstracted 'comparative sociology' searching for universal laws on the other. Each of these has to be rejected.

This brings me again to the themes of my final chapter. I would ask that this whole book be judged as a stimulus to further reflection rather than as anything approaching an exhaustive analysis of the major issues it raises. This plea for clemency on the part of the reader applies particularly, however, to the concluding sections of the book, which are frankly propaedeutic. None the less, I would insist that they are inescapably bound up with the main body of my arguments. Anyone who rejects Marx's evolutionary scheme, and a good deal of the substantive content of his materialist conception of history besides – as I do – yet remains sympathetic to other aspects of his work, must pursue the implications right through. If Marx's project be regarded as the furthering, through the conjunction of social analysis and political activity, of forms of human society in which the mass of human beings can attain freedoms and modes of self-realisation in excess of any they may have enjoyed before, who can dissent from it?

Certainly I do not, neither do I doubt the continuing relevance of Marx's writings to the pursuance of such a project. But such a stance demands a great deal of rethinking.

Abandoning Marx's evolutionism, it seems to me, both creates specific problems for Marxist political theory and at the same time clears the air for the possible resolution of others. Capitalism is not the summation – in contradictory form – of the 'universal history' of humankind. Consequently the transformation of capitalism by socialism can neither be adequately justified by appeals to 'historical necessity', nor can the disappearance of capitalism be regarded as some sort of panacea for all human ills. I am not suggesting that Marx regarded socialism as such a panacea; but one can hardly say that his views on the nature of the anticipated socialist society are free from ambiguity, or deny that they contain elements of utopianism. However, if we recognise that certain fundamental forms of exploitation do not originate with capitalism, or even with class divisions more generally, we are freed from trying conceptually to squeeze them within standard Marxist analyses. There are three main axes of exploitation of this sort, in my opinion. These are exploitative relations between states, particularly in respect of control of the means of violence; exploitative relations between ethnic groups; and exploitative relations between the sexes.

# 1

# The Time-Space Constitution of Social Systems

## The Theory of Structuration

In this opening section I shall describe the elements of a theoretical standpoint which informs the whole of the remainder of the book. Rather than attempting to recapitulate ideas which I have elaborated in some detail elsewhere,[1] I shall set out this standpoint – the theory of structuration – in propositional form. The theory of structuration was worked out as an attempt to transcend, without discarding altogether, three prominent traditions of thought in social theory and philosophy: hermeneutics or 'interpretative sociologies', functionalism, and structuralism. Each of these traditions, in my view, incorporates distinctive and valuable contributions to social analysis – while each has tended to suffer from a number of defined limitations.[2]

The chief features of the theory of structuration may be described as follows:

FIRST. A distinction is made between *structure* and *system*. Social systems are composed of patterns of relationships between actors or collectivities reproduced across time and space. Social systems are hence constituted of *situated practices*. Structures exist in time-space only as moments recursively involved in the production and reproduction of social systems. Structures have only a 'virtual' existence.

SECOND. Structures can be analysed as rules and resources, which can be treated as 'sets' in so far as transformations and mediations can be identified between the reproduced properties of social systems. In examining over-all societies we can attempt to identify *structural principles* or basic 'principles of organisation' involved in a multiplicity of transformation/mediation relations.

**THIRD**. A fundamental postulate of the theory of structuration is the notion of the *duality of structure*, which refers to the essentially recursive nature of social practices. Structure is both the medium and outcome of the practices which constitute social systems. The concept of the duality of structure connects the *production* of social interaction, as always and everywhere a contingent accomplishment of knowledgeable social actors, to the *reproduction* of social systems across time-space.

**FOURTH**. The stocks of knowledge drawn upon by actors in the production and reproduction of interaction are at the same time the source of accounts they may supply of the purposes, reasons and motives of their action. But the knowledgeability of social actors operates only partly in terms of discursive consciousness. On the level of the capabilities of the actor, the structural properties of social systems are embedded in *practical consciousness*: in 'knowing how to go on' in a whole diversity of contexts of social life. Practical consciousness, although not 'discursively redeemable' for the actor, has to be distinguished from unconscious sources of cognition and motivation.

**FIFTH**. To study the structuration of social systems is to study the conditions governing their continuity, change or dissolution. According centrality to the notion of social reproduction *does not* imply emphasising stability at the expense of radical discontinuities in system organisation. The inherent relation between production and reproduction involved in the idea of the duality of structure carries with it the implication that the seeds of change are present in every moment of the constitution of social systems across time and space. In the theory of structuration I aim to create a wholly *non-functionalist* style of social analysis. The attempt to exemplify such a style of analysis is one of my main aims throughout this book. This bears directly upon the sixth point below, since functionalist conceptions are by no means confined to 'orthodox functionalism' (Parsons, Merton, etc.) but appear prominently in Marxist thought.

**SIXTH**. The concept of social reproduction, as the preceding points should make clear, is not in and of itself an *explanatory* one: all reproduction is contingent and historical. Understood in any other way the notion of social reproduction easily tends to smuggle functionalist suppositions into sociology under another name.[3] In the theory of structuration there is no place for any version of 'functional explanation': the term 'function' is discarded altogether. The knowledgeability of actors is always *bounded*, by *unacknowledged conditions* and *unintended consequences* of action. These can be studied in the social sciences without attributing any teleological properties whatsoever to social systems.

**SEVENTH**. We can identify three 'layers' of temporality involved in the analysis of the structuration of social systems; each is also an aspect of the contingent character of social interaction. Temporality enters into: (a) the immediate nexus of interaction as contingently 'brought off' by social actors, the most elemental form of social reproduction, (b) the existence of *Dasein*, as the living human organism, the contingency of life in the face of death, and of biological reproduction, and (c) the long-term reproduction of *institutions* across the generations, the contingency of the transformation/mediation relations implicated in structural principles of system organisation. Institutions are practices which 'stretch' over long time-space distances in the reproduction of social systems. The structural practices of social systems 'bind' the temporality of the *durée* of the day-to-day life-world to the *longue durée* of institutions, interpolated in the finite span of existence of the individual human being. Most of what I have to say in this book is concerned with the level of institutional analysis, which methodologically brackets the strategic conduct of situated actors, treating rules and resources as chronically reproduced features of social systems. But given the earlier premises I have set out, this is written in the context of the (bounded) knowledgeability of social actors as always and everywhere the medium of the continuity of institutions.

**EIGHTH**. According to the theory of structuration, the components of social interaction are exhausted neither by its 'meaningful' nor its 'normative' content. *Power* is an integral an element of all social life as are meaning and norms; this is the significance of the claim that structure can be analysed as rules and *resources*, resources being drawn upon in the constitution of power relations. All social interaction involves the use of power, as a necessary implication of the logical connection between human action and *transformative capacity*. Power within social systems can be analysed as relations of autonomy and dependence between actors in which these actors draw upon and reproduce structural properties of *domination*.

**NINTH**. The integration of social systems can be analysed in terms of the existence of 'systemness' as *social integration* and as *system integration*. 'Integration' here has to be treated as 'reciprocity of practices', not as merely synonymous with either 'cohesion' or 'consensus'. Social integration refers to systemness expressed in face-to-face interaction, a primary manifestation of time-space *presence* in social organisation. System integration is concerned with systemness expressed as relations between collectivities, and while it therefore presupposes social integration, the mechanisms governing the latter cannot necessarily be derived from those involved with the former.

**TENTH**. *Contradiction*, treated as a structural feature of social systems, has to be conceptually separated from *conflict*, in two senses in which the second term may be understood: as division of interest between actors, or as manifest *struggle*. Contradiction can be most usefully defined as an opposition or disjunction between structural principles of a social system, such that the system operates in negation. That is to say, the operation of one structural principle presumes another which negates it.

One of my main objectives in developing the theory of structuration is to bring temporality into the heart of social theory, breaking with the division between the synchronic and diachronic which has played such a prominent part in both functionalist and structuralist traditions of thought. In *Central Problems in Social Theory* I established a preliminary treatment of time-space problems in social theory, a treatment which I shall elaborate further in what follows.

## Time-Space Relations

According to Talcott Parsons, *the* problem for sociological analysis, for social theory, is the 'problem of order'. In Parsonian sociology, 'order' is understood as the antithesis of 'disintegration', and hence the problem of order is treated as a problem of *social control*. Moreover, it is posed and responded to in functionalist terms: what are the principal functional exigencies which have to be met if order is to be achieved in society? I have no dispute with the assertion that 'the' problem of social theory is 'the problem of order'. But rather than understanding 'order' in opposition to 'disintegration', I oppose the term to chaos or formlessness.[4] The problem of order in social theory is how *form* occurs in social relations, or (put in another fashion) how social systems 'bind' time and space. All social activity is formed in three conjoined moments of difference: temporally, structurally (in the language of semiotics, paradigmatically), and spatially; the conjunction of these express the *situated* character of social practices. The 'binding' of time and space in social systems *always* has to be examined historically, in terms of the bounded knowledgeability of human action.

The appropriation of temporality for social theory of course poses some very considerable difficulties. Time and space have traditionally been seen not only as 'boundaries' to social analysis but have also been in a certain sense separated from one another in a disciplinary fashion. History, it is presumed, has as its special province the elapsing of time, while geography finds its identity in a pre-eminent concern with space. Each, then, is a bordering discipline for sociology, whose object is to analyse 'social structures' operating in the 'environments' of time and space. Time enters into social thought only in so far as it is equated with *change*, with 'dynamics' or the diachronic. The theory of structuration, as outlined above, necessarily rejects the logic of such a drawing of disciplinary boundaries, and the equation of time with diachrony or with social change. Time-space relations are portrayed as constitutive features of social systems, implicated as deeply in the most stable forms of social life as in those subject to the most extreme or radical modes of change.

The philosophical basis for this view has been pioneered by Heidegger, in his discussion of Being and time. But it is also relevant to mention analyses of time-space developed in post-Newtonian physics, which in certain respects bear more than a passing resemblance to the conceptions formulated by Heidegger in 'pure philosophy'. Heidegger's philosophy looks back beyond Kant to Leibnitz, and beyond Leibnitz to the Classical world. According to Leibnitz, we cannot speak of time and space as non-relational 'containers', because they are not, as such, 'existents'. We can only grasp time and space in terms of the relations of things and events: they *are* the modes in which relations between objects and events are expressed. In this context the Kantian positing of time and space as categories of mind was in some part a step backwards, for time and space are removed from the thing, from Being itself. Time and space become 'phenomena', as contrasted to the Classical view that all that is real exists in time and space.

As Heidegger stresses again and again in *Being and Time*, philosophy must return to the question of Being, obscured by the constant preoccupation of Western thought with epistemology. This preoccupation has manifested itself both in those accounts which have 'begun' from the subject and those which have 'begun' from the object. Thus the Cartesian *cogito* did not enquire into the *am* of 'I am', presupposed as a background to the cognising subject. Conversely, those philosophies which have concerned themselves with the nature of 'objects' or 'things' have remained, in Heidegger's terms, at the relatively shallow level of the 'ontic' rather than penetrating to the 'ontological'.[5] Being can only be rediscovered through the 'primordial horizon' of time, the means whereby both subject and object 'exist in time'. To speak of either a subject or object presumes an 'abiding through time':

> If Being is to be conceived in terms of time, and if, indeed, its various modes and derivatives are to become intelligible in their respective modifications and derivations by taking time into consideration, then Being itself (and not merely entities, let us say, as entities 'in time') is thus made visible in its 'temporal' character.[6]

In Heidegger's conception the 'nothingness' of 'non-Being', the 'nothingness that surrounds Being', should be understood neither as the 'emptiness' of space, nor the 'non-existence' of a disappeared past. Each of these suggests that the 'now' of Being can be localised. Time is not a derivative of space; and Being is not a fleeting sequence of 'nows'. The phrase that so scandalised the logical positivists, 'Nothing Nothings', indicates that time is manifest in the chronic reciprocity of Being and non-Being. Being exists in the coming-to-be of presence, which replaces both the idea of the 'present' and the 'point in space'. This theorem is expanded and developed in Heidegger's later writings, in which he rejects the priority he accorded to time over space in *Being and Time*.[7] 'Presence', however, should not be confused with the traditional notion of 'object in time' which Heidegger has specifically set out to criticise. As one commentator expresses it, for Heidegger 'future as the withholding of presence and past as the refusal of present grant and yield presence in a reciprocal relationship. *Presence* has replaced the present which can too easily be confused with the Aristotelian "now".'[8] We must resist not only the tendency to 'spatialise' time (Bergson), but also the notion that the calculation or 'measurement' of time-space gives us the clue to its true nature. We can 'characterise Being', Heidegger says, 'as presencing'. In this standpoint

> time-space no longer means merely the distance between two now-points of calculated time, such as we have in mind when we note, for instance: this or that occurred within a time-span of fifty years. Time-space is the name for the openness which opens up in the mutual extending of futural approach, past and present. The self-extending, the opening up, of future, past and present is itself prespatial; only thus can it make room, that is, provide space . . . prior to all calculation of time and independent of all such calculation, what is germane to the time-space of true time consists in the mutual reaching out and opening up of future, past and present.[9]

Time, Heidegger argues, should not be regarded as 'three dimensional' (past, present and future) but as 'four dimensional'; the fourth dimension is the 'presencing' which brings them together and holds them apart.

Although there are some sharp contrasts, this view also has some remarkable affinities with G. H. Mead's philosophy of time – a philosophy which has never figured prominently in the use of Mead made by the 'symbolic interactionists'. According to Mead, 'presencing' exhausts reality: the past always exists only 'in the present', as memory.[10] One of the interesting aspects of Mead's discussion of time is that, unlike Heidegger's writings, it was prompted in some large part by reflection about Minkowski's time-space as developed in physical theory. One should beware, of course, of thinking that Heidegger's 'four-dimensional' interpretation of Being has a great deal in common with the four-dimensional time-space of modern physics. But there is enough comparability to be able to draw out certain features of each relevant to analysing the time-space constitution of social systems. In the view of modern physics the four-dimensional cosmos is finite but unbounded. An immortal cosmonaut could circumscribe the cosmos, visiting every galaxy, without reaching a boundary. Four-dimensional time-space is difficult to 'think' or portray, because it cannot readily be presented visually. However, there is some indication in the recent writings of geographers that the non-Euclidean geometry of Riemman, Klein and others may provide clues for developing topological models of time-space relations superior to traditional Euclidean approaches.[11] According to Harvey, there is today some general agreement among theoretical geographers 'that "distance" can only be measured in terms of process or activity, in which time is one element; there is no independent metric to which all activity can be referred'.[12]

These ideas are very important in so far as they concur with Heidegger's conclusion that measurable time-space is derived – that is, *imposed* on time-space relations in Western culture – and should not therefore be confused with the nature of time-space as such. The circumstance that we recognise intervals of both time and space, and can measure them, has often cropped up in philosophical discussions of time-space.[13] The calculation or measurement of time and space have been taken to express their essential character. Time is thus presumed to be composed of 'instants', a space of 'points'. Since (in the terms of Zeno's paradox) every instant can be subdivided without end, it has often been supposed that time may be spoken of as composed of 'durationless instants', space as composed of 'dimensionless points'. In speaking of the 'saddleback of time', and replacing instants or points by intervals, William James and others tried to escape from these apparently paradoxical elements. The trouble with replacing the conception of instants with that of intervals was that it took over too much of the view it sought to supplant, supposing that the essence of time-space is to be found in its 'mensurability'. Each interval on the line of time-duration would seem to be durationless, thus reintroducing the notion of 'instant'.[14] To overcome this kind of difficulty we have to acknowledge, following Heidegger, that intervals are not instants, and neither is time-space 'composed' of them. Rather, intervals are *structured differences* that give form to content, whether this be hours on a clock, notes in a musical rhythm, or centimetres on a ruler. To say this, in other words, is to reaffirm time-space as 'presencing', rather than as 'contentless form' in which objects exist.

## Time and Consciousness

The temporality of *Dasein*, the human being, and that of the institutions of society in the *longue durée*, are grounded in the constitutive temporality of all Being. '*Dasein*,' as Heidegger points out, 'is not "temporal" because it "stands in history" . . . on the contrary, it exists historically and can so exist only because it is temporal in the very basis of its Being.'[15] But as compared with material objects, there are at least five major features of the human subject that distinguish human existence as peculiarly historical. (These are all in some part noted by Heidegger, but at this juncture I shall depart from Heidegger's own presentation where necessary.)

(1) The temporality of *Dasein* is finite, as a being that is born, lives and dies. This characteristic is shared, of course, with the animals. But only human beings live their lives in awareness of their own finitude. From the sociological point of view, the significance of the finitude of the individual human being is bound up with the complex relation between the emergence and sustaining of a 'subject' – an individual who is an 'I' interacting with others – and the *longue durée* of institutional time. Heidegger's conception of *Sein zum Tode*, however, is potentially misleading in two respects. One is that it concentrates too resolutely upon the individual as a 'futural' being, 'free for its own death', rather than seeing death (of others) as an everyday fact for those who go on living. The result is not only a moral philosophy of 'authenticity' and 'care' which has severe limitations,[16] but (from the point of view of sociological analysis) a failure to see the importance of the problem of the *generations* – of how the dead make their influence felt upon the practices of the living. Another possible shortcoming of Heidegger's conception, not unrelated to the first, is that it appears ethnocentric, excessively influenced by Western notions of death and guilt. Where death, for example, is a transition in an external cycle of rebirth, its relation to the

'authenticity' of life might be quite different from an outlook which has its roots in Judeao-Christian traditions. But however the relation between life and death be conceived, awareness of the finitude of the organic life-span is undoubtedly everywhere an anchoring feature of time-consciousness.

(2) The human agent, as a routine feature of the *durée* of day-to-day life in society, transcends the immediacy of sensory experience. The chronic interpenetration of presence and absence, the symbolic interpolation of the absent within the presence of the continuity of everyday activities, is a peculiar characteristic of human social life, as contrasted to that of the animals. Memory, of course, is not unique to the human organism. But the possession of a syntactically and semantically elaborated language permits, indeed demands, a transcendance of presence vastly greater than that open to any of the animal species. When we speak of 'memory', as Halbwachs pointed out long ago,[17] we should not think only of traces of past experiences in the brain of the individual. All societies have institutional forms which persist across the generations, and which 'shape' past experiences that date back well beyond the life of any particular individual. Understood as social *storage capacity* (one main basis of what I shall call 'surveillance'), I shall have a good deal to say about this later, and shall relate it to mechanisms of domination. So far as the individual's day-to-day experience of, and participation in the constitution of, social life is concerned, it is useful to employ Schutz's concept of 'shifting relevances'. A person's cognitive activity can be regarded as involving an interweaving of short-term purposes and longer-term projects. Long-term projects are often 'held in suspense', or lie dormant in the varied contexts of daily life; they nevertheless help to give over-all phenomenal 'shape' to the individual's existence. It is very important to understand that the *durée* of day-to-day existence is not composed of an aggregation of reasons, purposes, etc. A large amount of the literature concerned with the philosophy of action ignores the flow of daily experiences, and proceeds as though reasons and purposes are discrete 'components of consciousness'. However, as Schutz points out, we must recognise that the identification of 'a' purpose or reason for 'an' act presupposes a 'reflexive moment of attention' directed retrospectively at the flow of experience.[18] This is why I speak of the *reflexive monitoring of action* and the *rationalisation*

*of action* as chronic, processual features of human behaviour. These are crucial to practical consciousness; all (competent) actors in a society are expected to 'keep in touch' with why they act as they do, as a routine element of action, such that they can 'account' for what they do when asked to do so by others.

(3) The existence of the human being in society, as Marx made clear, is above all *historical*. Human beings do not just live in time, they have an awareness of the passing of time which is incorporated in the nature of their social institutions. This stands in the closest connection to the transformative capacity of human action; lacking a defined apparatus of instincts, human beings are 'forced' to master the material world in order to survive in it. Awareness of the passing of time, as the debate between Lévi-Strauss and Sartre has made clear, should not be equated with *historicity*, which is itself a creation of history and is probably specific to the modern West. By 'historicity' is meant a definite kind of time-consciousness, namely that human social energies can be actively controlled to promote progressive social change in a 'linear' fashion across time. This stands in strict contrast to what Lévi-Strauss calls 'reversible' time, characteristic of 'cold cultures'. The consolidation of historicity as a prevalent form of time-consciousness in the West has undoubtedly been closely associated with the invention of the clock; but more generally is expressed in a long-standing conceptual differentiation of 'time' in Western culture as an abstract quality. Most small-scale 'primitive' societies seem to lack such an abstract conception of time (or of space either). According to Evans-Pritchard, for example,

> strictly speaking the Nuer have no concept of time and, consequently, no developed abstract system of time-reckoning ... there is no equivalent expression in the Nuer language for our word 'time', and ... they cannot, therefore, as we can, speak of time as though it were something actual, which passes, can be wasted, can be saved, and so forth ... Certainly they never experience the same feeling of fighting against time, of having to co-ordinate activities with an abstract passing of time, since their points of reference are mainly the activities themselves, which are generally of a leisurely and routine character.[19]

(4) The time-experience of the human individual in society cannot only be grasped on the level of the intentionality of consciousness. There are internal 'storage' mechanisms in personality which are distinct from the 'recallable' traces comprising memory as such. That is to say, traces of the early experiences of the infant, involved in the formation of a 'basic security system' prior to a developed mastery of language, plus repressed ideational elements, link past with present on the level of the unconscious. The 'stratification' of personality is a temporal stratification, but one which also is intrinsically involved with the current activities of the social actor. The basic security system, or 'internal tension-management' system of personality, as I have tried to show in a previous study,[20] remains largely latent so long as the social frameworks within which the individual moves serve to sustain a sense of 'ontological security'. The *routinisation* of day-to-day life, most profoundly anchored in the 'deep' traditions of 'reversible time', is the single most important source of ontological security.

(5) It follows from what has been said about time-space relations in general that discussion of temporality can best be approached through grasping the interpenetration of presence or absence, the movement of individuals through time-space being seen as processes of 'presencing/absencing'. Different processes of presencing and absencing are achieved in the human body, its media of sensory interchange with the world and others, and the extensions of those media made possible by varying forms of technology. To stress this is a necessary corrective both to the Anglo-American philosophy of action and Heidegger's hermeneutic phenomenology, neither of which gives emphasis to the body as the focus of presence – although Heidegger's conception of the 'ready-to-hand' does relate to the manipulable aspects of the immediate environment of the person.

## Time-Space, Presence, Absence

As Hägerstrand points out, both the daily life of the individual and his or her over-all life's activity can be represented as 'a weaving dance through time-space'.[21] The term 'weaving dance', however, is a bit misleading, since most day-to-day life, as I have emphasised, is strongly routinised. It is the routinised, or largely taken-for-granted, character of life in society, in most contexts of time and place, which gives meaning to the phrases 'daily life' or 'day-to-day life' as a regular round of activities. In all societies the vast bulk of daily activity consists of habitual practices, in which individuals move through definite 'stations' in time-space.[22]

In recent years geographical authors have come up with a number of useful devices for analysing the time-space movements of individuals and collectivities. Thus Janelle, for example, has sought to chart locational changes in 'time-space convergence' between communities. The rate at which two cities are converging in time-space can be calculated by comparing, say, the length of an average journey by stage-coach between Edinburgh and London in 1780 with the length of the same journey made by aeroplane in 1980.[23] The time-space convergence effected by modern modes of transport is obviously one way of describing the 'implosion' of world society. But in spite of the emergence of such ideas, and of the importance of Hägerstrand's time-geography, I think it true to say that there is a lack of concepts which would make space, and control of space, integral to social theory.

In my view the most appropriate way of attempting to develop such concepts is by concentrating upon aspects and modalities of presence and absence in human social relations. Presence is a time-space notion, just as absence can refer to 'distances' in both time and space from a particular set of experiences or events. 'Presence', as both Heidegger and, following him, Derrida have made clear, should be understood neither as 'given object' nor as 'given experience'. Derrida's critique of the 'metaphysics of presence' must be listened to with some respect even though there are some major objections which can be brought against it.[24]

All social interaction, like any other type of event, occurs across time and space. All social interaction intermingles presence and absence. Such intermingling is always both complicated and subtle, and can be taken to express modes in which structures are drawn upon to incorporate the long-term *durée* of institutions within the contingent social act. Structures convey time across time-space distances of indeterminate length. In those societies which possess no writing, where there exists no physical 'imprint' of past time, the past is contained in the deep impress which tradition holds over the routinisation of daily experiences. But the symbolic mark, writing, is incomparably the most potent means of extending experience in time-space; by the same token, the advent of writing concretises certain basic dilemmas of hermeneutics alien to purely oral cultures.[25]

The human brain is, among other things, a storage device that contains both traces of past experiences and also the capabilities sustaining the reproduction of social systems. It would be a mistake, as I have previously pointed out, to think of memory as solely a record of personal experience (accurate or inaccurate). In all societies, including oral cultures, the memory traces of the individual incorporate past experiences of the collectivity. In oral cultures past–present relations are controlled by all members of the collectivity, who reproduce them in and through their mastery of the traditions embodied in the practices of the group. Of course, there are often 'specialists' in the elaboration of myth and legend, and in the spinning of stories. Such specialists may sustain their skills through a certain measure of secrecy *vis-à-vis* the rest of the community, particularly where these skills are associated with magical powers. With the advent of writing, or more generally the codification of words and numbers, the past can be *stacked* (tablets, files, documents, libraries, computer banks).

The concept of *presence-availability*[26] links memory (storage) and spatial distribution in the time-space constitution of social systems. All collectivities have defined *locales* of operation: physical settings associated with the 'typical interactions' composing those collectivities as social systems. I prefer the term 'locale' to that of 'place', more commonly used by geographers, because it is more than merely a 'positional' term. The locales of collectivities are integrally involved with the structural constitution of social systems, since common awareness of properties of the setting of interaction is a vital element involved in the sustaining of meaningful communication between actors (as indexical features of communication). I have drawn attention elsewhere to the importance of this for semantic analysis.[27] Locales may range from confined settings – the dwelling, office, factory, etc. – up to the large-scale territorial aggregations of nation-states or empires. A locale may be understood in time-space in terms of presence-availability. The 'small' community can be defined as one in which there is characteristically only a short distance in the time-space 'meshing' of interaction. The interactions constituting the social system are 'close' in both time and space: the presence of others is readily *available* on a direct face-to-face basis. Locales are normally *regionalised* on a time-space basis. By 'regions' within locales I mean aspects of the settings which are normatively implicated in systems of interaction, such that they are in some way 'set apart', for certain individuals, or types of individuals, or for certain activities or types of activities.[28]

I mean to use the concepts of presence-availability, locale and region or regionalisation with very general applicability. A 'home' or 'household', for example, may be analysed in terms of its time-space constitution by means of these notions. A home is typically a small-scale locale, with presence-availability of short distance, and – in modern Western societies at least – strongly regionalised internally by modes of activity. Rooms are usually categorised in respect of their characteristic usage in time-space, as 'living rooms', 'kitchens', 'bedrooms', etc. Larger-scale locales, such as cities, may be similarly analysed (and, of course, are composed of households plus other locales). The regionalisation of cities, it can be argued, under the influence of relatively free housing markets, is a major phenomenon involved in class structuration.[29] The same may be argued of the differentiation of the 'office' from the 'shop floor' in industrial organisations, and of course a multiplicity of other examples of time-space regionalisation could be offered as illustrative.

The shifting nature of the relations between the expansion of interaction over space and its contraction over time is obviously part and parcel of the 'time-space convergence' so prominent in the development of the contemporary social world. The global nature of social interaction in the modern era has gone along with the invention of new media reducing the distances involved in presence-availability. The telephone, and television video techniques, do not of course achieve the full presence of parties to interaction characteristic of ordinary 'face-to-face' encounters, but they do permit immediacy of time contact across indefinite spatial distances.

It is not my intention in this book to attempt to detail topological models for social analysis, important and interesting a task though this is in social theory – and one as yet only in a relatively rudimentary state of development. But two aspects of the regionalisation of locales are worth drawing particular attention to. One is that regionalisation is quite often closely associated with the episodic character of social interaction.[30] The *durée* of interaction is typically reflexively categorised by participants, and can also be so categorised by sociological observers, as a series of episodes that have beginnings and endings, or 'openings' and 'closings' in time-space. Episodes, of course, like the purposes and projects with which they are intertwined in the phenomenal experience of interaction, have overlapping time-space 'lengths'. That is why the term 'episode', or 'episodic characterisation', can be applied to trivial encounters equally well as to large-scale processes of institutional change.

Second, the regionalisation of locales is important in the concealment or visibility of social practices, a phenomenon of no small significance for the analysis of power relations. One mode of conceptualising the regional concealment/visibility of forms of social interaction, or episodes, is the differentiation of front and back regions suggested by Goffman. Many episodes are in some part 'staged performances' in which attitudes and behaviour are 'managed' in the front region in respect of those who form an 'audience' in the encounter in question. Goffman's own discussions of the management of performances in front regions are mostly concerned with small-scale locales, and take their examples from the contexts of Western societies.[31] But there is no reason to confine their application in either of these ways, however much it may be the case that certain features of the 'presentation of self' are peculiarly modern.

However, forms of regional visibility/concealment of social practices do not operate only in terms of the differentiation of front from back regions; and the modes of such operation are by no means always deliberately 'staged'.

## Institution, Collectivity, Society

I use the term 'social system' as equivalent to 'group' or 'collectivity'. 'Social system' has some advantages over the latter two terms, however, in so far as it is more precise; the 'systemic' nature of relations of interaction can be examined from various different aspects, and may take various guises.[32] Social systems are composed of interactions, regularised as social practices, the most persisting of these being institutions. These distinctions and relations are easy enough to formulate in an abstract vein, but how do they connect with that traditional focus of sociological concern: 'society'? How are we to conceptualise 'a society'?

We can first of all dispose of a relatively trivial issue, of a terminological sort. Some Marxist authors have held that the term 'society' should not be employed in social analysis, preferring to substitute for it the term 'social formation'. Nothing is gained by this tactic, however, unless the conceptual content of the latter term is made clear. The notion of 'society' has frequently been used in sociology in ways which I wish to reject; but so also has 'social formation'. I shall continue to speak of 'society', or (more accurately) 'societies', in this text, but I want to make my usage unambiguously distinct from various others. To put the matter specifically, there are three general conceptions of society which I propose to repudiate: that which portrays it as a system of 'functionally related parts' – a view found both in academic sociology and in Marxist writings; that which sees it as an 'expressive totality', the sort of view taken principally by authors influenced by Hegel; and that which regards it as a unity of 'levels' or 'instances', the standpoint most particularly associated with Althusser and his followers.

There are numerous objections which can be made against the familiar view that a society is a 'functional unity of parts', a view which has nearly always been more or less closely associated with the presumption that society can be compared with a biological organism. Some aspects, or versions, of this type of conception of society have been effectively criticised by functionalist writers themselves, most notably by R. K. Merton.[33] Merton's account of functionalism remains probably the most sophisticated general discussion of functional analysis.[34] But quite apart from the criticisms which can be made of any standpoint which depends upon the notion of function, Merton's critique of the 'postulate of the functional unity of society' fails to replace that postulate with any other interpretation of how a society might be regarded as a unity. His concept of a 'net balance of functional consequences', to be traced out in social analysis as the outcome of integrative versus disintegrative tendencies ('functions' versus 'dysfunctions'), does not answer the question of how society is to be conceptualised as a totality.

The idea that society forms an 'expressive totality' is in some respects quite different from the view of society as a functional unity, but there is one general resemblance between them. In both cases there is a fairly strong emphasis that societies (of all types) are unified by a coherent *consensus universel*. Each, in other words, tends to look to normative consensus as the main basis of the unity of the totality, society. But the mode in which this unity is understood is quite distinct in the two. Those who treat society as an expressive totality see the 'whole' as being in some sense present in its 'parts', whole and parts being connected in a dialectical relation. Thus Sartre says: 'A totality is defined as a being which, while radically distinct from the sum of its parts, is present in its entirety, in one form or another, in each of these parts, and which relates to itself either through its relation to one or more of its parts or through its relation to the relations between all or some of them.'[35] Although this sort of standpoint has been occasionally caricatured by Althusser, it has also been justifiably criticised by him. To trace the unity of a society to 'presence' alone – the expression of the 'whole' in the 'moment' –fails to generate a model of society which adequately recognises the disjunctures that exist in real societies, the strains or contradictions between different levels of the over-all social system.[36]

According to Althusser, the conception of society as an expressive totality cannot recognise the existence of 'structures of dominance, which is the absolute precondition for a real complexity to be a unity'.[37] For Althusser, social formations are 'overdetermined' wholes, characterised by the articulation of three 'levels': the economic, political and ideological. The economic level, 'in the last instance', determines the other two levels, but is at the same time overdetermined by them. A distinction is made between which level in a social formation is 'determinant' (in all cases, the economic) and which is 'dominant' (which may be either of the others). The economic level is not an 'essence', expressed in all other aspects of society, as (in Althusser's view) is the case in Marxist versions of the notion of an 'expressive totality'. Nor does the economic infrastructure simply determine or 'cause' the development of superstructures, as in 'economistic' versions of Marxism. The relation between the levels of a social formation is expressed instead in terms of what Althusser calls structural or 'metonymic' causality, which means that 'the structure is imminent in its effects'.[38]

The Althusserian view of the composition of social formations, since it is self-professedly developed as a resolution of the base/superstructure problem in Marxist thought, raises issues which are not necessarily posed by the first two conceptions of society. I shall put aside discussion of whether the differentiation between 'determinant' and 'dominant' instances can be sustained, depending as it does upon the conception of the 'last instance'. I shall simply assert that I do not believe it can be sustained. Althusser's conception of the totality is important, as contrasted to the two former interpretations, because it regards societies as more fractured or 'unevenly formed' than the others tend to do. But I do not think any of the main constituents of Althusser's analysis are adequately formulated: his idea of overdetermination; his exposition of 'metonymic causality'; or the thesis that the chief institutional orders of society are the economic, political and ideological. I shall make no attempt here to consider each of these in an exhaustive fashion, but shall consider only the following questions: (1) What sense can be given to the 'whole'/'part' relation in the structuring of societies? (2) What gives unity to a society, or (alternatively expressed) what makes a society worth calling *a* society, distinct from others? (3) How should the major institutions of society be categorised, or classified, in a generic way?

(1) Each of the three conceptions of society mentioned above suffers from failing to distinguish structure from system in the constitution of the totality. Functionalist theories conceive a society as a system of 'present' parts, analogous to the parts of an organic system. What is lacking in this view, in addition to deficiencies previously noted, is the idea of the duality of structure as 'binding' the interplay of absence and presence in the *durée* of social interaction. This is indeed a notion which links the moments or instantiations of social activity to properties of collectivities or social wholes (the structural properties of social systems). The moment/totality relation presumed here, however, is not an 'expressive one': that is to say, the 'part' does not in any sense 'contain' the whole, or even 'express' the whole. Nor is it a causal one, as Althusser argues. The recursive relation of moment and totality in the theory of structuration in fact *is best not seen as a part/whole relation at all*: the 'parts' of society are regularised

social practices, organised as social systems. In analysing point (2) below we have to consider what makes some social systems 'inclusive' enough to be called 'societies'.

(2) All societies *are* both social systems and also *consist* of social systems (structured in time-space). Of course, if the term 'society' is to be defined broadly enough to encompass both small or 'primitive' communities and very large-scale systems, we have to overlook some quite profound differences in modes of societal integration – differences which I shall be concerned with exploring in some part later in this book. I am offering here, therefore, a 'minimum' definition of a societal totality. Such a definition has to be understood against the background of the general account of the structuration of social systems set out previously, and the argument expressed in point (1) above.

A social system may be said to be a society or a societal totality if it embodies an intermingling of the following criteria:

(a) The association of the system with a locale comprising a 'social space' or 'territory of occupation'. Such a locale does not have to be a fixed, immobile area; still less does it necessarily involve the clearly demarcated boundaries characteristic of modern nation-states. Thus nomadic societies occupy definite, if only diffusely bounded, social spaces which they lay claim to, even if only in a temporary way. Most nomadic societies actually do not move in a random fashion, but along regular periodic time-space 'paths'.

(b) As the phrase 'lay claim to' implies, the sustaining of a *legitimated* series of prerogatives over occupied social space: especially the prerogative of the use of the material environment to provide sources of food, water and shelter.

(c) An 'institutional clustering' of practices among the participants in the social system, sustained through mechanisms of social/system integration. It is very important to emphasise again that integration should not be equated with a consensual acceptance of a 'common value system', though this is not precluded. A clustering of practices may be manifest even where there is considerable dissensus, or divergence of attitude and belief, among the members of the society (in terms of both discursive and practical consciousness).

(d) An over-all awareness, discursive and practical, of belonging to an inclusive community with a certain 'identity'. Two elements need stressing here. First, some accentuation of the term 'inclusive' is needed. A 'societal identity' tends to be an 'outer limit' of affiliation with others: it may often go wider than, although not necessarily be more strongly *felt* than, other more restricted group identifications. Second, we have once more to avoid the necessary presumption of consensus: consciousness that a collectivity has a certain identity, and that one is a member of that collectivity, is not the same as according it normative approval.

Certain qualifications have to be made about these criteria. First of all, *there are very few, if any, societies which have ever existed in isolation from others*; this applies to small-scale 'primitive' societal communities just as to modern nation-states, notwithstanding the common tendency of anthropological fieldwork to concentrate attention upon single societies. Second, although the study of varying types of societies and the relations between societies comprises a prime focus of sociological interest, it is obviously by no means the sole one. Many other types of structured collectivity, from dyadic associations up to large organisations, as well as relations which cut across societal totalities (such as, in modern times, between transnational corporations), can of course be the subject of sociological investigation. Third, of the four features of the existence of a society identified above, I give particular importance to the 'clustering' of institutions.

(3) Althusser distinguishes three 'levels' in a social formation. As critics have pointed out, it is by no means precisely clear how the term 'level' (or 'instance') is to be understood; nor is it evident why the three in question are regarded as the basic constituent elements of every form of society. At any rate, I shall not speak in this connection of 'levels', but rather of *types of institution*; and the classification of institutions I shall propose departs substantially from Althusser's threefold scheme.

A classification of institutions applicable to all types of society must be derived, in my opinion, from an analysis of the structural characteristics universally implicated in human interaction. I have tried to provide such an analysis in other sources,[39] and draw heavily upon these here. All human interaction involves the communication of meaning, the operation of power, and modes of normative sanctioning. These are constitutive of interaction. In the production of interaction actors draw upon and reproduce corresponding structural properties of social systems: *signification, domination* and *legitimation*. The resources constituting structures of domination are of two types, which I call *authorisation* and *allocation*: the former of these refers to capabilities generating command over persons, the second command over objects or material phenomena. These four structural features are implicated in the reproduction of all social systems, and simultaneously supply the basic logic for a classification of institutions. Such a logic expresses the moment/totality relation, providing a basic institutional categorisation which at the same time recognises the interrelation of structural components within concrete social systems or societies.

This institutional categorisation can be represented in the following way:

| | |
|---|---|
| $S - D - L$ | Symbolic orders/modes of discourse |
| $D(\text{auth}) - S - L$ | Political institutions |
| $D(\text{alloc}) - S - L$ | Economic institutions |
| $L - D - S$ | Law/modes of sanction |

where $S$ = signification, $D$ = domination, and $L$ = legitimation.

I use the term 'ideological' in a different way to Althusser, not to refer to signification as such, but as a concept linked to the critique of domination;[40] consequently, it does not appear in the above classificatory scheme. The dashes linking different sequences of $S$, $D$ and $L$ above indicate four different possible directions of institutional focus in studying societies. To analyse the institutional forms through which signification is organised is to analyse symbolic orders and modes of discourse; such an analysis must, however, also consider how symbol orders and modes of discourse interconnect with forms of domination and legitimation. The same argument applies to the other types of institution.

The above scheme indicates that there are symbolic, political, economic, and legal/repressive institutional elements in all societies. This leaves open, of course, room for wide variations in the articulation of collectivities in different forms of society in respect of institutionalisation. Two aspects of such articulation can be distinguished (these tend to be merged by Althusser and his followers). One is how far a society contains distinct spheres of 'specialism' in respect of institutional orders: differentiated forms of symbolic order (religion, science, etc.); a differentiated 'polity', 'economy', and legal/repressive apparatus.[41] The second is how modes of institutional articulation are organised in terms of over-all properties of societal reproduction: that is to say, 'structural principles'.

# 2

# Domination, Power and Exploitation: an Analysis

## Domination/Power Relations

One of the main emphases of the theory of structuration is that power is routinely involved in the instantiation of social practices. I advance this view in opposition to a prevalent tendency in sociology, common to various otherwise opposed schools of thought, to reduce power to a secondary characteristic of social life. Such is the case both with the various forms of 'interpretative sociology' and with 'normative functionalism', which treat the communication of meaning and normative sanctions respectively as the most fundamental components of social activity.

The interpolation of power as an inherent component of the constitution of interaction demands the overcoming of a dualism in established theories of power related to traditional subject/object dualism in philosophy and sociology. On the other hand, we find a range of conceptions of power, of which Max Weber's is the most widely employed, which treat power as the capability of an actor to achieve desired ends or goals. On the other hand, there are various notions of power which regard power above all as a property of collectivities: modern versions of this sort of standpoint include those developed by Parsons and Foucault. Each is associated with differing ideas of what *domination* is, and how it should be studied. Although Weber himself could not be included in this, many of those who have used his, or similar, conceptualisations of power have equated domination with 'decision-networks'. Domination is seen as expressed in the capabilities of networks of individual 'decision-makers' to realise their objectives in a particular range of serial contexts. One of the specific weaknesses of this sort of approach is that it is unable to cope with structural features of power, as involved in taken-for-granted spheres of 'non-decision-making'. The second approach, by contrast, tends to regard domination as expressing the structured properties of social systems. Its characteristic limitation is that power is seen as determined by, or emanating from, structures, rather than as operating in and through human action.[1]

If, however, we understand the couplet domination/power in the light of the duality of structure, the two approaches can be seen to be complementary. Resources treated as structural elements of social systems are drawn upon by actors in the instantiation of interaction. The power relations sustained in the regularised practices constituting social systems can be considered as *reproduced relations of autonomy and dependence in interaction*. *Domination* refers to structured asymmetries of resources drawn upon and reconstituted in such power relations. 'Domination' here is used in the sense of 'permitting dominion over', 'dominion' concerning the sway actors have over others, and over the material world they inhabit.

In social theory the term 'domination' is often used in a negative fashion, with the implication that it is an inherently noxious phenomenon. I shall not use the concept in such a way. The tendency to regard domination as inherently negative, and as intrinsically inimical to freedom of action on the part of those subject to it, is closely related politically to the idea that power is inherently *coercive*, and that its use inevitably implies the existence of *conflict*. Neither of these ideas withstands close scrutiny:[2] each usually reflects the assumption that power is not an integral and primary aspect of social life. There is, however, a contrasting thesis which does not see power as inherently coercive and conflictful, but which actually over-radicalises the role of power in social life, seeing social life as essentially formed by struggles for power. Foucault, I think, argues in this vein. None the less, his discussion of the concept of power is relevant here:

> If power were never anything but repressive [he asks] if it never did anything but say no, do you really think we should manage to obey it? What gives power its hold, what makes it accepted, is quite simply the fact that it does not just weigh like a force which says no, but that it runs through, and it produces things, it

induces pleasure, it forms knowledge, it produces discourse; it must be considered as a productive network which runs through the entire social body much more than a negative instance whose function is repression.[3]

Much the same point is made by Parsons in his various discussions of power, save that, unlike Foucault, he does not sufficiently emphasise that power is a double-edged phenomenon: that repression and coercion *are* prominent features of the operation of power.[4] At the heart of both domination and power lies the *transformative capacity* of human action, the origin of all that is liberating and productive in social life as well as all that is repressive and destructive.

In working out the main parameters of domination in society it is first of all necessary to indicate the chief types of resource drawn upon in power relations. I have claimed earlier that it is useful to distinguish *authorisation* from *allocation*. I mean this to be a wholly analytical distinction, as with the subdivisions of this basic differentiation I shall now propose. Domination, as a structural feature of social systems, always operates in conjunction with signification and legitimation in the concrete contexts of social life.

Allocation refers to man's capabilities of controlling not just 'objects' but the *object-world*. Domination from this aspect refers to human dominion over nature. Authorisation refers to man's capabilities of controlling the humanly created world of *society itself*. The major forms of allocative resource found in any society can be said to be as follows:

(a) Material features of the environment (raw materials, material power sources).
(b) Means of material production/reproduction (instruments of production, technology).
(c) Produced goods (artefacts created by the interaction of (a) and (b)).

The major forms of authoritative resource found in any society can be identified as follows:

(a) Organisation of social time-space (the temporal-spatial constitution of society).

(b) Production/reproduction of the human body (organisation and relations of human beings in society).
(c) Organisation of human life-chances (constitution of chances of self-development and self-expression).

None of these is a fixed resource, but all vary in different types of society: they are the media of the 'expandable' character of power within the societal totality. The three forms of authoritative resource are less self-explanatory than the allocative resources. By the 'organisation of social time-space', I refer to the localisation of practices in a society, where 'locale' is understood in the sense specified in the preceeding chapter. By the 'production/reproduction of the human body' I mean what Bertaux calls the 'anthroponomic' components of human society:[5] the distribution of human beings in society across time-space. Under (c), the 'organisation of life-chances', I mean the distribution of the capabilities of actors to achieve particular styles of life or modes of self-realisation in definite types of society. The forms of authoritative resource, like allocative resources, are not 'possessed' by individual social actors but are features of the societal totality. Like other structural characteristics of social systems, however, they only exist as resources in and through the very structuration of society which they facilitate or help to make possible. Taken together, the allocative and authoritative resources specified above are constitutive of the societal totality as a structured system of domination.

Thus far, of course, this scheme suggests only the barest outlines of a theory of domination and power. The resources indicated above have to be related both to the other elements of structure (signification and legitimation) and to several of the major concepts sketched out in Chapter 1. To connect the two types of resources to signification implies recognising their interlinking with the meaningful and normative components of society; this yields two aspects of domination in the structuring of social systems, *property* (allocative resources) and *authority* (authoritative resources). I shall analyse these in more detail later; both, however, obviously involve the mobilisation of *cognitively acknowledged* and *normatively sanctioned* resources within the institutional ordering of society.

**Transformation/Mediation**

Social systems are constituted of the situated practices of actors, and always express a 'mix' of intended and unintended conse-quences of action, reproduced in discernible patterns across time-space. While in the duality of structure, structure is treated as the medium and outcome of such situated practices, for purposes of *institutional analysis* (as mentioned previously) we may bracket intentional action, concentrating attention upon chronically repro-duced characteristics of social systems.

Structures can be analysed in terms of the transformations and mediations in human activity through which they are in turn sustained. *Transformation* and *mediation*: the two most essential characteristics of human social life. Transformative capacity, as mentioned earlier, forms the basis of human action – the 'could have done otherwise' inherent in the concept of action – and at the same time connects action to domination and power. Mediation expresses the variety of ways in which, in social systems, interac-tion is made possible across space and time. All interaction is 'carried' across time and space by media, organised structurally: ranging from the direct consciousness of others in face-to-face encounters to the modes in which institutions are sedimented in deep historical time, and in which social interaction is carried on across broad areas of global space. In the theory of structuration, transformation/mediation relations, as embodied in concrete social practices in definite forms of society, take the place of the concept of 'labour' as traditionally invoked in many versions of 'historical materialism'.[6] (Much more will be said about this subsequently.) To relate the 'real' transformations of the world implied in power relations to the 'transformational' nature of structures is not mere word play; on the contrary, the two senses of transformation are necessarily directly tied to one another by emphasising that structure consists of rules *and* resources. The substitution of transformation/mediation relations for 'labour' underlines the centrality of the Marxian notion of *Praxis* to social theory, without accepting the elision of labour and *Praxis* that is frequently made. I take *Praxis* to be an ontological term, expressing a fundamental trait of human social existence. To speak of human social activity as *Praxis* is to reject every conception of human beings as 'determined objects' or as unambiguously 'free subjects'. All human action is carried on by knowledgeable agents who both construct the social world through their action, but yet whose action is also conditioned or constrained by the very world of their creation. In constituting and reconstituting the social world, human beings at the same time are involved in an active interplay with nature, in which they both modify nature and themselves. In Hegel, 'labour' is used as an ontological idea in just this way; in Marx this very generalised notion of 'labour' is not always clearly distinguished from the more concrete sense of labour as the material production of goods. But it is important to differentiate one from the other in assessing Marx's 'historical materialism' – for I want to *accept* a 'materialist conception of history' *only* in the sense of accentuating the importance of *Praxis* as integral to human social life. I have very strong reservations, as I shall make clear, about the 'materialist conception of history', where that phrase is taken to mean that economic production or 'the economy' has a determinant role in historical change as a whole.

In institutional analysis we can distinguish three levels of abstraction in portraying transformation/mediation relations, as indicated in Figure 2.1.

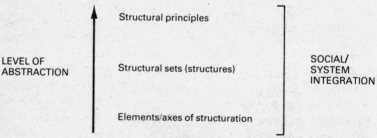

FIGURE 2.1

(a) The formulation of structural principles represents the highest level of abstraction of institutional analysis. To study the structural principles involved in the reproduction of a society across time-space is to analyse the modes of differentiation and articulation of the institutions which constitute that society. Structural principles are principles of organisation implicated in those practices most 'deeply' (in time) and 'pervasively' (in space) sedimented in a society. It is on this level that we have to analyse the 'base/superstructure' problem as a historical, rather than ontological, feature of the 'materialist conception of history'. The analysis of structural principles is closely bound up with questions of how societies should be typified or characterised.

(b) Less encompassing structural properties of societal systems can be studied as sets of rules and resources, specified in terms of 'clusterings' of transformation/mediation relations. Such structural relations are inevitably implied by more abstract analyses of structural principles. Transformation/mediation relations on this level can best be expressed as the mutual *convertibility* of rules and resources implicated in social reproduction. That complex of rules and resources we call 'money' provides a good illustration. Money, especially in developed 'money economies', meshes together an indefinite range of otherwise incommensurable phenomena, gearing them into reproduction cycles: the 'cycle of capital', famously described by Marx in the second volume of *Capital*, specifies the implications of this for some of the fundamental features of capitalism.

(c) On a more concrete level, the structural properties of institutionalised practices can be examined as elements or 'axes' of structuration. In *The Class Structure of the Advanced Societies* I distinguished various elements of class structuration. In arguing, for example, that the division of labour within the enterprise is a source of class structuration – among others – I wanted to indicate how the division of labour is centrally involved in the reproduction of class relations.[7] Like (a) and (b), this preserves an *epoché* upon intentional or strategic action, and treats structuration as the expression of 'impersonal' connections between structural properties.

Domination needs to be analysed on each of these three levels. In analysing structural principles involved in domination we are hence concerned with studying over-all interconnections between property and authority in the long-term reproduction of societies. In focusing upon structures of domination we are concerned with isolating sets of transformation/mediation relations which 'underlie' structural principles. Analysing domination from the third aspect involves identifying the major axes of structuration of power relations in a society. In case of misunderstanding, it should be explained that the differentiation of these three levels of institutional analysis is methodological, as is the differentiation of institutional analysis from the analysis of strategic conduct. There are no clear-cut boundaries separating them: each 'shades off' into the other on a gradation of increasing abstraction.

## Domination and Sanctions

Domination and power have to be separated conceptually from the sanctions connected with them. Like power, sanctions – or (more accurately) forms of sanctioning – have to be understood as chronic features of social activity. Sanctioning is anchored in the normative components of social interaction. The Parsonian conception of the 'double contingency' of interaction is very useful in grasping this. Interaction is constituted of the reactions of one actor to another and vice versa: the (contingent) responses of one actor are dependent upon the (contingent) responses of another or others. The activity of each person works as a sanction upon the conduct of the other. Most such sanctions operate on a taken-for-granted level, as (for instance) in the reproduction of language in and through everyday verbal discourse. Durkheim was right to argue that there are constraints built into the very fabric of social activity, integral to its nature (in his earlier writings he used 'constraint' interchangeably with 'coercion'). He was also right to point out that such constraints are not generally felt as such by those subject to them, because they are routinised features of day-to-day life. However, there are two basic flaws in Durkheim's account. He did not see that constraint and enablement are two sides of one coin, such that any theory which links constraint to the structural properties of social systems must treat structure as both constraining and enabling. But in addition, like Parsons after him, he supposed that routinised features of social life *ipso facto* express 'internalised' motivational commitments corresponding to them. In fact, as I have tried to show in some detail elsewhere, large areas of routine social reproduction are in a specific sense 'unmotivated',[8] and in many other contexts social actors have 'calculative' attitudes towards normative sanctions, since they are indifferent or hostile to the commitments entailed by them. Both these criticisms bear directly upon the significance of power in social relations. The inherent connection between constraint and enablement in the operation of sanctions is an expression of the relation of action–power–structure within the duality of structure, and hence also expresses asymmetries of power deriving from structures of domination. 'Calculative' or 'manipulative' attitudes towards normative sanctions are in turn extremely important empirically, in the many circumstances in which legitimation is not effected through strong motivational affiliation to a particular normative order.

To make these arguments is not of course to deny that motivational commitments relate to the reproduction of normative sanctions. It is to place seriously in question the thesis expressed by both Durkheim and Parsons, i.e. that system integration is achieved above all by the 'internalisation' of common values by the majority of the members of a society. None the less, there is a further aspect of Durkheim's analysis of norms which must be recognised as valid: that sanctions are not merely constraining because of 'negative' features such as the guilt, or fear of punishment, stimulated by their transgression. In his earlier works, especially *The Rules of Sociological Method*, Durkheim did see the constraining quality of 'social facts' as operating in a purely negative fashion in this sense – which was why he used 'constraint' and 'coercion' indifferently as synonymous terms. But later in his career he came to the view that norms have both positive and negative aspects – as associated with guilt or fear, but also with rewards (of a psychological or material kind): sanctions operate through inducement as well as coercion.

Drawing upon the above discussion, we can formulate the representation of the mechanics of sanctioning as in Figure 2.2.

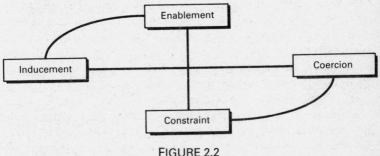

FIGURE 2.2

In this scheme the constraining and enabling aspects of sanctions are 'carried' through various possible interminglings of inducement and coercion. Inducement and coercion are no more exclusive of each other than are enablement and constraint. Desire has a compelling quality, just as coercion only has some hold over the action of those threatened by or subject to it because of its denial of positively valued attributes (in the case of violence, the preservation of life itself). The curved lines on the top-left and bottom-right sides of the diagram indicate two poles of sanctioning, with largely 'positive' elements concentrated in the combination of inducement and enablement, and 'negative' elements concentrated in the convergence of coercion and constraint. It should be pointed out that this scheme relates to the theory of structuration as a whole, not only to the level of institutional analysis. So far as institutional analysis is concerned, sanctions have to be studied in the conjunctions between legitimation and domination.

## The Problem of Exploitation

The problem of how exploitation should be conceptualised in social theory is of equivalent importance to that of how we should seek to analyse domination and power. Easily the most influential theory of exploitation in sociology is that of Marx, and this has to form the initial point of reference for any appraisal of the notion. In Marx, the question of exploitation (*exploitieren, ausbeuten*) is inevitably bound up with his over-all characterisation of the nature and development of class systems. In tribal societies, according to Marx, production and distribution are communal. In such societies the productive forces are relatively undeveloped; there is little or no surplus production. Classes only come into being with the expansion of the productive forces, such that a surplus is generated, appropriated by an emergent dominant class of non-producers. Class relations are hence inherently exploitative, since the ruling class lives off the surplus production of the subordinate class or classes. There is a major difference, according to Marx, between the exploitative relation involved between the two main capitalist classes and the class relations found in the prior types of class society, the Ancient world and feudalism. In the latter two types of society exploitation takes the form of the appropriation of the surplus labour by the dominant class. In the feudal *levée,* for example, the exploitative element is direct and open; a proportion of the production of the serf is taken by the *seigneur*. In capitalism exploitation is organised quite differently, and is concealed from view. The main task of *Capital* was precisely to solve the 'hidden riddle' of capitalist production: to show how an exploitative class relation is to be discovered at the very heart of the capitalistic production process. Capitalism, which for the first time in history severs the mass of the working population from immediate control of their means of production, turning them into 'formally free' wage-workers, is based upon the appropriation of surplus *value* by the dominant class. The 'hidden riddle' of capitalist production – that labour-power sells at its value and yet is still caught in an exploitative relation with capital – is deciphered through the identification of surplus labour-time as the source of profit accruing to capital.

I shall argue later in this book that the Marxian conception that, in capitalism, class relations intrude into the very centre of the production process is an extremely significant one. But I shall want to widen Marx's standpoint in so far as it involves the views that exploitation is (1) exclusively a feature of class relations, and (2) applicable only, within these confines, to human relationships. So far as (2) goes, I want to claim that the exploitation of nature cannot be treated as simply 'instrumental' or 'neutral' in regard of human interests. In Marx, nature appears above all as the medium of the realisation of human social development. The universal history of man is traced through the progressive elaboration of the productive forces, maximised in capitalism. It would not be true to say that from this standpoint nature is treated as merely inert or passive, since Marx emphasises that social development must be examined in terms of an active interplay between human beings and their material environment: 'By acting on the external world or changing it, [man] at the same time changes his own nature.'[9] But Marx's concern with transforming the exploitative human social relations expressed in class systems does not extend to the exploitation of nature. Certainly, in Marx's early writings, most notably in the *1844 Manuscripts,* one can find passages that suggest that nature is more than just the medium through which human history unfolds:

Nature is the inorganic body of man; that is to say nature, excluding the human body itself. To say that man *lives* from nature means that nature is his *body* with which he must remain in a continuous interchange in order not to die. The statement that the physical and mental life of man, and nature, are interdependent means simply that nature is interdependent with itself, for man is a part of nature.[10]

But the 'Promethean attitude' is always pre-eminent in Marx's writings, an attitude as unsurprising in the nineteenth century as it is indefensible in the twentieth century, when it has become apparent that the expansion of the productive forces can no longer be treated unproblematically as conducive to social progress.

Marx's linkage of exploitation to class domination is of course one aspect of the overriding importance he attributed to class and to class conflict. This again raises issues which will be analysed in subsequent chapters of this book, and which therefore have to be deferred for the time being. Here I shall simply assert that Marx tended to load the notions of class and class conflict with more conceptual burdens than they could possibly support. There are two aspects of this problem. One is the role Marx attributed to class in history, and the other, concomitant, issue is the question of what the 'classless' or socialist society will look like. If the exploitation of human beings by others begins with the first formation of class systems, then such exploitation will thereby disappear with the abolition of classes. But if, as I want to hold, exploitation exists before the emergence of class systems, and if within class systems not all forms of exploitation can be explained in terms of class domination, then the question of how exploitation can be transcended becomes correspondingly more complex.

I shall not deny that class relations are intrinsically exploitative, but shall suggest a more encompassing formulation of the notion of exploitation than that available in Marx. Exploitation, I want to propose, is most aptly conceptualised in relation to domination or *power*. In defining exploitation itself, we need not depart far from conventional English usage. According to the *Oxford English Dictionary*, 'to exploit' is 'to turn to account or utilise for one's own ends'. This is essentially the usage I shall suggest here. Exploitation may be regarded as domination *which is harnessed to sectional interests* (domination over nature or domination over human beings). (See Figure 2.3.)

This viewpoint links to the framework for the analysis of

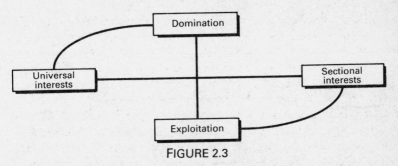

FIGURE 2.3

ideology which I have developed elsewhere.[11] The analysis and critique of ideology are concerned with showing how structures of signification are mobilised to legitimate the sectional interests of dominant groups, i.e. to legitimate *exploitative domination*. All forms of domination can be adjudged in terms of how far they are harnessed to the sectional interests of particular social categories, collectivities – or classes – and how far they serve the universal (generalisable) interests of broader communities or societies of which they are a part. The concept of interests raises numerous difficulties, which I shall not attempt to confront in this context. But it can be taken as axiomatic that sectional and universal interests are never wholly exclusive.

## Power and Control

All social systems, as I have said in Chapter 1, form reproduced relations of autonomy and dependence. In analysing the structural components of such power relations, it is always necessary to study connections between what, in an earlier study,[12] I described as 'the institutional mediation of power' as compared with 'the mediation of control'. I would now look upon these as two modes of analysing power relations, separated by a methodological *epoché*. When we bracket the institutional analysis of structures of domination, we can study how resources are manipulated strategically by actors in order to sustain control over the activities of others. Forms of control here simply refer to the modes in which actors apply knowledge (on any of the three levels of cognition distinguished before) to maintain asymmetries of autonomy and dependence in the reproduced relations constituting social systems (see Figure 2.4 overleaf).

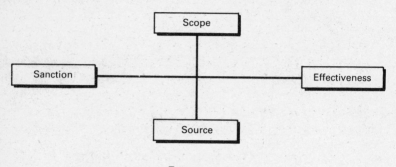

FIGURE 2.4

The *sources* of control that actors endeavour or are able to apply in social relationships can be analysed in terms of modes of appropriating allocative and authoritative resources to secure that control. Sources of control may be more or less 'manipulated' on the level of discursive consciousness by those involved, depending, among other things, upon how aware they are of the nature of the resources from which their power stems. All social actors, both the powerful and the relatively powerless, have some degree of *discursive penetration* of the conditions governing the reproduction of the social systems they produce and reproduce in their action. But resources are also chronically applied through the medium of actors' practical consciousness; and we can by no means treat unconscious forms of cognition as unimportant in this respect. These points are well illustrated in the study of suicidal behaviour. While there are a range of contexts in which suicides or attempted suicides occur, a considerable proportion of them can be under-stood as attempts to maintain and recover some measure of control over others through self-punitive acts. In some circum-stances the suicidal act is little more than a gesture, which the individual quite consciously employs as a means of attempting to influence the conduct of others; such suicide attempts usually do not seriously endanger the person's life. Even in such 'suicidal gestures', however, that which the person is capable of articulating about his or her reasons for the suicidal act may only partly tap what is tacitly involved in their practical consciousness of the nexus of circumstances leading up to the act. In more serious attempts at suicide there is frequently a confusion of conscious and unconscious elements involved which contribute to making many such attempts a 'gamble with death' in which the outcome is uncertain.[13]

By the *scope* of control I mean the range of persons and responses over whom or which actors seek to hold sway. Suicidal actions are limited both in affecting usually only those in the immediate circle of an individual's acquaintance, and in being necessarily sporadic events. Control which is extended in time and space – in other words, control of broad scope – is only possible in the context of institutionalised practices. But institutionalised forms of control obviously also vary widely in scope. A slave-owner has a considerably broader range of control over the lives of his slaves than a modern employer has over wage-labour. There is, of course, often substantial discrepancy between normative rights and obligations and the actual conduct of social life; the *effectiveness* of control always has to be analysed empirically, and is substantially affected by the *sanctions* which the actors in question can call into play.

It is very important to emphasise that there are no continuing relationships in any sphere of social life where the scope and effectiveness of the control which some actors have over other actors is complete. This is the basis for what I call the *dialectic of control* in social systems. However wide-ranging the control which actors may have over others, the weak nevertheless always have some capabilities of turning resources back against the strong. The dialectic of control is implied, I want to argue, in the logical connection between agency and power. An agent who has no options whatsoever is no longer an agent. An individual who is placed in solitary confinement, for example, might appear to be utterly powerless in the face of the scope of the control of his/her captors. But such is not the case, as hunger strikes, or 'the ultimate refusal' – suicide – indicate. Most circumstances of control, of course, are not nearly so all-embracing as those of captor and captive. This is more nearly a *limiting case* of imbalance of power than a type case. In the vast majority of circumstances of social life control is necessarily more restricted in scope and effectiveness. Hence the dialectic of control is more fluid, and those in positions of subordination may, in fact, be able to achieve considerable effective control over the contexts of their activity within social systems.

## Knowledgeability, Legitimation

In a good deal of modern sociological literature the term 'social reproduction' is invoked as though it were a magical touchstone, an explanatory concept of extraordinary potency. In fact, as I have emphasised in the previous chapter, it is not an explanatory notion at all: the reproduction of social systems is at every moment a contingent phenomenon which requires explanation. The conception of the duality of structure, operating in and through the (bounded) knowledgeability of human actors, is crucially important in avoiding the twin pitfalls of objectivism and subjectivism in explaining social reproduction. Theories of the former kind are prone to see the reproduction of society as something happening with mechanical inevitability, through processes of which social actors are ignorant. Theories of the latter sort tend, to the converse, to see social activity as a simple product of the skills of actors, a 'monological' view of social conduct which parallels Chomsky's syntactics in respect of language use. Such theories are in fact typically concerned with the production of social life rather than its reproduction across time-space, which remains unexplicated.

The notion of the duality of structure provides the groundwork for a theory of social reproduction because it involves the postulate that there is an inherent connection between the production and reproduction of interaction. This connection is not a logical one (as Winch's interpretation of social life suggests) but is grounded in the knowledgeability of social actors. Social life, as Max Weber pointed out long ago, is in most circumstances eminently predictable – perhaps more so than are events in the natural world. But this predictability is a skilled accomplishment of lay actors, not a phenomenon governed by mechanical forces. The predictable character of the social world is 'made to happen' as a condition and result of the knowledgeable application of rules and resources by actors in the constitution of interaction. The 'accomplished' character of the social world always involves 'effort' on the part of social actors, but is at the same time for the most part done 'effortlessly', as part of the routine, taken-for-granted nature of everyday life. The relations between practical consciousness and the structural properties of social systems are founded above all in the *routinisation* of day-to-day life. It is essential not to confuse the massive importance which the routine has in the reproduction of social life with 'blind habit' on the one hand or with engrained normative commitment on the other. In each case social actors appear as but dull automata, moving mindlessly through the contexts of their daily lives. On the contrary, the prevalance of the routine or taken-for-granted rests precisely upon the casually employed but very complex skills whereby social actors draw upon and reconstitute the practices 'layered' into institutions in deep time-space.

These observations have significant connotations for grasping connections between legitimation and domination in the constitution of societies. Theories of legitimation (like those of 'ideology' generally, with which they have been closely merged) have frequently suffered from two sources of limitation particularly characteristic of objectivistic approaches that have effaced the knowledgeability of the human subject.

(1) One concerns an issue I have already touched upon in discussing sanctions, the ties between motivation and social reproduction. The thesis that the system integration of society depends upon the 'internalisation' of common values obscures from view certain fundamental aspects of the knowledgeability of social actors. The taken-for-granted cannot inevitably be equated with the accepted-as-legitimate. The 'internalisation thesis' implies that an inherent connection between motives, norms and legitimation is involved in most of the activities of day-to-day life, as both the medium of their reproduction and the means of the over-all integration of society. An 'established social order' appears from this point of view necessarily as a 'legitimate social order'. But as large areas of routinised social life are not directly motivated, they form a 'grey area' between knowledgeability and commitment. Social life, in all societies, contains many types of practice or aspects of practices which are sustained in and through the knowledgeability of social actors but which they do not reproduce as a matter of normative commitment. One element in this is the prevalence of 'calculative' activities towards norms, which I have already referred to earlier. This is in a sense only the tip of the iceberg, since such calculative or manipulative attitudes operate primarily at the level of discursive consciousness.

So far as theories of legitimation (or 'ideology', as that concept is often understood) are concerned, the consequence is that there

is a considerably greater potential separation between the practices actors sustain in day-to-day social reproduction and the over-
all symbolic orders normatively sanctioned by dominant groups or
classes in particular societies. This comment applies to small-scale,
'primitive' societies with an oral culture as well as to large-scale
ones, and to the more powerful in a society as well as to the less
powerful.

From Durkheim onwards many social analysts have been prone
to exaggerate the degree to which 'primitive' oral cultures involve
a strongly integrated normative consensus; in Durkheim's case this
is in no small part a result of the theme of 'internalisation', which I
have tried to show is inherently suspect. 'Calculative' attitudes
towards normative sanctions are just as much part of 'primitive'
societies as they are of those more 'economically advanced' – and
are characteristic of societies in which the hold of religion is strong
as well as of those which are highly secularised. The disenchanted
do not have a monopoly of cynicism. This does not imply, of
course, that all societies can be lumped together in such respects.
In oral cultures, where the pervasiveness of tradition is a primary
feature of social life, the knowledgeability of practical consciousness is typically less uncoupled from an over-all symbol system
than in literate cultures, and especially in contemporary industrialised societies. The degree of uncoupling or 'distance' between
routinised social reproduction and the general 'legitimate order' is
undoubtedly strongly affected by the time-space distancing involved in the organisation of a particular society or type of society.
In large-scale, industrialised societies, increasingly linked on a
global plane, there are many forms of interaction of low presence-
availability, and many boundaries or dislocations between the
locales with which different social systems are associated. In such
circumstances the routines sustained via practical consciousness
may be in various possible ways disjoined from the normative
commitments legitimised in overarching symbol systems.

To make these arguments is to indicate one of the main reasons
why it is important analytically to distinguish social integration from
system integration. Social integration should not *ipso facto* be
equated with normative integration, but there is no doubt that
normative commitments tend to be more strongly and effectively
sanctioned at the level of face-to-face interaction. In small-scale
societies, where most interaction is marked by high presence-

availability, social and system integration are obviously more closely merged than in societies which stretch across long time-space distances. The disengagement of social and system integration tends inevitably to be closely connected with the uncoupling of day-to-day practices from the legitimations involved in the symbolic order of a society.

Authors who have overemphasised normative consensus and the ties between motivation and legitimation in societal integration have as a result characteristically failed adequately to analyse relations between legitimation and asymmetries of power. Those in subordinate positions in a society, particularly in large-scale societies, may frequently be much less closely caught within the embrace of consensual 'ideologies' than many writers – who certainly include Marxists, among others – assume.[14] The importance of this point is very considerable, and connects closely to the theme of the dialectic of control. At the same time, however, it should be noted that the 'distancing' of commitment to a legitimate order is not necessarily confined to the lower echelons in a society. If cynicism and a 'pragmatic' attitude towards norms are not confined to secularised societies, neither of course are they inevitably only characteristic of the less powerful in those societies. The notion of 'organisational fictions' – formulae which nominally command obedience but in fact are flouted in some degree by everyone (or perhaps manipulated by those in dominant positions to sustain their power) – has potential relevance to more encompassing elements of legitimation in society as a whole.

(2) Many theories of legitimation and of 'ideology' tend to presume that the cognitive components of symbol systems can be represented solely as beliefs, having a propositional form. The cognitive context of 'ideology' from such a standpoint is treated as a set of beliefs about a given range of phenomena which are held in common by most of the members of a society. Whatever objections may be raised against the conception of ideology advanced by Althusser (such objections are substantial, and include issues raised under (1) above), one of his important contributions is to stress that 'ideology' should refer to the whole content of day-to-day 'lived experience'. The cognitive elements that relate to legitimation do not consist solely of 'beliefs about' phenomena – beliefs about how society is constituted, or about 'how things should be run' – but have to be analysed also as

involved with the knowledgeability of practical consciousness. That is to say, the core of practical consciousness consists not only, to use Ryle's terms,[15] of 'knowing that' but also of 'knowing how'. If ideology be understood, as I have suggested earlier in this chapter, as the modes in which exploitative domination is legitimised, we certainly must include 'knowing how' within this category – both in regard of how the position of hegemonic groups is sustained and of how those in subordinate positions limit or resist their hegemony. 'Ideas' – or (more accurately) signification – are inherently embroiled in what people *do*, in the texture of the practicalities of daily life. Some of the most potent forms of ideological mobilisation do not rest upon shared beliefs (any more than shared normative commitments); rather, they operate in and through the *forms* in which day-to-day life is organised.

# 3

# Society as Time-Traveller: Capitalism and World History

At this juncture I want to move towards the more substantive concerns of this book, and to pose, in a preliminary way, the question of the *specificity* of industrial capitalism. By the 'specificity' I mean its distinctiveness. How different is capitalism, as a type of society, from other societies which have preceded it in history and which – more and more under the threat of dissolution – continue to coexist with it in 'underdeveloped' parts of the world? As a preliminary orientation, and at the risk of covering material that is wearisomely commonplace, it seems to be worth while examining the issue in Marx's thought. For Marx's theory of historical materialism, however deep-lying the flaws it may contain, remains the beginning-point for any discussion which aims at 'placing' capitalist society in history.

## Marx's Scheme of Social Evolution

Let us start out from what is most familiar of all in Marx's account of history: the evolutionary scheme within which Marx relates capitalism to prior 'epochs' of social development. Although various modifications – particularly important in respect of the so-called 'Asiatic Mode of Production' – were introduced by Marx later in his writings, he upheld the general outline of social evolution laid down in *The German Ideology* throughout his career. In *The German Ideology* the various stages in the development of human society are portrayed as phases 'of development in the division of labour [and] . . . different forms of property'.[1] The first type of society is tribal society, in which there is only a low development of the productive forces, and which includes hunting and gathering as well as small agricultural communities. 'The division of labour is at this stage still very elementary,' Marx says, 'and is confined to a further extension of the natural division of labour existing in the family.' This extension of the 'natural division of labour' in the family involves 'patriarchal family chieftains, below them members of the tribe, finally slaves'.

Tribal society is succeeded by the 'communal and state property' of the Ancient world, which (Marx argues) 'results from the union of several tribes into a *city* by agreement or by conquest, and which is still accompanied by slavery'. Communal property continues to exist, and indeed remains dominant 'Real private property', however, comes into being, and the more it develops, the more the institutions associated with the communal form are corroded. The expansion of private property goes hand in hand with an elaboration of the division of labour and a growing 'antagonism between town and country'; eventually the class relation between citizens and slaves becomes fully developed. In Rome the development of private property is on a scale not found again until the emergence of 'modern private property' in capitalism. Moreover, part of the small peasantry becomes expropriated to form a proletariat, though Marx adds that since it occupied an indeterminate position between citizenry and slaves, the proletariat 'never achieved an independent development'.

Whereas Ancient society began in the city, its successor, feudalism, has its origins in the countryside. 'This different starting-point,' according to Marx, 'was determined by the sparseness of the population at that time, which was scattered over a large area and which received no large increase from the conquerors [of Rome – the barbarian tribes].' The internal decline of the Roman Empire, followed by its overthrow by the barbarian invaders, also led to a regression in the level of development of the productive forces: 'agriculture had declined, industry had decayed for want of a market, trade had died out or been violently suspended'. Feudal property, 'like tribal and communal ownership . . . is again based on a community', in which, however, the 'Germanic military constitution provides the form of a class relation between nobility and the enserfed peasantry'. Once more, as the feudal system becomes more mature, there comes about an increasing division between the city and the countryside. None the less, in 'the heyday of feudalism', there was little division of labour. Each nation bore in itself the antithesis of town and country; the division into estates was certainly strongly marked; but apart from the differentiation of princes, nobility, clergy, and peasants in the country, and masters, joinerymen, apprentices, and soon also the rabble of casual labourers in the towns, no division of importance took place.

The towns and cities were vital to the first formation of capitalism. This took place, however, not in those urban communities which existed through much of the feudal period, but in cities which 'were formed anew by the serfs who had become free', and who became either craftsmen, day-labourers, or merely 'an unorganised rabble'. A crucial transition occurred with the expansion of production and commerce, giving rise to an urban mercantile class, which caused a growth in the connections of towns with one another; this 'soon calls forth a new division of production between individual towns, each of which is soon exploiting a predominant branch of industry. The local restrictions of earlier times begin gradually to be broken down.'[2] The association between towns was a major impetus leading the burghers to combine to defend their interests against the feudal aristocracy, a process which, in combination with other factors, eventually gave rise to the consolidation of the bourgeois class. The development of manufacture, in conjunction with the extension of commerce to America and the East Indies, bringing in large amounts of precious metals, helped advance the economic disintegration of feudal agrarian production, swelling the towns with a new proletariat.

There is, of course, one further stage of evolution, the crux of Marx's concern – the transcendence of capitalism by socialism. As Marx announces in the 'Preface' to *A Contribution to the Critique of Political Economy*,

The bourgeois relations of production are the last antagonistic form of the social process of production – antagonistic not in the sense of individual antagonism, but of one arising from the social conditions of life of individuals; at the same time the productive forces developing in the womb of bourgeois society create the material conditions for the solution of that antagonism. This social formation brings, therefore, the prehistory of human society to a close.[3]

In several paragraphs of the 'Preface', Marx establishes a relation between three key elements of his 'materialist conception of history': (1) the characterisation of the 'principal stages in the development of human society' thus outlined (to which, however, has to be added the 'Asiatic Mode of Production'); (2) the notion that a fundamental dividing-point in history, between the 'prehistory' and the 'true history' of humankind, is crossed with the advent of socialism; and (3) the conception that the movement of historical change which links (1) and (2) is to be found in the dialectic of forces and relations of production. This latter point is established in some of the most renowned lines in the whole of Marx's writings. In each particular type of society, at a particular phase of development, the productive forces come into conflict with the existing relations of production, such that these relations become limitations upon the further expansion of production. Marx continues:

> No social order ever perishes before all the productive forces for which there is room in it have developed; and new, higher relations of production never appear before the material conditions of their existence have matured in the womb of the old society itself. Therefore, mankind always sets itself only such tasks as it can solve; since, looking at the matter more closely, it will always be found that the task itself arises only where the material conditions for its solution already exist or are at least in the process of formation.[4]

The rudiments of this evolutionary view of history were established 130 years ago, and it would indeed be surprising if it could be accepted without substantial modification today. In what follows I shall not be concerned with attempting to replace Marx's scheme with a more elaborate or recast evolutionary picture of 'stages in the development of human society'.[5] Rather, I reject every type of evolutionary view of history. In this chapter, however, I shall be concerned mainly with the aforementioned question of the specificity of capitalism – a matter that is at any rate complicated enough in itself. I shall distinguish four principal areas of tension or difficulty in the portrayal of societal evolution sketched above. One concerns the theme that capitalism is the 'summation of world history', an ambiguously formulated conception in Marx in which the influence of Marx's debt to Hegel looms particularly large. The second relates to the 'internal' formulation of Marx's scheme: to inconsistencies which it embodies. The third raises sweeping issues which in this context I shall only be able to touch upon fairly briefly. It is the question of how far capitalism is specifically 'Western', expressing traits of European culture established well before its own emergence in the sixteenth and seventeenth centuries. Finally, we have to consider the 'materialist' underpinning of Marx's scheme: how far the forces/relations of production dialectic provides a universally applicable basis for the analysis of social change.

## Capitalism as the Summation of World History

The development of Marx's writings, as everyone knows, roughly followed the sequence of his personal career. Beginning with the critique of classical German philosophy in Paris, Marx became absorbed with French socialist traditions and from thence, in England, gave over much of the rest of his life to the detailed study of political economy. The result was a conception of history which embodied various fundamental strains or ambiguities, left unresolved by Marx himself. For Hegel, history can be interpreted (looking backwards) in the terms of the progressive advance of Reason, powered by the driving force of the dialectic: 'That Reason rules the world,' Hegel wrote, 'has been proved in philosophy.'[6] In 'standing Hegel on his feet again' Marx advocated an approach to history shorn of the epistemological framework within which it was interpreted by his predecessor. The study of the past was to become the study of 'real, living individuals' in the material contexts of their existence. Marx often wrote as though he were removing altogether every vestige of historical teleology:

> *History* does *nothing*: it 'does *not* possess immense riches, it does *not* fight battles'. It is *men*, real, living men, who do all this, who possess things and fight battles. It is not 'history' which uses men as a means of achieving – as if it were an individual

person – *its* own ends. History is *nothing* but the activity of men in pursuit of their ends.[7]

For Marx, none the less, the history of human society quite plainly retains a unity and a progression, to be analysed in terms of the dialectic of class conflict. There are two threads to this historical progression: the elaboration of the forces of production, and the expanding capabilities of human beings to understand and control the conditions of their life. These become bound together in the achievement of socialism, when humanity leaves behind its 'prehistory' at the same time as its full mastery of the material world comes to flower.

Marx's evolutionary categories have an essential role to play in the progressive movement of history which is thus identified. Each stage forms what Marx calls a 'progressive epoch' in 'the economic formation of society'.[8] Class is not for Marx a purely negative phenomenon, because the formation of classes injects the dynamic in history which has propelled humanity to the threshold of a society in which human beings will for the first time realise their 'true humanity'. The mechanics of the process are supplied in some of the key phrases in the 'Preface' to *A Contribution to the Critique of Political Economy* quoted above. Each succeeding type of society, from the Ancient world through to socialism, contains within it both the seeds of its own dissolution and the motive force to a movement to a 'higher stage'. Human beings only set themselves 'such problems as they can solve'. The evolutionary scheme set out by Marx is not a neutral historical record but an interpretation of the ascendancy of humankind to control over its own destiny.

Marx was not content, of course, with Hegel's notion that Reason in history can only be grasped retrospectively. The analysis of the developments which gave rise to capitalism was focused by Marx upon the immanent tendencies fostering the emergence of socialism. This emphasis simultaneously expresses the core of Marxism as a political philosophy linking theory and practice and creates the difficulties of 'determinism' and 'historical prophecy' which have continually dogged Marxist thought. I shall not be concerned with these problems directly here, however, but only with the implication of Marx's theme that capitalism contains within it the 'sum total' of the progressive forces of history (expressed in alienated or irrational form, but making possible the transition to a socialist society).

The theme that capitalism is the summation of world history – thus far – is, as I have mentioned, only ambiguously and incompletely elaborated by Marx. It is expressed in one form in Marx's early writings, in the idea that the worker, 'who is nothing, can become everything'; that capitalism maximises the contradictions involved in the development of the forces of production in the course of evolution, just as it prepares the ground for their final resolution. But it is also contained in the Marxian transferral of the dialectic to class struggle – for each stage in the 'progressive epochs' of human history both includes the achievements of the one which went before and is yet discontinuous from the preceding stage. Each form of society has to be analysed in its own terms, yet incorporates the advances made in previous forms of society.

As it contains within it the results of a progressive sequence of evolutionary change, expressed in contradictory form, yet also differs from the types of society which preceded it, capitalism is both continuous with previous history and yet discontinuous from it. I shall have a lot to say below about how the continuities and discontinuities of capitalism with other types of society should be conceptualised. For the moment it is important to note how significant the conception of capitalism as the summation of world history, co-ordinated within the transmuted Hegelian scheme which Marx establishes, is for the revolutionary rupture marked by socialism. Capitalism is the class society which is to put an end to class societies; it is a society which maximises human self-alienation, but in such a way as to open up the road to a new social order in which such self-alienation will be transcended.

Of course, the relation of the opening pages of *The German Ideology* and of the 'Preface' to the rest of Marx's texts is a debatable and controversial one. Towards the end of his life Marx reaffirmed his adherence to Hegel's dialectic, translated into 'its rational form'.[9] But he never wrote the general interpretation of dialectics he indicated he intended to produce.[10] We cannot say what alterations he may have made in his evolutionary conception if he had managed to develop a more elaborate or detailed dialectical account of history. As it stands, however, there are serious inconsistencies in Marx's arguments, even considered purely on their own terms. It is to certain of these that I shall now turn.

**Evolution: Continuities and Discontinuities**

Marx never abandoned the idea that a progressive evolutionary process can be traced out from the initial dissolution of tribal society to the developments which bring humankind to the threshold of socialism. As Lefort expresses it, 'Humanity is *one* in time. Despite pauses or regressions, there can be no doubt about the continuity of the drama.'[11] Marx wrote the 'Preface' to *A Contribution to the Critique of Political Economy* at the same period at which he was working on the draft notes of *Capital*, the notes that have today become famous as the *Grundrisse*. The *Grundrisse* contains a short section on the 'Forms which Precede Capitalist Production' (the *Formen*), by common acknowledgement the most subtle and sophisticated discussion of pre-capitalist (one should really say 'non-capitalist') social formations that Marx ever wrote. By the time he wrote the *Formen* Marx had clearly both amplified and altered the view on the development of human societies set out in the 1840s. In *The German Ideology* the sequence of societal development outlined is wholly European. But in the *Formen*, Oriental society, or the Asiatic Mode of Production, appears as the 'second form' of society developing out of tribal society.[12] This is, on the face of it, fully consistent with the account of evolution sketched in the 'Preface', where the progressive 'epochs' of history are listed as the 'Asiatic, Ancient, feudal, and modern bourgeois modes of production'.[13] Actually, however, a scrutiny of the ideas portrayed in the *Formen* indicates that certain tensions more or less latent in Marx's early accounts of social evolution emerge in a particularly acute way there.

These tensions have been well analysed by Lefort, and I shall follow the essential elements of his dissection of the *Formen* quite closely.[14] Lefort distinguishes two versions of history which appear in the *Formen*, a 'continuist' (evolutionary) and a 'discontinuist' one. The continuist version is the progressive, quasi-Hegelian interpretation of history described previously – the 'standard account' of Marxism. The discontinuist perspective, by contrast, places in question that whole mode of evolutionary argument: 'it does not appear here and there in the margins of what would be considered the main discourse; rather, it is the result of a different way of perceiving history and social life'.[15] Capitalism does not from the second standpoint represent the summation of world history. On the contrary, it stands out in relief from other types of society, as more radically distinct from them than they are from one another.

Marx's discussion in the *Formen* opens by contrasting one of the fundamental elements involved in capitalism – the existence of a mass of 'free' wage-labour – with production in all non-capitalist societies. Both in Europe and in the Orient, prior to the emergence of capitalism, the worker, as Marx puts it, is not in fact a *worker* at all. Labour is carried on within two overriding circumstances which govern the life of individuals. First, the individual producer 'relates to the objective conditions of his labour as to his property': there is a 'natural unity of labour with its material presuppositions'. The producer relates to nature as part of, and yet at the same time as an active contributor to, natural processes and events. Second, the individual 'relates to others [in the local community] as co-proprietors, as so many incarnations of the common property, or as independent proprietors like himself, independent private proprietors'. In both West and East 'individuals relate not as workers but as proprietors – as members of a community, who at the same time work'. The evident implication of these points, as Lefort says, is that labour is not at the origin of property – indeed, at one point Marx makes this perfectly clear. Tribal society turns out not to be the beginning-point of a progressive evolutionary scheme but the societal form out of which, in modified versions, Asiatic, Ancient and feudal modes of production all develop.

The underlying elements which unify all social formations prior to capitalism are founded in the 'naturally arisen spontaneous community' that persists in each type of social order. In such circumstances

Each individual conducts himself only as a link, as a member of this community as *proprietor* or *possessor*. The *real appropriation* through the labour process happens under these *presuppositions*, which are not themselves the *product* of labour, but appear as its natural or divine presuppositions. This form, with the same land-relation as its foundation, can realise itself in very different ways. E.g. it is not in the least a contradiction to it that, as in most of the *Asiatic* land-forms, the *comprehensive unity* standing above all these little communities appears as the higher *proprietor* or as the sole proprietor; the real communities hence only as *hereditary* possessors. Because the *unity* is the real proprietor and the real presupposition of communal property, it follows that this unity can appear as a *particular* entity above the many real particular communities.

This passage both establishes the general character of the views Marx proceeds to develop, contrasting capitalism with what went before it, and indicates the guideline of his analysis of the Asiatic societies. In 'Oriental despotism' communal property is organised within the self-sustaining village community; but the local community is duplicated by the 'higher unity' of the despotic state. The particular nature of the Asiatic social formations is traced by Marx to the relation between the community and the state, the latter being personified in the shape of a king-god. In the *Formen* this type of mode of production is not presented as the source of the development of Ancient society, which is instead another mode of movement out of tribal society. Like the Oriental type, Ancient society 'also assumes the community as its first presupposition' – in this case, however, the city rather than the self-sufficient village commune. In contrast to the account given in *The German Ideology* Marx accentuates neither the theme of the increasing proliferation of private property nor that of the expansion of the forces of production. The proprietal relation remains conditioned by the individual's membership of the community: 'Membership in the commune remains the presupposition for the appropriation of land and soil, but, as a member of the commune, the individual is a private proprietor. He relates to his private property as land and soil, but at the same time to his being as commune member.'

There is no reason to suppose that Marx abandoned the general elements of his analysis in *The German Ideology* in tracing how Ancient society disintegrated. But from the perspective of the *Formen*, there is even less basis than there was in the earlier work for maintaining that the Ancient world was riven by contradictory forces driving it on to a 'higher and newer form' of social organisation. Such a view can in any case only be justified if it is held that the dissolution of the Roman Empire, together with the Germanic clan community, formed a sort of symbiosis propelling 'history' forward. But even by reference to the principal criterion Marx offers in his progressive evolutionary scheme – the growth of the forces of production – such was admitted even in *The German Ideology* not to have been the case. In the early period of feudalism, Marx accepted, the productive forces regressed to a low ebb. In the *Formen*, feudalism or 'the Germanic form' is not represented as a resolution of the contradictions of the Ancient Mode of Production. Its core components are once again related to the communal characteristics of tribal society. Marx is vague about the conditions which lead to one type of development out of tribal society rather than another. But it seems evident that they do not bear any particular relation to the forces of production as such. In distinguishing the Asiatic from Ancient types of society, Marx says that the latter was the outcome 'of more active, historic life', as compared with the former; the factors shaping the emergence of Classical society were migrations and wars. The same factors are also mentioned in respect of the formation of the Germanic communities. But as a result of their sparse distribution in small groups, the commune only comes together for periodic gatherings. Communal land exists – and persists throughout the feudal period – but it is not the prime link between the individual and community. Rather than the village commune itself, the household is the main local centre of social life and of production. Private property actually appears here as more distinctly developed than in the Ancient world, if we follow the analysis of the *Formen* rather than that of *The German Ideology*. But the links between individual, community and land – although different from those in the other types of social formation – remain strongly established.

As Lefort points out, Marx leaves us in no doubt about the affinity of the three types of society, as differentiated from capitalism. It is worth quoting Marx at some length in this respect, at the point at which he draws together the threads of his discussion:

> In all these forms – in which landed property and agriculture form the basis of the economic order, and where the economic aim is hence the production of use values, i.e. the *reproduction of the individual* within the specific relation to the commune in which he is its basis – there is to be found: (1) Appropriation not through labour, but presupposed to labour; appropriation of the natural conditions of labour, of the *earth* as the original instrument of labour as well as its workshop and repository of

raw materials ... (2) but this *relation* to land and soil, to the earth, as the property of the labouring individual – who thus appears from the outset not merely as labouring individual, in this abstraction, but who has an *objective mode of existence* in his ownership of the land, an existence *presupposed* to his activity ... – is instantly mediated by the naturally arisen, spontaneous, more or less historically developed and modified presence of the individual as *member of a commune* – his naturally arisen presence as member of a tribe, etc.

If this does not actually split Marx's progressivist evolutionary scheme asunder, the least we can say is that it exists in considerable tension with it. Marx's evolutionary history, in the 'Preface' to *A Contribution to the Critique of Political Economy* and other sources, is linked to the dialectic of forces and relations of production: the productive forces, at a certain point in the development of a society, can no longer be contained by the pre-established relations of production, leading to their transformation. The analysis of the *Formen* runs counter to this, suggesting that – prior to capitalism at any rate – production is subordinated to the social relations connecting nature, the individual and the social community. Moreover, rather than implying that the forces of production have their own internal dynamic, as in his evolutionary view, Marx seems in the *Formen* to give primacy to 'ecological' factors (dispersal or concentration of populations) and to war in stimulating social transformation. '*Warfare*', he says, 'is ... one of the earliest preoccupations of each of these naturally arisen communities.'[16]

If the views developed in the *Formen* diverge so significantly from Marx's evolutionary conception of history, it is not surprising that they call into question the confident assertion of the *Communist Manifesto* that 'The history of all hitherto existing society is the history of class struggles.' Indeed, we must treat the very term 'class society' with some reservation if the concepts of the *Formen* are followed through. We find what might be called *class-divided* societies previous to the development of capitalism, but class divisions do not completely undermine the communal character of these societies. Class relations do not govern the basic character of production in either the Ancient world or in feudalism. Production remains tied to nature and to the 'natural community' in ways that are only finally broken through by the advent of capitalism – for the capital/wage-labour relation is thus quite unique, involving a process of separation of the realm of the 'economic' from other institutions unknown in prior forms of society. The slave or serf are not 'workers', nor is their 'labour' separated from their relation to nature and to the community.[17]

All this suggests that, far from being the summation of world history, the 'synthesis of previous syntheses', the development of capitalism marks a series of fundamental discontinuities with previous history. Capitalism, in some key respects at any rate, is more different from each of the other types of society Marx distinguishes than they are different from one another. Capitalism is distinctively a 'class society': the capital/wage-labour relation is predicated upon the dissolution of the ties between nature, community and the individual characteristic of other societal forms. From the side of wage-labour, this involves the eradication of 'the relation to the earth – land and soil – as natural conditions of production', and concomitantly of the 'real community' within which such production is ordered.[18] From the side of capital, what is involved is the commodification of property (the full alienability of property) and its circulation through the medium of money. These two processes suppose a 'period of the dissolution of the earlier modes of production'.[19]

## Capitalism as 'Western'

The distinctiveness of capitalism as a 'Western' phenomenon has unfortunately, since Max Weber, become embroiled in the largely fruitless debate about the role of 'ideas' in social change. To regard Weber's comparative work, as some have done, as a kind of quasi-experiment designed to test how far 'ideas' can influence the 'material' development of society does scant justice to Weber himself. Weber emphasised that a range of socio-economic phenomena separate the development of the Eastern civilisations from that of the West. The similarities of certain of Weber's views to some of those of Marx have been widely discussed, and I shall not seek to recapitulate these themes here.[20] Rather, I shall pose the problem of the 'Western' character of capitalism in relation to issues raised by the foregoing discussion of the *Formen*. The analysis of the *Formen*, I have suggested, seriously compromises not just the context of the evolutionary scheme which Marx initially introduced in *The German Ideology* but also its very nature. The implications of this were, however, not pursued by Marx himself, and were kept subordinate to his evolutionary conception.

In place of Marx's evolutionary view of history, I shall propose a non-evolutionary standpoint – one which none the less owes a great deal to Marx. Evolutionary models, as employed by many both before and since Marx, have been dominated by two connected theses which I shall want to reject. One is that a measure of the level of development achieved by any given society can be derived from how 'advanced' it is in terms of its capability of controlling the material environment – in terms, in other words, of the level of the development of the productive forces. In this respect Marx's evolutionary scheme shares a certain amount in common with social evolutionism as a whole. The second theme exists in ambiguous form in Marx's writings, given his emphasis (in some contexts) upon the dialectic of subject and object in history. It is the heavy concentration, in many evolutionary theories, upon social development as an 'adaptive' process, where 'adaptation' is conceived of in an almost mechanical fashion.[21] Any such conception falls foul of the theorem of the knowledgeability of social actors which I introduced earlier, and which certainly cannot be confined to those in the more 'advanced' societies.

I want to propose here an approach to history that understands social development in terms of *episodic* characterisations and what I shall call *time-space edges*. 'Episodes'[22] refer to processes of social change which have a definite direction and form, analysed through comparative research, in which a major transition takes place whereby one type of society is transformed into another. Episodes involve processes of structural transformation; but these do not have a mechanical inevitability to them. Two episodic transitions involved in the *Formen* are particularly relevant to my discussion here and in the remainder of the book. The first concerns modes in which tribal societies are displaced by, or transformed into, class-divided societies. The second concerns the episodic characterisation of modes of transition involving the emergence of industrial capitalism. I do not mean the notion of 'episode', thus formulated, to be a precise concept, and neither of course do I wish to claim that the two sorts of episodic occurrence just mentioned are the only ones of any importance in human history. In talking of time-space edges, as I mentioned in the Introduction, I wish to pay emphasis upon the simultaneous, interconnected, existence of different types of society. This helps to free us from the tendency of evolutionary thought to analyse societal development in terms of 'stages', and from the influence of 'unfolding models' of change. Varying forms of class-divided society have existed in conjunction with one another, with tribal societies, and with industrial capitalism. Time-space edges refer to forms of contact or encounter between types of society organised according to variant structural principles; they are the edges of potential or actual social transformation, the intersections between different planes of societal organisation. The term 'pre-capitalist' social formation is a misleading one in so far as it suggests that the various types of society discussed by Marx in the *Formen* wholly precede in time the emergence of capitalism (although most, of course, do).

When writing in an evolutionary vein Marx was prone to speak both as if the development of the productive forces were the basic driving-force of social change, and as if societies can be classified into 'stages' according to their level of elaboration of the productive forces. The latter presumption is discarded if we abandon an evolutionary view of history; and there are strong reasons to doubt the validity of the former. It will perhaps be sufficient in the present context to concentrate upon episodic relations between tribal and class-divided societies, a phenomenon which has been considerably illuminated by twentieth-century ethnological research. The category of 'tribal' or 'primitive' society is a very wide one, and it is evident from the anthropological fieldwork now available that there are considerable differences between societies which might be generally grouped within it. But it has also become clear that it is mistaken to regard all such societies as involving 'subsistence economies', if that term is taken to mean that a chronic material scarcity, or its threat, haunts the daily life of its members. Diamond is right to reject the thesis that there is an 'immanent logic' in surplus production. If 'primitive' societies do not produce a surplus, this is not necessarily because of an inadequate development of the forces of production.[23] As Sahlins argues, in at least many so-called 'subsistence economies', there is no principle of scarcity in operation. According to him, modern economics has invented 'scarcity', in the context of a system which puts a basic stress upon the expansion of production.[24] It is a mistake to treat hunting and gathering societies as 'impoverished'; and in most such societies people do not 'work hard' as compared with the modern industrial labourer. The quest for food is intermittent rather than chronic, and the rhythm of the day or of the periodic movement of the society is influenced more by ritual and ceremonial considerations rather than by material imperatives. Hunting and gathering societies include what Sahlins calls 'the original affluent societies'.

Sahlins extends this argument to include settled agrarian communities which, he argues, typically 'underproduce', in the sense that there is no generic pressure to maximise productive resources. Much the same standpoint is expressed by Clastres, who claims to show that members of 'primitive' societies are characteristically at least as able to provide for their needs as those in the most 'economically developed' capitalistic systems. Most primitive societies 'have at their disposal, if they so desire, all the time necessary to increase the production of material goods'.[25] They do not so desire, since the expansion of material production is not experienced as a driving impulsion. All this, it may be said, is quite consistent with some of Marx's emphases in the *Formen*, but not with the general presuppositions of his evolutionary scheme. It is not the forces of production which underlie the major episodic transitions prior to those associated with industrial capitalism. As Clastres goes on to point out:

> It would appear that . . . the Neolithic Revolution – while it did have a considerable effect on the human groups then existing, doubtless making life easier for them – did not mechanically bring about an overturning of the social order . . . it is the political break that is decisive, and not the economic transformation. The true revolution in man's protohistory is not the Neolithic, since it may very well leave the previously existing social organisation intact; it is the political revolution, that mysterious emergence – irreversible, fatal to primitive societies – of the thing we know by the name of the state.[26]

I shall return later to the question of this 'mysterious emergence', which has all the importance Clastres ascribes to it, even if we may doubt that it involves processes which are irreversible. At this juncture, however, it is relevant to turn briefly to the class-divided societies designated by Marx as the Asiatic Mode of Production. Of the various non-capitalist social formations distinguished by Marx, the Asiatic has perhaps been subject to more discussion recently than any other – in some part because of the influence of the *Formen*. It is not my intention here to review this literature, which can hardly be said to have reached any worthwhile consensus.[27] There is no doubt that Marx's analysis of the Oriental societies is both illuminating and seriously flawed. It is the societal type most under tension in his account. As the only specifically 'non-Western' type of society Marx discusses, the simultaneous recognition of its differences from the other types and its interpolation as the first 'progressive epoch' in an evolutionary scheme create pronounced difficulties. It cannot be pretended that these are adequately resolved by Marx himself. Here it is sufficient to indicate the nature of some of these difficulties:

(1) There are strongly defined 'Europocentric' overtones in Marx's various analyses of the Oriental societies, noted by many subsequent commentators. The idea that the Asiatic societies are despotic, given particular prominence by Montesquieu, and the Hegelian contrast of the dynamic character of the West as contrasted to the 'stagnant' East, were appropriated in a fairly direct way by Marx. Marx certainly was not free from what has been said of European liberal thought in general, distinguished by an inclination 'to look down on Asia . . . as barbarous, in spite of all its pomp and show, because it allegedly had no respect either for the rights of private property, or for the liberties of the individual'.[28]

(2) The evaluation of the Asian societies as stagnant – as demonstrating a peculiar 'unchangeability', as Marx puts it in *Capital*[29] – is only at all defensible in the context of the evolutionary scheme, in which the development of the forces of production is the index of the level of evolution. The conception that Oriental society is a sort of historical 'dead-end' in the progression of humankind again appears as a distinctly Europocentric one.

(3) Even if we confine attention to the forces of production, there seem serious empirical limitations to Marx's assessment of the unchanging character of the East. As Weber, among others, has shown, in both India and China at different periods there occurred

a significant degree of economic development, as indicated by the expansion of manufacture, trade and the accumulation of capital. Private property also seems to have been of considerable importance, particularly in China.

(4) To pose the question of the 'unchangeability' of the Asiatic societies from the point of view of 'why they developed so far and no further' is inadequate – and again betrays the strong influence of evolutionism: 'the unchangeability of Asiatic societies', Marx says, 'is in such striking contrast with the constant dissolution and refounding of Asiatic states, and their never-ceasing changes of dynasty'. [30] The question for Marx is – as it became in a somewhat different guise for Weber – what explains the barriers that prevented the Eastern societies from moving towards the formation of capitalism? But an equally significant question, if we accept that there is no inevitable 'forward' movement to history, is how was it that the Oriental societies did not relapse back or 'disintegrate' back into congeries of tribal societies? Marx's arguments do not really address this question at all. If the state has so tenuous a connection with the 'infrastructure' of the village communities, if it is subject to 'constant dissolution', why does it not disappear altogether?

(5) The former point is related to a fifth one of great potential importance. How are we to interpret the nature of the state in the Asiatic Mode of Production? How does the state achieve and sustain its 'despotic' power? One element of Marx's seeming answer to this question has become famous – that the state administers irrigation works which it would be beyond the capability of the local community to control. We cannot be sure from the textual evidence just how much importance Marx attributed to this factor, but in any case there is reason to doubt that there is an intrinsic connection between hydraulic works and the centralised state. Leach's study of Ceylon has been often quoted in this respect. According to Leach, the very extensive irrigation works which were developed in the ancient state of Sinhala were not associated with any kind of centralised 'despotism'. The works were built over a very long period, and not according to any central plan; they were mostly constructed locally, without the large-scale mobilisation of labour-power.[31] Even if it were the case that the rise of the state in the Oriental societies was closely entangled with hydraulic operations, this

would introduce a circumstance not easy to interpret in the light of what Marx says elsewhere about the state as the expression of class contradictions.

(6) This brings us to a final problem. How specifically 'Asiatic' is the Asiatic Mode of Production? The question is one of great importance, whatever the rights or wrongs of Marx's discussion of the generic character of the major Eastern social formations, India and China. It opens up the issue of the nature of the early civilisations of the Near East, and of forms of state in South America and Africa. Contemporary debate on the matter was initiated by writers such as Suret-Canale, who attempted to apply the concept to pre-colonial Black Africa, and has been carried on by Godelier among numerous others. Godelier's analysis is a suggestive and important one, however questionable it may be in certain aspects. As Godelier points out, we might construe Marx's arguments in the *Formen* as suggesting that the Asiatic Mode of Production is one possible type of transition from classless to class (or, in the terminology I shall use, class-divided) societies. Godelier rightly emphasises that such a thesis cannot plausibly be sustained if we do not criticise Marx's own analysis, especially in regard of the supposedly 'stagnant' character of the Asiatic societies. In Godelier's words,

> The image of Asia stagnating for millenia in an unfinished transition from classless to class society, from barbarism to civilisation, has not stood up to the findings of archaeology and history in the East and the New World ... What was born in Greece was not civilisation but the West, a particular form of civilisation which was finally to dominate it while all the while pretending to be its symbol.[32]

If the Oriental societies themselves are not mere 'stagnant' barbarisms, neither were those of early Egypt and Mesopotamia, nor the pre-Columban empires of South America. Marx nowhere accords these societies more than passing mention. But one can hardly deny that they mark major episodic transitions in history. In them we find precisely what Marx singled out as of overriding importance: an expansion of the productive forces, or of human control over nature; but we also find the emergence of writing, science, codified law and numerous other novel cultural phenomena; and above all, the formation of the state.

## Forces and Relations of Production

The dialectic of forces and relations of production plays a basic role in Marx's 'materialist' conception of history' as outlined in the 'Preface' to *A Contribution to the Critique of Political Economy*.[33] In Marx's evolutionary scheme we are offered a series of developmental stages in which a similar pattern repeats itself: the growth of the productive forces leads to an increasing tension with an existing set of relations of production, eventually culminating in a revolutionary transformation of society. Two types of argument in Marx's writings are relevant to assessing this notion. There is, first of all, a general theoretical thesis which Marx sometimes seems to advance about the primacy of production over other elements of social life. Production, he says, is the first exigency of human life, the necessary basis upon which all other social institutions are built; hence we must infer that changes in the forces of production are the main medium of social transformation. But this argument, if taken at its face-value, is clearly invalid. It certainly does not follow that, because material production is necessary to sustain human existence, the social organisation of production is more fundamental to explaining either the persistence of, or change in, societies than any other institutional forms. Marx himself appears to recognise this explicitly at one point in the *Formen*, in the course of criticising Proudhon. The idea, Marx says, 'that human life has since time immemorial rested on production' is 'only a tautology'.[34]

The second type of context relevant to evaluating the thesis that it is on the level of production that the driving impetus to social change is to be found is, of course, that of the concrete discussions Marx offers of particular types of social formation. But here, as I have indicated previously, there are major inconsistencies between Marx's evolutionary scheme and the views developed in the *Formen*. These views express quite a radical break with the forces/relations of production dialectic. Just as, Marx suggests, there is no 'economy' in non-capitalist societies – in the sense that this presupposes an institutional separation from other sectors of society which only occurs in capitalism – so in these societies production is neither distinctly separate from communal organisation nor is its expansion the focus of social change. '*The original conditions of production*,' Marx asserts vigorously, '*cannot themselves* originally be *products* – results of production.' It is exactly this process, i.e. how production comes to be the motor of social transformation with the advent of capitalism, which we need to explain:

> It is not the *unity* of living and active humanity with the natural, inorganic conditions of their metabolic exchange with nature, and hence their appropriation of nature, which requires explanation or is the result of a historic process, but rather the *separation* between these inorganic conditions of human existence and their active existence, a separation which is completely posited only in the relation of wage-labour and capital.[35]

As with other ideas in this chapter, I suggest that it is the themes of the *Formen* which are worthy of further elaboration rather than those involved in Marx's evolutionary interpretation of history. The forces/relations of production dialectic is not a miraculous device that somehow holds the answer to disclosing the underlying sources of social change in general. Nor can the contradictory character of social formations be understood in these terms – except in the case of capitalism. The forces/relations of production dialectic, I shall argue, has peculiar reference to capitalism as a type of society.

# 4

# Time-Space Distanciation and the Generation of Power

Three commonplace assumptions tend to be found among those who have advocated evolutionary schemes in the social sciences – whether or not the authors concerned have been influenced by Marx. These can be stated as follows: (1) human societies tend to develop from relatively simple forms of organisation to more complex ones; (2) the sources of major processes of societal change are primarily endogenous in character; and (3) the most fruitful comparisons between different types of society are to be made between those that are 'close together' on the presumed evolutionary scale, however such a scale is arranged. I want to place each of these assumptions in question in what I have to say in this and subsequent chapters. Quite apart from their involvement in evolutionary theories which suggest that there is some sort of 'adaptive logic' propelling human societies along a path towards increasing complexity, there is good reason to distrust the terms 'simple' and 'complex' as applied to classifying societies. Many 'primitive societies' have very complex modes of kinship organisation, and all possess languages of a structurally differentiated kind. Rather than using the terminology of simple/complex, I wish to introduce the notion of *time-space distanciation* to analyse some of the phenomena with which evolutionary theorists have been concerned. By 'distanciation' here I mean to get at the processes whereby societies are 'stretched' over shorter or longer spans of time and space. The generic concern of the theory of structuration is with how social systems 'bind' time and space. But it is obvious that societies differ greatly in terms of the extent of time-space 'stretches' which they span; and we can ask how this comes about.

The issues posed by the second assumption referred to above

are more significant than they might initially appear. It relates not just to sources of social change but also to what 'societies' are conceived to be. The debate between 'evolutionists' and 'diffusionists' is a familiar one in the anthropological and archaeological literature. But both sides in this controversy have tended to operate with similar models of what a society is like: a social system clearly distinct from its 'environment' of other societies. The main question at dispute has been how far change originates 'internally' or 'externally'. What this fails to address is the character of the interconnections in which virtually all societies exist, or have existed, with others. The 'totalising' elements distinguished in Chapter 1 (pp. 44–8) which mark a society off as a peculiarly encompassing form of social system are never complete. The nexus of relations – political, economic or military – in which a society exists with others is usually integral to the very nature of that society.

The third idea mentioned above flows readily from evolutionary theory but has no justification once we abandon evolutionism. Position upon an evolutionary scale becomes replaced by distance or proximity in time-space. The latter, as I have just indicated, cannot generally be adequately studied as the 'succession' of one type of society by another, since throughout 'civilised' human history we find the coexistence of societies living along time-space edges. Distance in time or space, on the other hand, becomes no bar to fruitful comparative analysis.

**Time-Space Distanciation**

The structuration of every social system, however small or large, occurs in time and space, but none the less also 'brackets' time-space relations. This intermingling of presence and absence is inherent in the nature of the constitution of social systems: every society participates in some form of dissolution of the restraints of time and space. The study of how such a dissolution is achieved is the proper concern of the analysis of time-space distanciation. In this section I shall be concerned with how time-space distanciation is involved with the generation of power.

According to the theory of structuration as outlined earlier, power is generated in and through the reproduction of structures of domination, which includes the dominion of human beings over the material world (allocative resources) and over the social world (authoritative resources). I shall take up the question of allocative resources in some detail in the next chapter, in relation to the problem of class domination. In this chapter I shall concentrate attention upon modes in which authoritative resources are implicated in distanciation, taking the time-space edges between tribal and class-divided societies as my main empirical focus.

The underlying thread of my argument is as follows. Power is generated by the transformation/mediation relations inherent in the allocative and authoritative resources comprised in structures of domination. These two types of resource may be connected in different ways in different forms of society. It certainly is a mistake to suggest, as at least some interpretations of Marx's 'materialist conception of history' would have us believe, that the accumulation of allocative resources is the driving principle of all major processes of societal change. On the contrary, in non-capitalist societies it seems generally to be the case that the co-ordination of authoritative resources is the more fundamental lever of change. This is because – or so I shall argue – authoritative resources are the prime carriers of time-space distanciation.

Consider the time-space organisation of the smallest of human societies, band societies of hunters and gatherers. Such societies, of course, are marked by the predominance of presence, or of very high presence-availability. Extension in space occurs via the foraging activity of individuals who may spend periods of up to several days away from the remainder of the group. But the main, and distinctive, mode of spatial organisation is to be found in the perambulatory activity of the group as a whole. The spatial movement of hunting and gathering societies, it should be made clear, is not adequately understood as simply concerned with the production of material goods. These groups, like larger nomad societies, may lack fixed settlements but they do typically lay claim to the legitimate control of a domain as their 'territory of operation'. The periodic movement of the whole society may be seen as one way in which the members of that society transcend spatial limitations of presence. If 'territoriality' is taken to mean first and foremost the formation of a type of authoritative resource – claim to legitimate dominion over a given spatial extension – it must not be associated only with the settlement of villages or cities.

Still less would it be correct to suppose that claim to legitimate control over territory is only found where there is some kind of state apparatus; what normally appears in this case is the insistence upon clear-cut administrative control of a territorial area (developed to its fullest extent only in nation-states).

Extension in time in band societies is achieved primarily via two overlapping sets of phenomena: the grounding of legitimation in tradition, and the fundamental part played by kinship in societal structuration. Kin relations are embedded in time, in that they link living individuals to the dead, whether or not this is formalised in lineage systems or ancestor worship.[1] But kin relations also help locate the living temporally, by marking phases of the life-cycle. The kinship system, together with religion, provide the main axes around which tradition coagulates. The connections between tradition, time and time-consciousness in non-literate societies are so important that it is worth spelling them out in a little detail. Tradition, which is the most elemental form of social reproduction, involves a particular type of time-consciousness, but it would probably be mistaken to regard it as involving a particular type of consciousness *of* time as such. In societies that are dominated by tradition, neither 'tradition' nor 'time' tend to be distinguished as separate from the continuity of events which they help to mould. We must have some reservations about Max Weber's conception of the 'traditional' as a type of legitimation. According to Weber, in this type 'legitimacy is claimed . . . and believed in by virtue of the sanctity of age-old rules and powers'.[2] This formulation, particularly in the context of Weber's contrast with more 'rational' modes of organisation, is a potentially misleading one. It suggests that tradition is itself a legitimising force, and thereby implies that 'tratitional legitimation' has no rational basis; that what is done today is done merely because it is 'age-old', because it has always been done. But people do not generally believe in the age-old for its own sake: they believe in it because they regard it as embodying distinctive and precious value-standards and forms of knowledge. This is why 'tradition' as such is a chimera, seen apart from the concrete beliefs and practices which are embedded in it.

The level of time-space distanciation characteristic of band societies is low. The mobile character of the society does not involve a mediated transcendence of space: that is to say, it does not, as in large societies, involve regularised transactions with others who are physically absent. The differentiation of presence and absence is not incorporated in the structuration of the societal community. The distanciation in time that can be secured in any non-literate society is similarly quite restricted. Tradition in a broad way maintains contact with a distant past, in the sense that similar beliefs and practices are continued across the generations. But the influence of tradition specifically acts to overcome a severance of 'present' and 'past': the past is not recoverable except in so far as it is implicated in the present (more accurately, in the continuity of 'presencing').

These considerations point to the importance of *storage capacity* to time-space distanciation and the generation of power. We may distinguish two forms of storage, corresponding to the two types of resources that enter into structures of domination. One is the more obvious of the two: the storage of 'material' or allocative resources. Storage capacity is much more important to the production of a 'surplus' than technological change in the instruments of production. But the storage of allocative resources turns out also to be less significant than the storage of authoritative resources as a whole. I shall try to amplify these claims shortly. To talk of 'storage' of material resources is more complex than may appear at first sight. Storage here involves not simply the physical containment of material goods (which is its least interesting form). The term should rather be understood as implying a range of time-space control. The two types of productive system most often mentioned in the archaeological literature as associated with the formation of 'civilisations' – agriculture in general, and irrigation agriculture in particular – each increase storage capacity, as contrasted to hunting and gathering. In agriculture the earth itself is regarded as a 'store' of potential produce; the garnering of products here involves biting quite deeply into time, since even relatively rudimentary forms of agriculture necessitate advance planning of a regularised character. Irrigation agriculture, where it involves the human construction of waterways, canals, etc., both demands and makes possible a greater co-ordination of time-space relations.

Storage of authoritative resources involves above all *the retention and control of information or knowledge*. There can be no doubt that the decisive development here is the invention of writing and notation. In non-literate societies knowledge is stored through its incorporation in traditional practices, including myth-telling: the only storage 'container' in such circumstances is the human memory. The time-space distanciation made possible by writing (and, in modern times, by mechanical printing) is much greater. There have, of course, been civilisations without writing – most notably the Inca, who employed *quipus*, knotted cords, as a mnemonic device. But such examples are exceptional. Writing seems everywhere to have orginated as a direct mode of storage: as a means of recording information relevant to the administration of societies of an increasing scale. In the early phases of development of Sumer, for example, writing seems to have been used exclusively to record and tally administrative details: 'Tallies and tokens, wage-lists and ration lists, lists of supplies and monthly accounts – these are the documents we have in tens of thousands.'[3] Listing, collating – what are these but the first origins, and always the main foundation, of what Foucault calls 'surveil-lance'? The keeping of written 'accounts' – regularised informa-tion about persons, objects and events – generates power that is unavailable in oral cultures. The list is the most elementary form of information coding, and therefore of information storing. The significance of lists, and of the differences between them and oral communication, have been well brought out by Goody.[4] A list is a particular type of 'container', not just an aid to the memory, but a definite means of encoding information. Lists do not represent speech in any sort of direct way, and contrast with the flow of oral communication; the early development of writing thus signals a sharper break with speech than might be imagined if we suppose that writing originated as a visual depiction of the spoken word.[5] In Sumer, listing led eventually to the further development of writing as a mode of chronicling events of a 'historical' nature. Kings adopted it in order to list or record their achievements in government and in war. These 'event lists' form the first known 'written histories', and eventually built up to span a large number of generations.

If storage of allocative and authoritative resources plays an essential underlying role in the promotion of time-space distancia-tion so also does the differentiation of centre/periphery relations. The *city*, as a religious, ceremonial and commercial centre, is a distinctive feature of all societies characterised by extensive time-space distanciation. When Spengler wrote that 'World history is city history' he may have been overstating the case, but not too unduly. Suppose we set out an over-all classification of major types of society as follows:

> Band societies
> Settled agricultural communities
> City-states  ⎫
> Empires  ⎬  'Civilisations' (class-divided societies)
> Feudal societies  ⎭
> Capitalist societies  ⎫
> Socialist societies  ⎬  Industrialised societies

In *all* these forms of society, following the first emergence of civilisations, the city, in divergent relations with the countryside, has played an influential role. The connection between agrarian communities and cities is one I shall take up in the following section. But in the light of the pervading influence of evolutionary theories it is worth again emphasising the significance of time-space edges in societal development. It is not just the case, for instance, that hunting and gathering societies have coexisted with early agricultural communities or city-states: each of the types of society indicated above has coexisted simultaneously with every one of the others (with the possible exception of feudalism, depending upon how narrowly the concept of 'feudal society' is formulated).

The city, as Mumford has shown brilliantly, may be regarded as a special form of 'container', a crucible for the generation of power on a scale unthinkable in non-urban communities. In his words,

> the first beginning of urban life, the first time the city proper becomes visible, was marked by a sudden increase in power in every department and by a magnification of the role of power itself in the affairs of men. A variety of institutions had hitherto existed separately, bringing their numbers together in a common meeting place, at seasonable intervals: the hunters' camp, the sacred monument or shrine, the palaeolithic ritual cave, the neolithic agricultural village – all of these coalesced in a bigger meeting place, the city . . . The original form of this container [the city] lasted for some six thousand years; only a few centuries ago did it begin to break up.[6]

The enclosure of cities by walls enhances the metaphor of the container. How far is Mumford correct, however, to presume that the agricultural village preceded the origin of the city? Mumford's work has done a good deal to free us from the misleading presumption that the expansion of 'productive forces' is the chief mobilising factor in social change. But in one respect he might not have gone far enough in questioning established views in archaeology.

## Urbanism, Agriculture, Trade

These established views, in their broad outlines at least, have been strongly influenced by the writings of Childe, who in turn drew his inspiration from Marx. Marx's insistence upon 'the prime importance of economic conditions', Childe wrote in 1936, 'is gaining acceptance in academic circles remote from the party passions inflamed by other aspects of Marxism'.[7] Certainly, the ideas Childe established on this basis have been generally accepted by many who have otherwise no connection with Marxism at all: perhaps in some part because an emphasis upon the determining role of production has a compatibility with the main source of evidence, material artefacts, that archaeological research has to rely on in seeking to understand societies that no longer exist.

Childe's writing is strongly steeped in evolution: there is a continuity, according to him, between natural and social evolution. The notion of increasing 'adaptation' to the demands of the material environment has a central part to play. The major stages in societal development distinguished by Childe are each triggered by economic transformations. The palaeolithic or 'old stone age' period is characterised by hunting and gathering, and is succeeded by the 'neolithic revolution' of agriculture and stock-breeding. The latter was eventually followed by the 'urban revolution', the formation of city-based civilisations. These stages, in Childe's view, are 'moments in an organic process of economic accumulation and of scientific and technical advancement'.[8] Childe recognised, of course, the significance of the growth of religious and kingly power in the development of the early civilisations; but his analysis accentuates rather forcibly the economic conditions and consequences of these phenomena as of decisive importance.

The idea that the 'neolithic revolution' necessarily precedes the emergence of cities is one that seems so indisputable, on the face of it, that it is not surprising that for many years it was presumed by Childe and almost everyone else to be axiomatic. That the city developed out of the neolithic village, in some way or another, seemed perfectly obvious. It is no longer so obvious, however – partly as a result of archaeological discoveries since Childe's time which have shown urban settlements to have existed at much earlier dates than was previously thought. The most famous of these sites is that at Çatal Hüyük, which dates from 7000 to 6000 B.C. Çatal Hüyük is the earliest neolithic site yet found, and at the same time the earliest city. This conjunction serves as the principal stimulus to Jacobs's questioning of the conception that the agricultural village preceded the first development of the city. Her thesis – that cities come first, rural developments later – is of course a controversial one, and I shall not accept her views in their entirety.

Jacobs combats what she calls 'the dogma of agricultural primacy' on the basis of a generalised claim about the economic productivity of the city as compared with the countryside. Cities have certainly been long seen as the centres of civilisation, but are often regarded as parasitic economically upon the surrounding countryside – both in their early origins and in their relation to rural areas once they have come into being. The city, however, Jacobs suggests, has been throughout history the characteristic source of innovations which have then been incorporated in rural production; and the emergence of the city was the stimulus initiating the 'neolithic revolution', rather than the other way around. The notion that first came agriculture, then settled agricultural communities, then cities, in an 'adaptive' progression, ignores the facts that settlement and agriculture have nothing in particular to do with one another, and that palaeolithic hunters and gatherers did have fixed settlements. The supposition that hunting and gathering and fixed settlements are incompatible is perhaps an example of too much 'reading back' from the mobile bands described by anthropologists:

The old idea that permanent settlements were impossible until after agriculture was invented is contradicted by so much hard evidence that many archaeologists no longer subscribe to this idea, although few scholars in other fields seem, as yet, to be aware of this reassessment. The world is dotted with various kinds of palaeolithic leavings which indicate that hunters had permanent settlements ... I would suggest that permanent settlements within hunting territories were ordinary features of pre-agricultural life. They would have been as natural for men as burrows are for foxes or nests are for eagles. Almost all activities would have been carried on in the settlement and it would also have served as the base for work carried out in the field – hunting, foraging, defending the territory, and raiding adjoining territories ... This implies that permanent settlements which grew as cities were, from the first, city-states. There would have been no such thing as a pre-agricultural city without a surrounding territory belonging to the city.[9]

According to Jacobs, settlements such as Çatal Hüyük provided the milieux in which agricultural technology was first developed and the 'neolithic revolution' initiated. As Sahlins and Clastres have suggested for more recent times, she argues that early hunters and gatherers did not necessarily lack the capability of producing a 'surplus'. But even if such were not the case, it would not follow that the creation of cities depended upon the prior production of 'surplus' food, because we know that cities have often developed in societies in which hunger was chronic and in which famines occurred periodically. In Jacobs's assessment, cities such as Çatal Hüyük can be regarded as having developed first of all primarily as trading outposts, thus leading to an expansion of manufacture; some of the techniques developed in urban manufacture were then applied to the cultivation of food to support a growing population. One implication of this analysis is that there were no cities which arose in isolation. In prehistoric, as in modern times, it seems probable that cities only developed in relation to other cities, involved in a network of connections with one another as well as with the surrounding rural areas.

If Jacobs's thesis is correct, it takes us some way from the conventional standpoint in regard of early city development. But perhaps it is worth while returning to some of Mumford's ideas in order to criticise some of her emphases. She is no doubt right to point to the economic productivity of the city as a general phenomenon. However, while her interpretation dispels the notion that a surge in the forces of production brings about the changes that lead to the rise of the city, she continues to lay stress upon the economic role of cities in the ancient civilisations. But this is as dubious in itself as the views she attacks. For the economic power generated by the early cities seems of lesser significance than political and military power, centred first in theocratic and later in monarchical control, which in the vast majority of cases appears to have been most consequential in their formation and subsequent development. Mumford's view is that ancient cities were above all 'containers' of religious and later royal power, the temple and the palace. It was these, he argues convincingly, which (by fair means or foul) attracted people from a distance, including traders; the drawing power of the city brought the merchants, rather than vice versa.[10] There seems no reason to suppose that this was not true of the very first urban settlements that may have developed directly within hunting and gathering economies.

### Legitimation and Time-Space Distanciation

The level of spatial dispersion found in city-states is often relatively low: both the early Sumerian and the Greek city-states were small, some of the latter being quite tiny. It will be part of my argument here that while empires are often seen as resulting from, and no doubt often have resulted from, the fusion of several city-states, there is a qualitative break between the two types of societal organisation. The argument can be expressed in terms of the relations between time-space distanciation and various aspects of sanctions which I distinguished in Chapter 2.

If the expansion of storage capacity is the principal means of the generation of power in time-space distanciation, this is not a phenomenon without 'costs' in regard of societal integration. In societies of high presence-availability, social integration is obviously largely coterminous with societal integration as a whole. Most city-states, like band societies and settled agricultural communities, can be classified within this category. Here the 'society' is based in the locale of the 'community', and the terms can be used virtually interchangeably. A 'society' in this sense is a 'community' in two ways: in terms of time-space proximity, or high presence-availability; and in terms of cultural homogeneity, founded in the similarity and continuity of traditional practices and the significance of kinship as a medium of collectivity organisation.

The consequence of this is that the power generated within city-states is usually legitimised through the mechanisms of community: it is 'traditional legitimation', given the limitations of this phrase noted previously. The power-centre that is the city has as its nucleus, both physically and socially, the theocratic order of the temple. The physical domination of the city by the temple, as in ancient Sumer, no doubt had a very direct symbolic value in reinforcing established beliefs and practices among the populace: it was simultaneously an incarnation of both power and of tradition. In the third millenium B.C. Sumer held about a dozen city-states, most having a walled city surrounded by small hamlets. The temple, on its *ziggurat*, stood out not only above the city but also over its surrounding area. According to Sumerian religious thought, each city belonged to its main god, to whom it had been allocated on the day the world was created. The secular power of the gods was none the less limited, and depended upon the uncoerced adherence of the free populace.[11] Legitimation in such circumstances is founded more upon inducement than upon coercion.

In Sumer, as probably in most cases elsewhere also, the consolidation of the city-states within an imperial domain came about substantially as a result of military campaigns: wars waged not just between the city-states themselves, however, but between city-states and 'barbarian' groups of various types. At least one characteristic type of transition between city-states and empires seems to have involved the solidifying of military command 'within' the society in question through military expansion 'outside'. Thus Sumerian history indicates that at the beginning military leaders were probably chosen and appointed by the governing assembly of citizenry for particular military tasks or expeditions. But the power thus acquired was employed to develop the trappings of monarchy, and increasingly to either shift the stronghold of power from the temple to the palace, or to merge the two in the divine person of the king. The army became the bulwark of monarchical, and imperial, power internally, at the same time as it was the means of the creation of empire externally.

Prior to the emergence of industrial capitalism in the West, world history was fought out along the time-space edges linking the various 'barbarisms' with differing forms of city-states, and feudal and imperial societies. Empires compose really the only examples of large-scale centralised societies before the advent of capitalism.[12] Efforts at centralisation were normally consciously made by rulers, who attempted to produce homogeneous modes of administration and political allegiance within particular territories. But it would be a major error to suppose that the level of centralisation of power was usually anywhere near as great as in the industrialised societies. As with the latter, in empires mechanisms of system integration become increasingly detached from reproduction founded in social integration. But there are fundamental contrasts between the nature of system integration in each case. I shall attempt to interpret these via the views on legitimation and domination I set out earlier on.

Before the arrival of capitalism there was no large-scale society in which the village community did not remain a basic unit, however strongly developed the urban areas in that society may have been. Certainly there were significant differences, to use Marx's term, in how far local agrarian communities were 'self-sufficient', having their own 'internal division of labour', and how far alternatively they were involved in systems of market exchange. But even where, as in Rome, *latifundiae* became common, the hold of the local community and its traditions over the mass of the agrarian labouring population was not broken. System integration was not achieved through social integration, but almost in spite of it. The point is made, albeit perhaps overdrawn, by Eberhard:

> In earlier societies it did not matter of which race, religion or culture the rulers were. They lived their own life in their palaces and cities. They did not interfere with the life of other groups, communities, classes, layers, except that they forced them to make contributions for their support – for which they promised 'protection'. And the members of the lower layers, too, did not care who ruled them, nor did they care what people in other layers did, how they looked, which language they spoke.[13]

How was system integration sustained in imperial societies? Three sets of factors seem most important: the use of coercive sanctions, based on military power; the legitimation of authority *within ruling elites*, making possible the establishment of an administrative apparatus of government; and the formation of economic ties of interdependence. Military power has virtually always been decisive not only in the creation of empires but also in whatever continuity of existence they might have enjoyed. To emphasise this might appear to be a banality, if it were not for the influence which consensual theories of 'order' have had in the social sciences. However great and grand emperors and kings have been, and however much their rule has been enveloped with symbols of legitimation, they have been remote figures from the vast majority of the population subject to their government. The segmentalised character of imperial societies, indeed of all non-industrialised societies of any size, by virtue of the persistence of the local community, inevitably involved a 'two-tier'[14] organisation, in which the normative distance between centre and periphery always remained considerable. The persistence of localised communities, and of the modes of organisation of kinship and tradition that characterised them – phenomena which of course have assumed a variety of particular forms – *are the chief foundations of the dialectic of control in non-capitalist societies*. The power of those who needed to extract coercively taxation, or other forms of tribute or services from populations subject to their rule, did not penetrate many aspects of daily life, which were nourished from other sources.

This is not to say that the legitimation of power was unimportant in the system integration of imperial societies; but its significance is to be found primarily in terms of how far it helped to consolidate the ruling apparatus itself. The 'two-tier' character of imperial societies indicates that some discretion has to be applied when concepts of 'despotism', whether Asiatic or otherwise, are employed. 'Despotism', as it has been used from Montesquieu onwards, has at least two connotations. One is that rule is arbitrary, in the sense that the dictates of the ruler are not effectively confined by acknowledged traditional practice or by impersonally formulated laws. The other is that the ruler has very sweeping, or 'absolute', control over the activities of his subject population. Each of these is easily exaggerated when used to describe imperial societies, if it is not acknowledged how distinct their organisation is from that of the industrialised societies. The ruler is less dependent upon the normative allegiance of his subjects at large than upon the loyalty of the administrative and military apparatus: in so far as his command over that apparatus depends upon the adherence of its members to the legitimised codes of his rule, he is not able to flout these codes indiscriminately. This is true even of the most extreme forms of personalised rule, such as that which Weber calls 'sultanism'.[15] The second aspect of despotic power is also inherently limited. The ruler may have command over the lives of his subjects in the sense that if they do not obey, or actively rebel, he can put them to the sword. But the 'power of life and death' in this sense is not the same as the capability of controlling the day-to-day lives of the mass of the population, which the ruler is not able to do. 'Despotism' has to be clearly separated from *totalitarianism*, which is much more far-reaching in the level of authoritative command over a subject population; and which depends, or so I shall argue subsequently, upon a much greater extension of the possibilities of surveillance than is ever available in societies where storage of information and the 'monitoring' of the activities of the population are relatively undeveloped.

Economic interdependence is the least important of the three sets of factors mentioned above in the system integration of imperial societies. Non-capitalist societies *are not* modes of production, even though like all societies they obviously *involve* modes of production. If technological or economic change are not the main levers of societal transformation prior to the emergence of capitalism, nor are they the most significant media of integration. In the case of imperial societies this is readily demonstrated by the lack of fit between political and economic boundaries, and between political and economic institutions. In empires, the extension of the territories claimed by the administrative apparatus, won through military power or its threat, constantly overran whatever unified forms of economic interdependence existed.[16] In terms of types of productive system, there are no clear differences between imperial societies and other less inclusive non-capitalist social formations. There seems no need to develop these points at any length since they have been elaborated by many other writers.

## Class-divided Society

Power, I have argued earlier, is generated by the intersection of authoritative and allocative resources: the first is expanded through the extension of social control of time-space, the second through control of nature. Marx's 'materialist conception of history' undeniably gives pride of place to relations with nature in influencing societal change. As an over-all interpretation of history, it does not pass muster. No use is served by defending it in a blindly dogmatic way; it should be discarded once and for all. There is no doubt that the abandoning of the 'materialist conception of history', together with Marx's evolutionary scheme, has serious consequences for the picture which Marx drew of capitalism and its transcendence by socialism. But these must be faced and thought through by anyone not just interested in producing yet another 'refutation of Marx'.

If we repudiate the 'materialist conception of history', what role does class division play prior to the development of capitalism? For Marx, private property is the basis of class division – without private property, no classes – and is at the same time bound up directly with the origins of the division of labour and the state. According to the text of *The German Ideology*,

> Division of labour and private property are … identical expressions: in the one the same thing is affirmed with reference to activity as is affirmed in the other with reference to the product of activity. Further, the division of labour implies the contradiction between the interest of the separate individual or the individual family and the communal interest of all individuals … out of this very contradiction between the interest of the individual and that of the community the latter takes an independent form as the *state,* divorced from the real interests of individual and community, and at the same time as an illusory communal life, always based, however, on the real ties existing in every family and tribal conglomeration.[17]

Although we cannot be sure that Marx shared his views, Engels regarded the emergence of private property as preceding the formation of states. According to Engels, states developed as a means of protecting the newly acquired property rights of individuals against the traditions of communal ownership. The emergent state 'not only sanctified the private property so little valued and declared this sanctification to be the highest purpose of human society'; it also 'set the seal of general social recognition on each new method of acquiring property and thus amassing wealth at continually increasing speed'.[18]

Engels's account is considerably more 'Europocentric' than that developed by Marx in the later stages of his career: the 'Asiatic Mode of Production' does not appear in Engels's analysis, which is confined to Europe and which treats Athenian Greece as a generalisable model for the transition from tribal societies to societies with classes. In Marx's eyes, nevertheless, fully fledged class societies are only identifiable in European history; the 'Asiatic Mode of Production' is not a class society but one that has become arrested at an early phase of development out of tribal orders. The main reason why Marx reaches such a conclusion is evident in his various discussions of this issue. It is because there are limits placed upon the independent development of private property by the coexistence of the 'self-sufficient' village communes on the one side, and a state apparatus on the other. But there is a major inconsistency introduced by this thesis – for if the state has its origins in the defence of private property, as the means whereby one developing class sustains its hegemony over another, how does it come about that the state should inhibit the formation of private property and classes proper? On what basis was the state established in the first place?

If classes only existed in European history, by Marx's own analysis there would only be three types of class society: the Ancient, feudal and capitalist. But if classes are to be found in the Asiatic societies – leaving aside for the moment the question of what constitutes a 'class society' – they might also exist in a sociologically significant sense in other civilisations also. This issue has been much debated in the literature. One school of thought (to which Wittfogel, among others, belongs) holds that the concept of class needs to be reformulated to bring it into line with the manifest importance of the state apparatus in non-capitalist civilisations. The notion of class adopted by Marx, according to Wittfogel, 'emerged in a society [nineteenth-century capitalism] that was decisively shaped by conditions of property'. The example of what, according to his view, are 'hydraulic societies' demon-strates that we must recognise 'state power as a prominent determinant of class structure': 'The men of the state apparatus,' he proposes, 'are a ruling class in the most unequivocal sense of the term; and the rest of the population constitutes the second major class, the ruled.'[19] This view, then, gives an emphatic answer to the question of whether class societies have existed outside the European context. It has proved surprisingly popular with those who, unlike Wittfogel, are not disillusioned with Marxism as a whole, and who draw quite different political implications for contemporary socialism than those depicted by Wittfogel. But it is nevertheless a view which does not withstand scrutiny – for reasons that have nothing specifically to do with the validity or otherwise of Wittfogel's claims about the significance of irrigation agriculture in the types of society he discusses. It might be justifiable to say that the state can act as a 'prominent determinant' of class structure, but this is quite different from treating the state officialdom as a ruling class. This sort of conception opens the way to all the confusions of so-called 'elite theory'.[20] The concept of class was taken by Marx to refer to the sectional forms of domination created by private ownership of property. As such, it can be readily distinguished from other structural sources of power in society, however much Marx himself might have tended reductively to suppose that class domination is the origin of political power.

It will be my argument here that Marx was right to have reservations about the significance of class as a structural feature of the Asiatic societies, on grounds that apply also to the ancient civilisations of the Near East and to those of Meso-America and Peru. But he was wrong, I think, to suppose that Greece and Rome, or European feudalism, were distinctly different in this respect: that is, that they were 'class societies' whereas the others were not. In none of these societies was control of private property the most significant basis of power, nor indeed was the distribution of allocative resources more generally. On the basis of scholarly advances made since Marx's time, one may say with confidence that he underestimated the level of development of private property, in land or in manufacture, in both India and China. Wittfogel accepts that 'in many hydraulic societies there existed considerable active [productive] private property'.[21] This appears to have been true even in the case of Peru, to judge by recent archaeological discussion. Peru has often been regarded as an 'agrarian socialist society', involving the suppression of private property and a centrally planned economy.[22] But it seems likely that this is a misinterpretation, based on an uncritical reading of the main sources from which our knowledge of the Inca derives, the manuscripts of Spanish priests, traders and soldiers. Private property in land appears in fact to have been strongly developed.[23]

Private property, in various differing forms, therefore seems to have been as widespread in non-capitalist civilisations outside Europe as in the European societies. There is no clear rationale for the claim that, as a basis of class formation, the development of private property assumed a peculiar importance in Europe. But, conversely, nor is there any justification for supposing that an 'early' consolidation of the state apparatus in the Asiatic societies separates them conclusively from the West. Marx was probably in the respect too much influenced by the idea of 'oriental despotism' in the East: for authoritative resources were the main basis of both political and economic power, though not of course in exactly the same concrete ways, in both East and West. Marx's reservations about the role of class divisions in the Eastern civilisations, in other words, apply in some substantial degree to the history of Europe also. This is why I choose to employ the term *class-divided society* to refer to the non-capitalist civilisations.[24] By a 'class-divided society' I mean a society in which there are classes, but where class analysis does not serve as a basis for identifying the basic structural principle of organisation of that society. I shall subsequently contrast class-divided society with the *class society* ushered in by capitalism. The elaboration of this distinction, however, presumes examining what 'property' is in more detail, a problem I shall take up in the following chapter.[25]

# 5

# Property and Class Society

Marx's 'materialist conception of history' is predicated upon the primacy of allocative resources in societal organisation through the universal applicability of the forces/relations of production dialectic. The formal correlate of this dialectic is the 'abstract model' of class domination which applies to each of the types of class society that Marx distinguishes.[1] Marx's abstract model of class is a dichotomous one. In the class societies, two basic classes exist, differentiated in terms of ownership of the means of production or private property. Those owning the means of production as their private property are able to use their ownership to exploit the labour of others through the appropriation of a surplus product. Identifying the dichotomous class division supplies the analytic master-key to unlocking the power relations inherent in a class society, as the division of classes is a division of both property and power. Class division implies a relation of structured dependence and conflict, since each class exists in 'asymmetrical reciprocity' with the other, yet at the same time has interests which are opposed to those of the other. Class 'conflict' in its most basic sense refers to the opposition of interests structured into a mode of production, and may be distinguished from active struggles, of whatever kind, that may arise between classes.

All class relations are intrinsically exploitative, since the dominant class appropriates surplus production (surplus labour) to its own ends. But the mechanism of exploitation differs in varying types of society. In societies prior to capitalism, exploitation occurs either through some form of *corvée* labour, slavery, or through the direct appropriation of the surplus product. Exploitation here, Marx agreed with the physiocrats, is naked and direct. With the advent of capitalism, in which labour-power sells at its market value, the mechanism of class exploitation is not so immediately apparent – indeed, as I have mentioned before, Marx regarded it as the 'hidden riddle' of capitalist production. The riddle is solved through uncovering the origins of surplus value as the source of profit appropriated by the capitalist class.

All this is numbingly familiar, and I recapitulate it here only as a background for taking up two problems that are partly latent in this general account as regards the significance of allocative resources. One concerns the nature of the process whereby surplus is extracted; the second concerns the very nature of property itself, the principal issue with which I shall be occupied in this chapter.

## Exploitation and Surplus

What is the 'surplus product' which figures so prominently in the Marxian account of class domination? The notion fits fairly snugly within the assumptions of Marx's evolutionary scheme, since the expansion of the forces of production is presumed to bring about a burgeoning creation of material wealth, this being appropriated as private property by a nascent ruling class. Marx seems to owe the idea of surplus production to the physiocrats, for whom it was closely connected with the critique of the feudal aristocracy as a 'sterile' or non-productive class.[2] In Marx's hands the concept becomes one to be applied broadly to class societies, including both the Ancient world and (transmuted as 'surplus value') in capitalism. I have already pointed out earlier in the book that there is no need to suppose that those in societies which could potentially expand production would choose to do so; as know-ledgeable human agents, they may see their priorities elsewhere. But how can a 'surplus' be defined? There seem two possibilities, if we consider that 'surplus' refers to 'surplus of material products'. We could perhaps say surplus production exists when, in a particular society, more is produced than is demanded to meet the bare physical needs of survival of the members of that society. But there are various difficulties with this – if, at any rate, it is to be made integral to the theory of class domination as formulated by Marx. In the first place, there are or have been very few societies in the world in which everyone has existed chronically at or near starvation level. The majority, if surplus is defined in relation to the bare minimum necessary for physical survival, have produced some sort of surplus. In the second place, if we concede that there is no mechanical inevitability that those who could produce more will do so, the potential for surplus production becomes more significant as a gauge of 'material wealth' than the goods that are actually produced and utilised. Finally, there is no shortage of instances where ruling elites lived in extreme luxury, while large numbers of their subject population starved.

A surplus could, however, be defined as production which exceeds that which is necessary to sustain a traditionally sanctioned or habitual way of life. If we define 'surplus' in this way, it reinforces the conclusion that the creation of surplus production is unlikely to have been a driving impetus of great significance in history, since the binding force of tradition is strong. Apart from this, however, it becomes unclear why the appropriation of surplus production should be regarded as exploitation at all, if the producers have no need for the goods involved.

These comments apply to the non-capitalist class societies, or what I have called the 'class-divided' societies. Within capitalism, according to Marx's theory at any rate, one might suppose that the situation is clearer than that described above. For surplus value can be measured, in relation to the working-day of the labourer: it is that which is 'left over' when the cost of the labour-power has been paid for by the employer, and which goes to the latter. Here it would seem that there can be an economic definition of surplus. So there can be – but with one crucial proviso. The 'surplus' can be defined economically in capitalism only because the 'economic' there becomes peculiarly significant, as contrasted to class-divided societies, *as a medium of power*. I take this to be one of the mainstays of Marx's critique of classical political economy: that the 'free' exchange of labour-power and capital in the context of the capitalist market in fact allows the capitalist class coercive power over wage-labour. It is this insight that needs to be generalised historically, and applied to class-divided societies as well as to capitalistic ones. That is to say, even though 'surplus production' consists of material goods, it can only be defined *as* a surplus in terms of the *asymmetrical distribution of power between classes*. A 'surplus' is simply that which one class manages to extract from another.

If this is a common phenomenon of all class systems, we must also make clear, in this case following the lines of Marx's analysis quite closely, how the mechanisms of surplus extraction differ between class-divided societies on the one hand and class societies on the other. The major source of difference is an extremely significant one, and I shall have more to say about its implications later. In class-divided societies the extraction of surplus production is normally backed in a direct way by the threat or the use of force. Class division rests less on control of allocative than of authoritative resources, usually backed by the potential or actual use of violence. Control of the means of violence may be largely centralised in the hands of a monarch or imperial ruler, or may be more decentralised under the sway of local warlords. This is not particularly relevant for the question at issue, however. In class-divided societies the economic power involved in class relations is rarely either achieved or sustained by solely economic means. This is above all the case with class relations involving agrarian production, which of course has been in all non-capitalist societies the pre-eminent basis of economic life. In capitalism, by contrast, the dominant class acquires its position by virtue of the economic power yielded by the ownership of private property. As the fundamental axis of the capitalist mode of production, the capitalist labour contract has no counterpart in class-divided societies. I shall regard this as underlying everything that follows in this chapter. The extraction of surplus value in capitalist economies is founded upon the economic constraint deriving from the dependence of the propertyless wage-labourer upon those who have access to capital. In class-divided societies, except in those instances where large-scale centralised irrigation schemes were the basis of agriculture, the economic dependence of the agrarian producer upon the dominant class was slight or attenuated.

All of this is transformed by the advent of capitalism; the severing of the wage-worker from control of the means of production places him/her in a situation of necessary economic dependence upon the employer. The phrase 'asymmetrical reciprocity' which I used earlier is intended to capture this: in a capitalistic society the worker needs the capitalist just as the capitalist needs labour-power, while at the same time there is an endemic conflict relation between them.

## Allocative Resources: Private Property as Capital

The capitalist labour contract is founded on the market encounter between the owners of capital and the possessors of 'mere' labour-power. Marx laid great stress, of course, upon the second of these elements, presuming as it does the expropriation of masses of the peasantry from the land, a process 'written in blood and fire' across the face of post-feudal Europe. In relation to the writings of those who saw the origins of capitalism purely from the perspective of the accumulation of capital, this emphasis is enormously important. But what Marx wrote about capital (and about *money*) is significant in its own right. I want to refer here to those aspects of Marx's analysis relevant to issues of time-space mediation raised previously.

Just as there are tensions between Marx's evolutionary scheme and certain of the views expressed in the *Formen*, so there are between the over-all features of Marx's class theory, described briefly at the opening of this chapter, and his interpretation of the class structure of capitalism. Class domination in general is organised in terms of ownership of private property of the means of production, used to glean a surplus from the active producers. But Marx's examination of capitalism as a social and economic system also shows that 'private property' – or allocative resources – in capitalism is in certain basic respects fundamentally different from that characteristic of non-capitalist societies. Here again we must to some degree use Marx against himself, to insist that capitalism is more distinct from other types of societies than he tended to indicate in his evolutionary scheme. The concept of 'property' was never analysed in detail by Marx, and it would be necessary to discuss it at some length were one to attempt a satisfactory elucidation of the notion. For my purposes here it is enough to specify a minimal categorisation of how 'property' might be analysed. First of all, *property has a content*, property *is* something. The chief form of private property in the means of production in class-divided societies is *land*, even if the formation of money capital through commerce and agriculture may be a far from negligible phenomenon. In capitalism the main forms of private property are factories, offices, machinery, etc., however much land (itself capitalised) might remain a necessary productive resource. It is difficult to underestimate the sociological significance of this difference, and Marx provides us with a framework for analysing it – again, especially in sections of the *Grundrisse*. 'Property', of course, also implies normative rights of control of material resources. Here we can usefully recognise variations in the level and types of alienability of resources. It has usually been the case in class-divided societies that those who owned land,[3] and profited from the labour of others upon that land, were subject to limitations on how far it could be either legally transferred or sold on a market. Class-divided societies tend to be characterised by the elements indicated at the top left-hand corner of Figure 5.1, the economy of capitalism by those at the bottom right-hand corner. The pervasive importance of the land in non-capitalist societies is brought out by Marx in the following passage:

> Among peoples with a settled agriculture – this settling already a great step – where this predominates, as in antiquity and in the feudal order, even industry, together with its organisation and the forms of property corresponding to it, has a more or less landed-proprietary character; it is either completely dependent on it, as among the earlier Romans, or, as in the Middle Ages, imitates, within the city and its relations, the organisation of the land. In the Middle Ages, capital itself – apart from pure money-capital – in the form of traditional artisans' tools, etc., has this landed-proprietary character. In bourgeois society it is the opposite. Agriculture more and more becomes merely a branch of industry, and is entirely dominated by capital.[4]

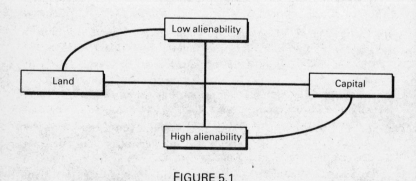

FIGURE 5.1

In all forms of class-divided society the most prevalent modes of social association occur in communities of high presence-availability. This is as characteristic of imperial societies as in smaller societal units. Although there have been various types of city-states whose wealth has been built through trade and commerce, by and large it is true to say that trade exists in the interstices of class-divided societies. Trading relations are carried on between communities that always sustain a high degree of local autonomy. The pre-eminence of agrarian production in such settings means much more than merely the predominance of immobile property. As Marx stresses in the *Formen*, and repeatedly returns to in other parts of the *Grundrisse,* in non-capitalist societies production is geared to what he calls the 'natural relation' with land and with the local community. Agrarian production inevitably follows the rhythms of the seasons, and involves the producer in continuous and subtle mediations with nature. Even though the main line of social differentiation in class-divided societies is between country-side and city, the city characteristically preserves a direct confor-mity with the contours of the natural environment.[5] What is true of space is also true of time and time-consciousness. In feudalism, as in other class-divided civilisations, the mass of the population only knew two unquestionably fixed moments of the day, sunrise and sunset. Among elites, calendars provided often precise calcula-tions of the passing of days, weeks and years; but precision in time-calculation within the course of day-to-day activity was neither known nor desired.[6]

In distinguishing use-value from exchange-value, and in showing money to be the medium of 'pure exchange-value', Marx demon-strates how money expresses and makes possible the disembed-ding of social relationships from communities of high presence-availability. Money, one might say, is the specific enemy of presence; its value is wholly parasitic upon exchange. As Simmel points out, money

is completely formless: it does not contain within itself the slightest suggestion of a regular rising and falling of the contents of life; it offers itself at every moment with the same freshness and efficiency; by its far-reaching effects and by reducing things to one and the same standard value, that is by levelling out, countless fluctuations, mutual alterations of distance and proximity, of oscillation and equilibrium, it levels out what would otherwise impose far-reaching changes upon the possibil-ities for the individual's activities and experiences.[7]

Simmel is mistaken, however, in so far as he treats money itself as the agent producing such consequences, rather than relating the utter dependence of the capitalist economy upon money to the analysis of commodity production, as Marx does, and hence to the class structure.

Commodity production, even of the 'simple' form, involves the commensurate exchange of incommensurables. The goods which compose commodities have use-values, but the exchange-values that actually define them as commodities differ from one another only quantitatively – money expressing this quantification. A commodity, Marx says, is 'an equivalent' and as such 'all its natural qualities are extinguished'; 'it no longer takes up a special, qualitative relationship towards other commodities, but is rather the general measure as well as the general representative, the general medium of exchange of all other commodities'. The product, as a commodity, becomes translated into a moment of exchange. All commodities thus have a double existence, as 'natural product' and as exchange-value. The process of circulation of commodities, Marx reasons, can only reach an advanced level – as involved in a fully fledged capitalist economy – if exchange-value becomes detached from products and exists alongside them as a commodity, i.e. money. The development and universalisation of money, Marx points out, in a definite way parallels the emergence of writing, since both trace out a progressive distanciation from the objects to which they 'refer'.[8] Writing, one might argue, manifests such a distanciation in the movement from pictures to abstract marks that have an 'arbitrary' relation to the object-world.[9] Money also begins as objects or products that have use-value which become implicated in exchange; but it progressively becomes detached from the use-value of its content. Marx rejects those theories of money which seek to anchor its value in a specific content, such as silver or gold. The true essence of money is to be found in the intrinsically 'worthless' form of paper money, not in those forms which might seem to have some qualities that can be connected to use-values. Money becomes a commodity only because it represents or symbolises the exchange-value of all other commodities.

The Money–Commodity–Money relation is the fundamental component of the circulation of capital within the capitalist economy. The development of 'worthless' money is crucial to this, since money in this form maximises the transformation/mediation relations expressed in the widespread commodification of products. Money makes possible the circulation of exchange-values across very large time-scale distances. It only does so because it permits the expression of exchange-value in the shape of prices. Other types of commodity exchange, such as barter, payment in kind, or feudal services, do not constitute circulation: 'To get circulation, two things are required above all: *Firstly*, the precondition that commodities are prices; *Secondly*: not isolated acts of exchange, but a circle of exchange, a totality of the same, in constant flux, proceeding more or less over the entire surface of society.[10]

Money is a medium of circulation, but also permits the storage of wealth on a massive scale. Weber's analysis is perfectly compatible with that of Marx at this point. Two features that Weber singles out as especially significant in the formation of capitalism can be seen as devices aiding the storage of money capital: the invention of double-entry book-keeping, and the co-ordination of credit facilities. The circulation of commodities involved in a fully fledged capitalist economy involves extension in space and extension in time. Money permits the acquisition or disposal of goods between persons who are widely separated in space and time. Double-entry book-keeping allows the adjusting of inflows and outflows that occur over long spans of time-space. Credit facilities permit what Weber explicitly calls 'storage of value', meaning by this the delaying of obligations against future promise of payment.[11] The conjoining of such book-keeping and the provision of credit is the core of banking, such an important institution in organising both circulation and storage of money.

## Allocative Resources: Capital and Wage-Labour

The dissolution of feudalism and its replacement by capitalism, Marx argues, involves two sets of processes: the accumulation of capital on the one hand, and on the other the creation of 'free' wage-labour. He pours scorn on those who imagine either that the origins of capitalism can be understood wholly in terms of capital accumulation, or who suppose that capital accumulation itself brings about the development of a propertyless labour force. The stockpiling of money that was the basis of the 'original accumulation' of capital was in some relatively minor part implicated in the disintegration of feudalism, via the formation of commodity markets. But the 'labour market', a distinctive phenomenon of capitalism, was largely the outcome of other processes (in England, the enclosure movement) that were only contingently associated in Europe with the growth of monetary wealth.[12] How and why these processes occurred, of course, is a matter of continuing debate, and I do not propose to enter into this debate here. What is vital in Marx's analysis is the manner in which he shows that the structural set M–C–M, in the capitalist economy, relates the convertibility of capital to the convertibility of labour (labour-power). The structural set Money–Labour Contract–Profit assumes the same form as the Money–Commodity–Money relation.

This isomorphism comes about because labour-power itself becomes a commodity and hence enters directly into the transformation/mediation relations presupposed by exchange-value. There can be no doubt that Marx was entirely justified in stressing the radical nature of the historical transition brought about by the expropriation of producers from their means of production. The process of expropriation obviously decisively altered the character of what 'labour' is under capitalism, as contrasted with all class-divided civilisations. Rural labour, as noted earlier, always formed an integral element of the 'natural relation' with the local community and the land. Labour-power, as a commodified form, relates to labour in this traditional sense much as money relates to the use-values of the goods for which it is exchanged. As a commodity, labour has a similar double existence to other commodities, as on the one hand the expenditure of human skills and abilities, and on the other a 'cost' to capital, defined in terms of its value in exchange.

The underlying constitutive component of both goods and labour that permits their common existence as interchangeable commodities, according to Marx, is *time*. Every commodity, including labour-power itself, is 'the objectification of a given amount of labour time'.[13] The 'socially necessary labour time' governs the value of commodities, and is the standard measure of exchange-value. Units of time are what makes the value of commodities divisible and quantifiable. The quantification of time is thus that very foundation of the universalising character assumed by the exchange of commodities. In economic calculation, accounting, and so on, commodities are transformed into quantitative measures of value on paper. On paper, as Marx says, this process proceeds by mere abstraction; but 'in the real exchange process a real *mediation* is required, a means to accomplish this abstraction'.[14] *This means is supplied by the fact that commodities in exchange exist only as exchange-values, which in turn depends upon the temporal equation of units of labour.* To determine how much bread is required to exchange for a yard of linen, in Marx's example, the bread must be equated with a particular quotient of labour-time. The same must be done for the linen. Each of the commodities must be equated with something other than itself. This 'something' is not an object but a relational phenomenon based upon the quantified scale of labour-time:

> The commodity first has to be transposed into labour-time, into something qualitatively different from itself (qualitatively different (1) because it is not labour-time as labour-time, but materialised labour-time; labour-time not in the form of motion, but at rest; not in the form of the process, but of the result; (2) because it is not the objectification of labour-time in general, which exists only as a conception [it is only a conception of labour separated from its quality, subject merely to quantitative variations], but rather the specific results of a specific, or a naturally specified kind of labour which differs qualitatively from other kinds), in order then to be compared as a specific amount of labour-time, as a certain magnitude of labour, with other amounts of labour-time, other magnitudes of labour.[15]

The nature of Marx's argument should be made clear here. Time, in the context of the inevitable passing away of the human organism, is a scarce resource in all types of production system, and hence in relation to labour in general. 'Economy of time,' as Marx laconically puts it, 'to this all economy ultimately reduces itself.'[16] However, the calculation and co-ordination of exchange-values by labour-time is a specific feature of the commodification of economic relations introduced by the convergence of money capital and the formation of wage-labour characteristic of capitalism. As compared with surplus production in class-divided

societies, surplus value is assessed solely in terms of the quantification of the working day. In non-capitalist economies the producer
may have to allocate part of the working day, or more commonly a
certain number of working days in a given period of time, to
productive activity the results of which are appropriated by the
exploiting class. But this has only a specious similarity to the
quantified labour-time implicated in the production of surplus
value. In capitalism a specific temporally bounded 'working day' is
introduced, subdivided into units of time, and used as a bargaining
medium between worker and employer. Struggle over time is the
most direct expression of class conflict in the capitalist economy;
the length of the working day is not determined by tradition or
convention but by the outcome of such struggle. 'Time is
everything,' Marx says, 'man is nothing; he is at most the
incarnation of time. Quantity alone decides everything: hour for
hour, day for day.'[17]

The 'double existence' of labour-power as a commodity differs
from that of other commodities in two highly significant ways.
First, labour-power is the only commodity which itself produces
value, and thus has a very special part to play in the generation of
profit in relation to the capitalist. Second, the 'other side' of
labour-power (that side of its existence in which it is not a
commodity) is not merely the use-value of a material good but a
living human being with needs, feelings and aspirations. Labour-
power is a commodity like any other – but resists being treated as a
commodity like any other. The ownership of property, as capital,
confers a range of rights upon employers, creating power over
those whose only 'property' is their labour-power, and who are
compelled to negotiate a monetary wage in a labour market. Given
the purely economic nature of the capitalist labour contract,
labour-power is regarded as a 'factor of production' and a 'cost' to
the employer. But labour-power consists of the concrete activities
of human beings, working in definite industrial settings, who resist
being treated as on a par with the material commodities which they
produce.

The interlocking of capital and wage-labour in a relation of
dependence and interest conflict is the *chief basis of the dialectic of
control* in the productive order of the capitalist economy. This is a
matter of fundamental importance in separating capitalism from
class-divided societies. In the latter it is the resistance of the local

community, tradition and kinship circles to the penetration by relations of absence which sustains a definite measure of control of the exploited over their conditions of day-to-day existence. The vast extension of time-space mediations made structurally possible by the prevalence of money capital, by the commodification of labour and by the transformability of the one into the other, undercuts the segregated and autonomous character of the local community of producers. Unlike the situation in most contexts in class-divided societies, in capitalism class struggle is built into the very constitution of work and the labour setting. In the context of the productive organisation, whatever sway the wage-worker gains over the circumstances of labour is achieved primarily through attempts at 'defensive control' of the work-place: informal norms of production, the threat of or actual collective withdrawal of labour, absenteeism, and so on.

## Capitalism as a Class Society

In calling capitalism a class society, and thereby distinguishing it as a social system from class-divided societies, I mean to emphasise principally two things: the primacy accorded to the 'economic', and more generally to the transformation of nature; and, following from the above disucssion, the intrusion of exploitation and class domination into the heart of the labour process. The connections between these two characteristics are to be found in the transform-ations indicated above, whereby the dominant form of property becomes capital and where simultaneously the only 'property' possessed by the majority of the population consists in their market capacities: the nature of the labour-power which they are able to offer as a marketable resource to achieve a money wage. In such circumstances, class relations, founded upon private own-ership of the means of production in 'asymmetrical reciprocity' with propertyless wage-labour, have a centrality in the dynamics of power far beyond anything found in class-divided societies.

Whatever the role Puritanism – and indeed certain codes of Christianity more generally – may have played in the early origins of capitalism, it is indisputable that, once well established, capitalist society is associated with a chronic impetus to technolog-ical innovation and 'economic growth' unparalleled in previous history. There seems equally little doubt that Marx was right to locate this impetus in the dynamic nature of production governed by price, profit and investment. If this appears something of a banality on the face of things, it becomes less so when seen in the light of the rival theory which for a long while dominated sociology, the 'theory of industrial society'.[18] For the theory of industrial society (and its latter-day affiliate, linked to a conception of a supposedly 'post-industrial' world) has no account of the mechanism generating the changes it diagnoses: technology appears as its own prime-mover.[19]

In capitalist society, as differentiated from class-divided civilisations, ownership of private property is both the means of appropriating a surplus product (in the shape of surplus value) and at the same time a fundamental lever of social change. Private property, as capital, is a mechanism of social organisation and mobilisation; it is involved in the reproduction of the societal totality in a very much more significant sense than ownership of either land or of mercantile capital in class-divided societies. For, once established, the capitalist economy depends upon maintaining levels of investment that will allow productive enterprise to be carried on at a profit; and in turn the creation of profit is the condition of renewed investment. This means that allocative resources assume a new prominence, in relation both to the constant pressure to material accumulation, and also as the very centre of the mode whereby such accumulation is realised.

The commodification of economic life in capitalism, as I have tried to show above, proceeds in two – connected – ways. On a 'lateral' dimension, the expansion of capital, and especially its predominant transformation into money capital, involves a massive expansion of product markets. On a 'vertical' dimension, with the widespread expropriation of labour from control of the means of production, labour-power becomes separated from the 'content' of work itself, from the actual operations the worker performs. One major outcome of the conjunction of these two extensions of transformation/mediation relations is that *the extraction of surplus becomes part of the very process of production*. In class-divided societies a peasant may have to give over a certain period of labour, or a proportion of production, to the dominant class. Even where state-administered irrigation systems existed, the process of labour was not significantly penetrated by the exploitative relation. Class-divided societies of all types were based predominantly upon peasant production; there is far less difference between the modes of peasant labour found in the class-divided civilisations over five millenia than there is between peasant labour and the labour of the capitalist wage-worker. It is of the first importance to see that the intersection of the commodification of exchange and of labour-power is what made industrialisation possible, not the reverse.

There were only two ways, broadly speaking, in which the 'management' of labour occurred in class-divided societies. One, to which I have already made some considerable reference, hardly counts as 'management' in anything like the conventional sense at all. This is linked to what has been by far the most common means of exploitative control: it is where, in agrarian production, the producer is 'managed' only to the extent of having to participate in *corvée* labour or to cede products to an exploiting class. The second form, which comes closer to capitalist-industrial production in respect of involving the 'management' of a labour force, is where there is mass co-ordination of labour, on plantations or for building projects (the construction of temples, roads, etc.). Slave labour has typically been prominent in such circumstances, though by no means universally so. The second type of exploitation of labour has sometimes involved the creation of 'human machines', particularly where labour has been harnessed for the pursuance of specific large-scale projects. These human 'mega-machines',[20] however, have (a) not been controlled by commercial or manufacturing classes; (b) have only been organised in a sporadic way, and (c) have not *integrated* labour-power with the technological form of the labour task. Human labour was co-ordinated in the manner of a machine, but not treated as an element of the organisation of technology itself. The latter, as the work of Braverman in particular has helped to clarify, is a basic characteristic of the capitalistic labour process.[21]

There is no doubting the importance of the changes ushered in by the 'Industrial Revolution', beginning in Britain and subsequently spreading across the world. But two factors have conspired to substantiate a strongly established view that the Industrial Revolution is to be basically seen as a related series of technological innovations. One is the supposition that it was changes in technique which were the main impetus leading to the spread of factory production, and more generally to the pervasive separation of the home from the work-place. But the development of the factory seems to have been more closely associated with a perceived need to discipline wage-labour by submitting workers to direct means of surveillance.[22] It is not at all difficult to see how this connects to the process of the penetration of the productive process by class relations analysed above. The formation of the capitalist labour contract, as I have mentioned previously, is sanctioned neither by norms of obligation or fealty, such as existed in feudalism, nor by the direct threat of force. The only sanction, possessed by employers as a whole rather than by individual employers, is the need of expropriated workers to have some form of paid work – *der stumme Zwang*, the 'dull compulsion' of economic relations, as Marx described it. The concentration of workers within a distinct and separate work-place, a specific locale in which production is carried on under direct supervision, permits the employer control over labour-power which would otherwise be difficult to achieve.

A second basis for exaggerating the technological innovations of the Industrial Revolution is to be found in historians' frequent acceptance of the Victorian view of the overriding significance of mechanical innovations made in the late eighteenth and early nineteenth centuries in Britain. Such a standpoint belittles an extensive history of invention dating at least as far back as the eleventh century, but certainly not merely internal to Europe. Trade and warfare with the then more technologically advanced civilisations of the Near and Far East led to a far-reaching resurgence of technical activity. From Byzantine culture came developments in textiles, pottery and mosaics; from the Islamic world, irrigation, chemicals and horse-breeding; from China, porcelain, silks, paper-making and gunpowder.[23] The exploitation of the Americas greatly augmented the range and supply of raw materials, and helped to further major technical refinements of mining and smelting industries. In mining, and in military organisation of the sixteenth and seventeenth centuries, we find many of the most important antecedents of both the technology and the social discipline subsequently incorporated in factories:

By the sixteenth century . . . mining and smelting had become advanced industries, in the sense that many operations were highly mechanised ... many of the principal mechanical inventions were derived from the mine, including the railroad, the mechanical lift, the underground tunnel, along with artificial lighting and ventilation ... Mining originally set the pattern for later modes of mechanisation by its callous disregard for human factors, by its indifference to the pollution and destruction of the neighbouring environment, by its concentration upon the physico-chemical processes for obtaining the desired metal or fuel, and above all by its topographical and mental isolation from the organic world of the farmer and the craftsman, and the spiritual world of the Church, the University, and the City.[24]

In the army barracks, and in the mass co-ordination of men on the battlefield (epitomised by the military innovations of Prince Maurice of Orange and Nassau in the sixteenth century) are to be found the prototype of the regimentation of the factory – as both Marx and Weber noted.

The particular history of European technology, however, is of less consequence for the standpoint I have developed in this chapter than the disembedding of technological innovation from its traditional subordination to other institutions. Whatever may have been the chain of events producing this result, it was integrally bound up with the twin processes of commodification that created a class society out of a class-divided one.

## The Separation of the Economic and the Political

The institutional separation of the 'economic' from the 'political' has long been treated as a major characteristic of capitalism by many authors, both Marxist and non-Marxist. But we must take some care in working out the implications of this. In class-divided societies, although at the local level the 'economic' is embedded in the institutional framework of community life, in a certain sense production relations are much more distinct from the 'political' – in the form of the state – than they are in capitalist societies. The state may organise and sanction the extraction of surplus production, but it is quite marginal to the production process itself. There is therefore a definite sense in which economic and political relations are more closely integrated in capitalism than they ever were previously.

As it stands, however, this is a misleading conclusion because the 'economic' and the 'political' do not have the same meaning with the development of capitalism as in non-capitalist types of society. This is obvious enough in the light of what has been said previously about the expansion of commodification involved in the formation of the capital/wage-labour relation as the centre-point of the production system. But it is highly important to avoid (a) supposing that the role of the capitalist state, even in early capitalism, has ever been limited to that of providing an administrative and legal apparatus guaranteeing the contractual relations forged in the economic sphere; and (b) imagining that the separation of economy and polity can be understood as hinging upon the competitiveness of commodity markets. Each of these notions was closely associated with classical political economy, and the critics of political economy, including Marxist writers, have by no means been free of them.

Point (a) raises a host of difficult historical and analytical problems, which I have no intention of confronting in the current context. It seems difficult to deny, however, that Weber was right in insisting upon the essential significance of the 'absolutist state' in Europe for the rise of capitalism, and in holding that absolutism was quite different from the 'despotism' of the Asiatic or other imperial societies. European absolutism not merely coincided with, but was closely dependent upon, the consolidation of a 'civil society' based in the semi-autonomous urban communes. It would be an error to regard the absolutist state just as a transitional phenomenon between the collapse of feudalism and the establishing of capitalism. The absolutist rulers played as great a role in dismantling the normative framework of the *Stände* as did the growth of the independence and wealth of the 'bourgeois' towns. All this, of course, was recognised and commented upon by Marx. Marx's analysis suggests that the bourgeoisie combined with the absolutist monarchy to complete the overthrow of feudalism, rebelling against the absolutist rulers once their own power had increased sufficiently. However, the desire of capitalistic elements to secure an expansion of markets in goods and labour is presumed to have been a major mobilising force underlying this process, such that the bourgeoisie were interested in restricting the scope of state power. This seems not only an over-simplification but also directly related to an underestimation of the scope of the activities of the state in early capitalist society. The absolutist state contributed more to the consolidation of capitalism than aiding in the elimination of the feudal dispersal of powers. So far as the administration of the economy of an emergent capitalism 'internally' was concerned, these contributions involved particularly the centralisation of the system of paper money; 'externally', states energetically pursued policies of military aggrandisement that swelled the wealth of the major countries of Western Europe. It is a commonplace today to emphasise that capitalism, from its beginnings, was a 'world system', in the sense given to that term by Wallerstein – a world system decisively different in certain ways from imperial societies.[25] But it is equally important to recognise that it also began as a state system within Europe of a kind that seems to have had no close parallel among class-divided civilisations in other times and places.[26] There is no need to argue that this was simply 'functional' for capitalism, to acknowledge the wholly obvious fact that the capitalist societies came into being as territorially bounded states.

Adoption of view (b) above has far-reaching consequences for how the maturation of capitalism is portrayed. As a general characterisation, it can be said that this view considers the defining feature of a capitalist economy to reside in the competitive production of goods. The 'autonomy' of the economic is taken to be the *same thing* as the competitiveness of commodity markets: economic life, free from the intervention of the political sphere, is controlled by regulative principles of economic exchange alone. In this conception the separation of the 'economic' from the 'political' only aptly describes capitalism in its nineteenth-century form, and then mainly with reference to countries such as England and the United States rather than to those like Germany, in which there was a greater degree of 'state direction' of economic development. With the increasing concentration of industry, the centralisation of national economies, and the expanding role of the state in economic life, so it is reasoned, the economic again becomes united with the political. Poulantzas has commented accurately upon this standpoint:

A whole tradition of political theory, based on an ideological delimitation of the autonomy of the political from the economic (i.e. the theoretical tradition of the nineteenth century, which involves precisely the theme of the separation of civil society from the state), mistakes this autonomy for that specific non-intervention of the political in the economic which is characteristic of the form of the liberal state and of private capitalism. On this interpretation, because of its marked intervention in the economic, the contemporary state in state monopoly capitalism involves an abolition of the respective autonomy of the political and the economic characteristic of the capitalist mode of production and a capitalist formation.[27]

The separation of the economic from the political should be regarded *as based in the capitalist labour contract* rather than in the nature of product markets. This is completely compatible with the Marxian view that the fundamental character of capitalism does not derive from the expansion of markets as such, but from the conjunction of such expansion with the commodification of labour-power. The capitalist labour contract serves as a major nexus of transformation/mediation relations, or structural sets, converting allocative resources (control of private property as capital) into authoritative resources. Being limited to an economic transaction, the labour contract formally denies the worker any rights of participation in the authoritative apparatus of decision-making within the enterprise. The counterpart to this is the assignment of specifically 'political' rights to a sphere of 'citizenship' distinct from the authority system of the industrial enterprise. From this view, even in the 'classical capitalism' of nineteenth-century Britain, the economic and the political were never separate in the sense of being detached or uncoupled from one another – as I have pointed out, this would be a more apt characteristic of class-divided societies than of capitalism. The separation of economy and polity is best described as one of *insulation*, whereby relations between capital and wage-labour are kept 'non-political', by the severance of industrial conflict from party struggles within the state. This is the core of validity in the conception of the thesis of the 'institutionalisation of class conflict' as formulated by Dahrendorf, Lipset and others two decades ago.[28] For them, however, the differentiation of 'class struggle in industry' and 'class struggle in the state' represented the transcendence of nineteenth-century entrepreneurial capitalism as analysed by Marx (see below, pp. 212–14).

# 6

# Time, Labour and the City

In the previous chapter, on the basis of Marx's analysis of capitalism as a system of commodity production, I have argued that 'private property' in capitalist society has an altogether different sense and significance to that in class-divided societies. Class conflict (in the sense of endemic opposition of class interests in a situation of 'asymmetrical dependence') and active class struggle have a centrality in capitalism which they do not have in class-divided societies. It should be recognised how much this view contrasts with the 'theory of industrial society' (see pp. 122–3 above), as elaborated first of all by Saint-Simon at the turn of the nineteenth century, in variant forms by Spencer and Durkheim at a later period, and in relatively recent years by a variety of prominent authors. According to this conception, the notion of class applies with the specific reference to non-capitalist societies such as European feudalism and the Classical world. In feudalism there is a non-productive, militaristic dominant class, which holds sway over the mass of the producers. With the advent of industrialism, however, there is no class of non-producers: everyone, both workers and employers, participate in the system of industrial production. The new industrial order is not an inherently class society, and writers such as Durkheim interpreted the class struggles of the nineteenth century in Western Europe as expressions of the strains created by the transition from an agrarian to an industrial order, not as integral to that new order itself.[1]

However, there is an essential core of truth here in the difference that is singled out between capitalism ('industrial society') and those societies which I have called 'class-divided'. And it is one that Marx did not sufficiently underline, at least in those passages in which he sketched out his evolutionary scheme of the dialectic of forces and relations of production – for in class-divided societies the dominated class or classes do not 'need' the dominant class to carry on the process of production. A peasant producer may have to cede a 'surplus' to a dominant class, in return perhaps for the rather dubious reward of 'protection' from military predators, but what the peasant does in the labour process can quite readily be carried out (save where centralised irrigation works are involved) by a free peasant – as is in fact the case in small, independent agrarian communities. Once the mass of the labour-force has been expropriated from the land – a phenomenon of course unknown before capitalism and one whose sociological significance, as I have stressed before, can hardly be overstated – this situation obviously no longer holds good. The worker needs an employer to gain a livelihood, just as the employer needs labour-power in order to carry on production. Rather than this signifying the end of class, I have argued, it actually involves the intrusion of class relations into the very heart of production. Dependence, as I have tried to make clear, does not exclude conflict of interest or active class struggle. Rather, the opposite is the case. In class-divided societies, open class struggle is generally only sporadic, though it may be very violent. Peasant rebellions might be turned against either local warlords or landlords, or alternatively against state officials, generating various types of confrontations and movements.[2] But in the class societies of capitalism, class struggles are a chronic feature of the organisation of production, centred ultimately on the reduction of 'labour' to 'labour-power' as the key to the extraction of surplus value.

If the analysis offered in the preceding chapter is correct, time, as a separable 'dimension' of human life, intersecting with the 'substance' of human activities as situated in a separable 'space', is focal to the organisation of capitalistic production. When we say 'time is money', when we refer to 'spending time', etc., these phrases mean more than the commonplace that time, for human beings with a finite life-span, is a scarce resource. The *commodification of time* is the underlying connecting link between the massive expansion of the commodity form in the production of goods, on the one hand, and the commodification of labour (as labour-power) on the other. The commodification of time means that time is drawn into the 'double existence' which is the predicating quality of every commodity. Time as lived time, as the substance of the lived experience of *durée* of Being, becomes accompanied by the separated dimension of time as pure or 'formless duration'. With the expansion of capitalism, this is what time seems to come to *be,* just as money seems to be the universal standard of value of all things. Time as pure duration, as disconnected from the materiality of experience, comes to be perceived, in direct opposition to the actual state of things, as real, 'objective' time, because like money it is expressed in a universal and public mode. This universal and public mode, again like money, is nothing other than its own quantification as a standard measure standing at the axis of a host of transformation/mediation relations. The commodification of time, and its differentiation from further processes of the commodification of space, hold the key to the deepest transformations of day-to-day social life that are brought about by the emergence of capitalism. These relate both to the central phenomenon of the organisation of production processes, and to the 'work-place', and also the intimate textures of how daily social life is experienced.

In class-divided societies, as indeed in non-capitalist societies of all sorts, the classification of time socially is never separated from the *substance* of social activities. A great deal has been written about time and time-consciousness in both tribal and class-divided societies, and I shall only draw sparingly upon it here in order to provide a general illustration of the points at issue. One indication of the unusual nature of the isolation of time as mensurable duration, and its differentiation from space, is to be found in linguistics. According to Tuan, of the three terms 'time', 'space' and 'place' (the latter meaning what I have called 'locale'), only the third can be translated into most non-European languages without difficulty.[3] This conforms to what Evans-Pritchard has to say in his famous discussion of Nuer time-reckoning, which I have already quoted (above, p. 36).[4] For the Nuer, the year is the longest unit of time-reckoning; they speak of last year, this and next year, but otherwise time is calculated by reference to significant events.[5]

The emergence of class-divided societies, I have argued previously, is inseparably involved with the 'binding' of time-space relations made possible by writing. This has almost universally been accompanied by the creation of calendars, accompanied by cosmological investigations. Control of time here, and in capitalism, is intimately connected with the authoritative control of subject populations. But it would be quite wrong to suppose that such cosmological time-reckoning is a direct, simpler, forerunner of the commodified time of capitalism. In the first place, access to such time-measurement, like writing itself, is the monopoly of the select few. In the second place, it does not penetrate the routines of daily life, even among elites, whose day is not more precisely delineated temporally than those of the subordinate classes. Third, and most decisively, time is not separated from the substances or qualities that are organised in and through it. On the contrary, the identification of temporal ordering cosmologically is the very locus of divine power, yielding access to the religiosity of things. Not for nothing does Krishna, in the *Bhagavad Gita*, reveal himself as divine with the words 'I am time'.[6]

Of all class-divided civilisations, the Maya seem to have been most preoccupied with the cosmological ordering of time.[7] Each day of the year for them was divine, and each was carried by a specific god. The cosmological calendar developed by the Maya, as is well known, incorporated correction formulae for the years that were more precise than the leap-year system introduced about a millennium later in Europe by Pope Gregory. In spite of this extraordinary achievement, the Maya do not seem to have formulated a unitary concept of time, as a single phenomenon borne by the gods; temporality remained embedded in the particularities of the individual deities.

The commodification of time in early capitalism, like much else, was probably in some part the outcome of long-term features of European civilisation – in this case, of the influence of Christianity. The temporal thematics of Christianity appear to be in especial contrast to the temporality of that other great 'seed-bed' of Occidental culture, ancient Greece. While distinct conceptions of time can be traced out in different schools of Classical philosophy, the dominant one was probably the theogonical interpretation of *Kronos*, as unending time – a framework of thought that seems to have shared a good deal in common with the Persian idea of *Zurvān Akarana* (the cycle of eternity).[8] Max Weber's claims about the influence of Christian value-standards upon the subsequent formation of capitalism can here be focused upon conceptions of time. Some scholars have argued plausibly that the doctrines of the crucifixion and the redemption encourage a linear rather than a cyclical or 'eternal' interpretation of time. The crucifixion is a single event, not subject to repetition; the possibility of redemption offers a potential direction to time, as unfolding towards a definite culmination of human existence. According to Whitrow, prior to the development of Christianity only among the Hebrews and in Zoroastrianism is there found either a teleological conception of the universe or the notion that history is progressive. The emphasis upon the non-repeatability of events, however, is specifically Christian.[9] Augustine's struggles with the concept of time in *Confessions* and *The City of God* – time as at once the most self-evident and yet divinely ineffable quality of experience – document an effort to get at an expressly linear formulation of time-consciousness.

The impact of Christianity in these respects should not be overstressed, however. Throughout the medieval and immediately post-medieval period in Europe time was not generally perceived by the ecclesiastical authorities as a single parameter, but rather as a set of segmented qualities of the seasons and divisions of the Zodiac. Cyclical notions of time continued to vie with linear conceptions. Most important, time continued to be interpolated within the qualitative differentiation of material and social phenomena, rather than assuming its 'double existence' as mate-riality and commodity.

The commodification of time in the emergence of capitalism was as closely integrated with specific technical innovations – particu-larly, of course, those involved in the construction of clocks – as was the so-called 'Industrial Revolution'. Mumford has suggested, in fact, that it is the clock rather than the steam-engine that should be regarded as the epitome of capitalist industrialism. Power-machines existed well before the arrival of capitalism; their systematic harnessing to the creation of a novel system of production, he suggests, was only made possible by the invention of clocks. In the clock is to be found 'a new kind of power-machine, in which the source of power and its transmission were of such a nature as to ensure the even flow of energy throughout the works and to make possible regular production and a standardised product'.[10] Mumford sees the clock, rightly enough I believe, as vital to the co-ordination of machinery and labour-power. But the increasing intrusion of the precise time-measurement made possible by clocks, I should want to say, goes even deeper than this. The public, objectified time of the clock is the very expression of the commodification of time. Time as 'measured duration' *is* commodified time, time as freely exchangeable with all other time, time distinguished and separated from the substance of Being.

The clock, much more than power-machines, is the foremost example of that conjunction of science and technology that has become such a distinctive feature of the capitalist economy. Precise time-measurement was both a prime stimulus to, and contributing element in, the standardisation of other dimensions of measurement – given concrete form when the Royal Society issued exact standards of length, volume and weight in the seventeenth century.[11] In common with many other technical innovations that contributed to the rise of capitalism, clocks did not originate in Europe. The Chinese possessed mechanical clocks centuries before they were known in Europe – where they appear to have been independently invented at a later date. It is not known who invented spring-driven clocks. The architect Brunelleschi is reputed to have been making them as early as the turn of the fifteenth century. But the first spring-driven clocks were mainly flat, round-table clocks; the incorporation of spring-drive in compact and portable time pieces did not come about until some two centuries afterwards.[12] Not until a successful pendulum clock was invented by Huygens in the middle part of the seventeenth century was there a time keeper that could perform continuously and accurately for years on end.

There is no point in tracing out the history of time pieces in any further detail here. Nor is it my purpose (at any point in this book) to enter into the endless debates about the weightings of contributory factors to the rise of capitalism. My main argument concerns the significance of the creation of time with a 'double existence' in which, as in other processes of commodification associated with capitalism, the universal, abstract, quantifiable expression of time comes to predominate over the qualitative organisation of time processes characteristic of all non-capitalist forms of society. The clock is the material carrier of this phenomenon, but the important thing is to trace out its consequences for social life in capitalist society.

Since the quantification of time, as an abstract dimension

independent of any other content, is at the heart of the twin processes of the commodification of labour and products, it is hardly surprising how closely this theme connects with the organisation of work discipline in the capitalistic work-place.[13] This therefore relates back to the significance of 'management' as an integral feature of the capitalistic enterprise.

## Labour Discipline and the Capitalistic Work-place

As Marx repeated again and again, what is distinctive to capitalistic production is the encounter of 'free' wage-labour and capital, as the axis of the labour process. The 'management' of 'free' labour-power, concentrated in factory and in office, has no real precedent in class-divided societies. This is not to say, as I have pointed out earlier, that there were not a variety of different examples of the large-scale, disciplined co-ordination of human beings prior to the development of capitalism. In the last chapter, however, I made the claim that the surveillance of labour instituted in the capitalistic work-place was not primarily the outcome of technological change. This is a matter of great significance for the 'capitalism' versus 'industrial society' debate, and in this section I shall amplify the claim rather more.

One of the most important historical sources for analysing the origins of modern labour discipline, at least in England, is Pollard's work, *The Genesis of Modern Management*.[14] Let me include a substantial quotation from this book, because it encapsulates some fundamental issues. Contrasting other historical examples with capitalist management within the business enterprise, he writes:

did not the ancient Egyptians build their huge pyramids, or the Chinese their wall, or, more recently did not Louis XIV inaugurate a magnificent system of main-road building in France? If the control of large masses of men was in question, had not the generals controlled many more, over the ages, than the manager of even the largest industrial company? ... All those developments, it must be admitted, preceded the industrial revolution, often by several millennia, and it is equally true that the entrepreneurs and managers of the industrial revolution learnt one or other aspect of their work from them. The innovation, and the difficulty, lay in this: that the men who began to operate the large industrial units in the British economy from the middle of the eighteenth century onwards had to combine these different objectives and methods into one. Like the generals of old, they had to control numerous men, but without powers of compulsion: indeed, the absence of legal enforcement of unfree work was not only one of the marked characteristics of the new capitalism, but one of its most seminal ideas.[15]

The 'difficulty', as Pollard describes it, was nothing less than that of transmuting one way of life into another.[16] In class-divided societies labour which required surveillance – such as with the large-scale projects described by Pollard – was quite exceptional; the mechanisms of exploitation of surplus production, to repeat the argument of the previous chapter, did not depend upon the direct control of the labour process. The point is not only that, with the transference from traditional agrarian to industrial labour, the worker lost control of the means of production. Labour which is integrated with the natural rhythms of climate and the soil, and embedded in communities of high presence-availability, has quite a different character from the regularised operations inherent in the capitalistic organisation of work. The massive dislocations which the transference of the mass of the labour-force from one to the other involved (and which continue today in numerous areas of the world) have by now been well documented. In England as in most Continental countries, the putting-out system was a principal intermediary between agrarian (or traditional craft) labour and industrial work. It is, of course, a misconceived view of the 'Industrial Revolution' in England which sees it as the swift conversion of a population of country folk into factory hands. More than fifty years after the arrival of steam-power, domestic industry was increasing at as rapid a rate as factory industry. At the mid-nineteenth century the factory operative was still very much outnumbered by the commercialised domestic worker.[17]

Domestic or small workshop production, as E. P. Thompson has pointed out, had little of the regularity achievable within the factory or large centralised work-place. In various respects it preserved a closer dependence upon the vagaries of nature, as well as allowing the worker greater control over the labour task.

Inclement weather could not only disrupt agriculture, building and transport but also, for example, the actual process of such an occupation as weaving, since the completed articles had to be stretched out to dry in the open. The length of the working day was variable: in some part because of workers' own inclinations or capacities, in some degree because of variations in the supply of raw materials or in demand for products. Moreover, mixed occupations survived in England for some considerable period after the widespread development of capitalistic industry. Domestic workers participated at certain periods of the year in agriculture, for example; and Cornish tin-miners were involved part of their time in the fishing industry. Thompson remarks that whenever such workers were in control of their working lives, intense periods of activity typically alternated with 'bouts of idleness'. Most traders 'honoured Saint Monday' (a practice which has hardly disappeared entirely today in any area of industry: perhaps one might say that Saint Monday drives a 'Friday Car').[18]

The transmogrification of agricultural and domestic workers into factory or office workers involved two major types of change in habits or in the routinisation of daily life. One of these marks life outside the factory, or rather the relation between work and non-work. This is the separation of the home from the work-place. We should not think of this simply as a material separation of the household and the work-place, but rather a reorganisation of the time-space relations in the 'time-geographical paths' followed by individuals in their daily lives.[19] The notion and the fact of the 'working day', calculated by worker and employer alike in terms of commodified time, became central to the worker's experience, and ever after has remained a focus of class struggles. Two opposed modes of time-consciousness, 'working time' and 'one's own' or 'free time', became basic divisions within the phenomenal experience of the day. These may be 'filled' with activities, but in neither case do these activities stand in organic relation to the rhythms of nature – a matter I shall develop further in my subsequent discussion of capitalism and urbanism. Weber reminds us that the separation of household and work-place is not completely unique to capitalism: the bazaar system of the Islamic cities of the Near East, for example, according to Weber, 'rests throughout on the separation of the castle (*Kasbah*), bazaar (*suk*) and residences'.[20] But he is quick to point out that this separation was quite different in substance from that involved in the division between home and work-place in capitalism. Characteristically, he emphasises the distinctive separation, in the West, of household and business for accounting and legal purposes. But if we accept that, underlying the capitalistic accounting of the enterprise, are the processes of commodification described earlier, making possible the routinised extraction of surplus value, this analysis complements the remarks I have made above.

Certain further implications or consequences of the separation of the household and work-place should be mentioned here as having far-reaching social ramifications. The process of separation drastically affected the character of the relations between the sexes (although the details of the changes involved, in Britain and the other European countries, remain controversial), and helped to create the distinctive phenomenon of 'housework'.[21] Domestic industry still tended to preserve a considerable measure of interdependence between men, women and children. The rise of the separate capitalistic work-place, however, dissolved this interdependence a step further than had already occurred through the prior disintegration of peasant production: 'It was this process – the decline of family and domestic industry – which shattered the interdependent relationship between husband and wife, which led to the identification of family life with privacy, home, consumption, domesticity – and with women.'[22] Recognising this, of course, should not lead us to forget the fact that throughout the history of capitalism since the dominance of the centralised work-place women workers have made up a major proportion of the labour-force.

The other sets of changes, of course, concern the issues raised by Pollard – the incorporation of large sectors of the work-force within the disciplined order of factory production. The methodical surveillance of labour contracted as sheer labour-power posed fundamental problems of discipline for early factory managers. The easier and irregular routines of domestic labour had to be replaced by the 'time discipline of the mill clock and the foreman's job watch'.[23] This was accomplished by varying mixtures of inducement and coercion. In the factories, pioneers such as Arkwright experienced great difficulty 'in training human beings to renounce their desultory habits of work, and identify themselves with the unvarying regularity of the complex automaton'; he 'had to train his workpeople to a precision and assiduity altogether unknown before, against which their listless and restive habits rose in continued rebellion'.[24] Working-people were by no means unaware that many industrial units were modelled upon work-houses or prisons. There were not infrequently direct connections between factories and these organisations, both in Britain but particularly in certain Continental countries. Pollard suggests that the strength of these connections has been generally underesti-mated by historians. The employment of unfree labour was not at all insignificant in the labour-force in the late eighteenth and early nineteenth centuries.[25]

It is a major part of my argument in this book that the capitalist labour contract, and the extraction of surplus value, in contrast to the extraction of surplus production, do not involve the immediate control of the means of violence by employers. But in the interstitial phases of the consolidation of capitalistic production in Britain, employers did often hark back to the more traditional methods of maintaining control over the extraction process. The 'volunteer' force raised in 1794, and consisting mainly of gentry, farmers, shopkeepers and 'employers on horseback', was supposed to help thwart the possibility of French invasion, but also operated as an internal security force. Regular troops were in action internally until beyond the Chartist period.[26] Foster has shown that, in Oldham,

> Within only a decade of building their first factories Oldham's employers had been forced to put on army uniforms and use their sabres ... the suddenness of this breakdown, far from being coincidental, stemmed directly from the inability of the old-style social structure to sustain the new pressures of *industrial* capitalism.[27]

And this demanded the daily 'imprisonment' of labour within the capitalistic work-place.

What occurred in Britain was not necessarily recapitulated elsewhere; as the leader in many of the changes described here, the circumstances of transition to factory production certainly involved unique features. The question of how far Britain was a 'special case', which from several angles is of considerable importance to theories of the development of capitalism – not the least of which is Marx's heavy reliance upon materials drawn from Britain in *Capital* – is not one that I shall consider here.[28] I wish to stress, however, that the analysis offered here conforms closely to the thesis developed by Marglin about the origins of factory discipline.[29] Marglin specifically poses the question: how far was the success of the factory in supplanting domestic labour sheerly the result of its technological superiority, associated with the new sources of mechanical power? His answer is that factory production spread primarily because it made possible the surveillance of labour that substituted the employer's control of the labour process for that of the worker.[30]

## Capitalism and the City

An essential thesis of this book is that the city cannot be regarded as merely incidental to social theory but belongs at its very core. Similarly, 'urban sociology' is more than just one branch of sociology among others – it stands at the heart of some of the most fundamental problems of general sociological interest. To understand this it is crucial to place urbanism in a comparative context, that of the opposition between class-divided societies and capitalism, and along the way it is necessary to break with some hitherto well-established theories of urban life. Fortunately, this is not quite as formidable a task as it might have appeared even a decade ago, because a new critical edge has been introduced into urban theory by recent Marxist authors on the city, most notably Lefebvre, Harvey and Castells. I shall not follow exactly the same conceptions as they develop, but with two of the main premises of their writing I am in entire agreement. These are: first, that the city cannot be adequately theorised in isolation from the analysis of societal totalities; and second, that urbanisation associated with capitalism cannot be assumed to be a direct continuation or expansion of cities in non-capitalist societies.

The elucidation of these ideas means looking again briefly at the role of cities in class-divided societies. I have no wish to underestimate the wide range of forms of societal organisation subsumed under the term 'class-divided societies'. In the typing of non-capitalist societal totalities there are still very deep divisions among historians and among anthropologists. The concept of 'feudalism' has been perhaps the most contentious of these – debates about the characterisation of traditional China in particular are almost comic in respect of the divergent views which they have provoked. As Granet remarked a long while ago, 'Le mot "féodal" est un terme expressif, commode – et dangereux.'[31] But there can be no denying that all class-divided societies have involved some form of urban organisation. We have to give some considerable attention, however, to what 'urban' is taken to mean here, since definitions of 'the city' have varied widely – and how 'the city' is conceptualised is obviously vital to theories of the urban component of society.

We can classify definitions of the city in three ways: (a) there are those definitions which seek to have a universal character, i.e. to apply to 'urbanism' at all times and places, (b) there are those definitions which, regardless of how far they make claims to universality, have tried to supply substantive criteria of what it counts to be 'urban', and (c) other definitions, again regardless of how far they claim universality, concentrate more upon what might be called the 'relational form' of urbanism, in which the city is conceptualised in terms of its role within the wider society. In the light of the comments I have made just previously, it is not surprising to find that concepts of the city falling under (c) have been less common in 'urban sociology' than those belonging to (b).

Of views of urbanism that belong to the first category – universal conceptions of urbanism – by far the most influential within sociology has been that of Louis Wirth. For Wirth the minimal definition of a city is a 'relatively large, dense, and permanent settlement of socially heterogeneous individuals'.[32] Wirth's argument, of course, centres upon the significance, in such settlements, of urbanism as a 'way of life', involving a preponderance of impersonal or 'secondary' contacts with strangers. Wirth's discussion, which shows considerable affinities with Tönnies's portrayal of *Gesellschaft*, has by no means lost its relevance today: that is to say, to the capitalist city. But as a general conception of the city, or of urban life, it is simply a non-starter. It has, of course, been criticised by those who point out that *gemeinschaftlich* relations tend to persist rather strongly even within the very large urban agglomerations of modern times. Its most severe limitations, however, derive from the fact that several of the cardinal characteristics attributed by Wirth to urbanism as a whole are not found in most cities in non-capitalist societies. As one author on non-capitalist urbanism succinctly puts it, 'Whatever merits it may yet retain, it ultimately reduces the city to a Western and relatively recent phenomenon.'[33]

Among more substantive definitions of the city, Max Weber's formulation has pride of place. Weber's discussion of the city is complex, and as one would expect of a scholar of such encyclopedic knowledge, sensitised to a vast range of comparative materials. In view of the range of Weber's learning, it is rather surprising how much his characterisation of urbanism is based upon the medieval and post-medieval cities of Europe.[34] Cities elsewhere (Weber concentrates upon traditional China and India for the most part) tend to be regarded as marginal types – to such an extent, as I shall indicate, that a large proportion of settlements in diverse class-divided societies would be denied full urban status if his criteria were adopted. Weber's conception of the city places particular emphasis upon the autonomy (administrative and political) of the city from the broader authoritative organisation of the society of which it is a part: 'the city must . . . to some extent be a partially autonomous organisation, a "community" (*Gemeinde*) with special administrative and political institutions'.[35] In addition to this criterion, Weber draws special attention to the existence of local markets: 'A city . . . is always a market centre'; and to the significance of the city as a garrison or fortress, a phenomenon which he sees as virtually ubiquitious in non-capitalist societies, and which he connects closely to the administrative-political autonomy of the city. The upshot of this, as Weber is prepared to concede, is that, as a communal settlement, the city 'in the full meaning of the world [has] appeared as a mass phenomenon only in the Occident'.[36]

Although Weber's analysis, unlike that of Wirth, is concerned primarily with non-capitalist cities, his characterisation of the urban is almost as restrictive for the study of traditional cities as is that of Wirth. What Weber has to say about European cities, especially in the post-medieval period, is very valuable as a contribution to understanding the rise of capitalism, and he illuminates in a penetrating and indeed indispensable way contrasts between Western and Eastern settlement patterns. But for probing the character of the city in class-divided societies in general his conception cannot be allowed to stand as it is. The main reason for this is the rarity, outside Europe,[37] of significant administrative-political autonomy of cities – with the exception of city-states, which, however, do not really fit with Weber's criterion either, since they are not entities within a wider society. But Weber's emphasis upon cities as the location of markets is also problematic, again reflecting perhaps an excessive reliance upon European experience. Although Weber is not very specific in the context of his discussion of the city about what he means by a market, it seems probable that he was thinking of an autonomous price-fixing market of the kind that, on a massive basis, became a dominant feature of the emergence of capitalism. The work of Polanyi and others has shown, however, that such markets have been quite unusual in cities in class-divided societies, or indeed in the economic systems of such societies more generally.[38]

The third type of definition, the relational, does not necessarily exclude elements of the other two, but places the emphasis upon how the city connects to other (social/spatial) features of the environment outside the urban area itself. Some such conceptions have been very general in form; a more precise version, however, is to be found in central-place theory, originally worked out by Christaller.[39] Central-place theory is usually presented as an economic account of the city, and although there are various versions of it, most seem to fall in category (a) as well (c): that is, they are posed as universally valid accounts. Central-place theory, in its most elemental form at any rate, treats cities as particular sorts of economic centres, providing certain definable advantages in the retailing and distribution of goods. The main notion of central-place theory is that cities, as 'high-level centres' that provide specialised goods, have more extensive maximal hinterlands than do 'lower-level centres' that provide common goods in chronic demand. A hierarchy of places develops in which specialised goods are only available at high-level centres, or cities, which are consequently able to serve as the organising economic foci of large hinterlands.

There are major difficulties with this conception, however, especially if it is seen as generating a universal interpretation of settlement patterns. It presupposes the existence of autonomous price-fixing markets in much more specific a way than Weber's definition of the city does, as its assumptions are explicitly those of rational consumers in a framework of neoclassical economics.[40]

Since it is based upon economic theory, it also rests heavily upon the general thesis that the development of cities is to be understood primarily in economic terms. Other, more technical, objections can be made to central-place theory within its chosen frame of reference of neoclassical economic theory. But these are hardly relevant in the present context, since the above-mentioned considerations severely limit the appropriateness of central-place theory to class-divided societies, whatever judgements one might make about its usefulness to capitalist cities.[41]

These things having been said, there is one element of the type of approach marked by central-place theory which is highly important, though it has no intrinsic connection with the content of that theory as such. This is the idea that the city is what in geographical terminology is 'a generator of effective space', or what I have called earlier in the book a *storage container*, that permits time-space distanciation well beyond that characteristic of tribal societies. My remarks on this will be confined for the time being to the city in agrarian or class-divided societies. One of the most striking features of the literature on these societies, both specific and more generalised, is that the 'city', the 'state' and 'civilisation' tend to be treated in the same breath – often being used as more or less interchangeable terms. I shall not formalise the concept of 'civilisation' here, and shall have a lot to say about the state in the following chapters. But I do want to accept that the connections between these three terms, as employed in the archaeological and anthropological literature, are in no way fortuitous. The city *in relation to the countryside* is the indispensable locus of the transformation/mediation relations (structural principles) involved in the differentiation of class-divided societies from tribal societies. Without cities, there are no classes and no state.[42]

An impressive array of comparative evidence on the non-capitalist city has been brought together by Sjoberg, in his well-known work on the subject.[43] Although there are major objections that can be made against aspects of Sjoberg's analysis, and certain of his generalisations can definitely be brought into question,[44] some of his views are close to those I wish to emphasise. Sjoberg stresses, as I have done earlier, that the city is to be understood first and foremost in relation to the generation of power. He explicitly downplays links between economic factors and urbanisation as decisive for the origin of cities. Such factors, he says (in my opinion rightly) are

> not as crucial for urbanisation as most historians have contended; contrariwise, large-scale economic enterprise is highly dependent upon an effective power structure. We can find no instance of significant city-building through commerce alone ... We must [he argues], if we are to explain the growth, spread and decline of cities, comment upon the city as a mechanism by which a society's rulers can consolidate and maintain their power.[45]

When Marx says in *The German Ideology* that the most fundamental division of labour prior to capitalism is that between city and countryside, he makes a point that has been largely ignored by those interested in developing or elaborating his ideas.[46] The economic differentiation between city and countryside is greater than within each of these taken separately: that is to say, while in most cities in class-divided societies there is a considerable division of labour (an artisanate, warriors, priests, etc.), this is an urban phenomenon, not characteristic of the society as a whole. The contrasts between agrarian economic organisation and the economic forms of the city also constitute modes of symbiotic dependence – in which, if Jacobs is right, the city may have played even more of a leading role than has been generally thought. But Marx's proposition is far more telling if it is not construed on a purely economic level. The city is the generator of the authoritative resources out of which state power is created and sustained. The meaning of this has to be made clear, in the light of what I have said about Weber on the 'autonomy' of the city. If cities in class-divided societies do not typically enjoy significant 'administrative-political autonomy' from the rest of the society of which they are a part, it is because they are the basis of whatever administrative-political integration is achieved in that society as a whole. As I have already emphasised, the administrative order of the state in class-divided societies never penetrates the traditional organisation of local agrarian communities in the same manner as occurs subsequent to the development of capitalism.

In class-divided societies cities are crucibles of power. Virtually everywhere the generation of power in the city has been expressed in religious terms: the temple is socially and physically the centre-point of urban organisation. The most plausible theory of the autogenesis of cities (and therefore of city-states), which broadly conforms to the theses of both Mumford and Wheatley, is that cities initially emerge around what the second of these two authors calls 'ceremonial centres'.[47] The control of extensive areas of territory, however, demands the specialisation of an administrative and military apparatus. The conjunction of religious and military power explains two of the most pervasive (although not wholly universal) spatial characteristics of cities in class-divided societies: the pre-eminent central area, dominated by physically impressive religious and government buildings; and the existence of city walls. Mumford has pointed out that the city walls give physical shape to the 'container' of power. As another observer has remarked, 'Up to a century ago, in most of the world a city without walls was as rare as a European garden without a fence is today.' The same commentator points out that the English word 'town' is related to the German *Zaun*, meaning 'fence'.[48]

The pace of life in cities in class-divided societies is slow. If time is not commodified and 'the pre-industrial urbanite, compared to industrial man, does not think of time as a "scarce commodity"',[49] neither is there usually a high level of commodification of space. The alienability of land within cities in non-capitalist societies has varied widely, but everywhere it has been hedged by restrictions of numerous kinds. Non-capitalist cities have rarely been 'planned' in anything akin to the modern sense of 'town planning', but there are remarkable similarities in patterns of land use among cities in widely divergent times and places. These are given their over-all form by the two dominant features already mentioned: the monopoly of the centre by ceremonial and administrative build-ings, and the presence of the city walls (in many cities in class-divided societies there have been two sets of walls, the inner section of public buildings and market-place also being walled). The dwellings of the elite also usually tend to be concentrated in the centre of the city – although they may own rural residences as well; communications within the city are not rapid, and there is not a great deal of daily mobility of population across different areas of the city. The less privileged groupings live towards the outer limits of the urban area, with outcasts or pariah groups scattered on the periphery, not always within the city walls, though they may claim the protection of moving into the interior of the city when under external attack. Some class-divided civilisations, of course, have possessed quite developed road systems linking different cities or regions. But in all non-capitalist civilisations, if one discounts mass migrations of populations in times of warfare, plague or famine, travel was a specialised affair. Although there have been societies in which large military forces could be moved with some dispatch over considerable distances, travel for the most part was hedged with difficulties and dangers. An eighteenth-century German saying advised a journey over north German roads as the best way, next to marriage, of learning fortitude.[50]

A major part of the argument I shall develop in the next two chapters is that, with the advent of capitalism, the city is no longer the dominant time-space container or 'crucible of power'; this role is assumed by the territorially bounded nation-state. This idea at first seems paradoxical: for does not the development of capitalism bring in its train a spread of urbanisation upon a scale unprecedented in history? After all, it has been estimated that, in what I have called class-divided societies, cities nowhere comprised more than 10 per cent of the population.[51] We often read statements such as the following: 'Before 1850 no society was predominantly urbanised. By 1900 only one, Britain was. Now all industrial nations are highly urbanised, and the process is accelerating throughout the world.'[52] Underlying such a pronouncement – which refers to facts whose significance is profound and undeniable – is the apparently innocuous assumption that most people used to live in agrarian settings and now, increasingly, they live in urban ones. The writer presumes a continuity in what the 'city' or the 'urban' is, using some sort of implicit conceptualisation belonging to the first category of definitions that I mentioned above. This kind of assumption has penetrated very deeply in social theory, since it is also accepted by a whole range of conceptions which oppose *Gemeinschaft* (rural) to *Gesellschaft* (urban), and which from both socialist and conservative perspectives bemoan the swamping of 'community' by the rising tide of impersonal urbanism.[53]

The symbiotic but differentiated relationship between city and countryside (in various diverging forms) is basic to the time-space organisation of class-divided societies, and thus to the mobilisation of power. With the maturation of capitalism, however, three sets of changes affecting the city occur: (a) the city is supplanted by the nation-state as the dominant power container; (b) the contrast between the city and countryside is a fundamental axis of the structuration of class-divided societies – but this contrast is *progressively dissolved* with the advent of capitalism, at least within the developed capitalist societies themselves; and (c) the factors influencing the social patterning of urban life are for the most part quite different from those involved in cities in non-capitalist civilisations. Taken together, these represent a profound discontinuity between the city in class-divided societies and capitalist urbanism. The mass migrations from the land into urban areas associated with the rise of capitalism mark not just a population movement from one type of social milieu to another, but an *over-all transformation of those milieux themselves*. The development of capitalism has not led to the consolidation of the institutions of the city, but rather to its eradication as a distinct social form.[54]

The most tangible expression of this change is the disappearance of the city walls, the physical enclosure of the power container. The obsolescence of the city walls signifies major alterations in the control and deployment of military power as well as economic transformations in land use. So far as the former of these is concerned, it is important once more not to overstress the significance of sheerly technological developments. Certainly, advances in destructive firepower progressively reduced the effectiveness of city walls as a means of defence; but standing behind these technological advances, as I shall argue subsequently, was the increasing consolidation of the means of violence in the hands of the state. The economic transformations that undermined the traditional character of the city, as Marx emphasised, began in the countryside rather than in established urban areas themselves. The commercialisation of agriculture, and the commodification of agrarian property, drove a wedge into the pre-established rural/urban dichotomy. Modern history, Marx says, is 'the urbanisation of the countryside'.[55] The new industrial centres, for the most part, were not created on the same sites as already established urban communes. In the early period of formation of capitalism, in the late seventeenth and early eighteenth centuries, the guild organisations in the traditional cities prevented money capital from being turned into industrial capital: 'Hence in England an embittered struggle of the corporate towns against those new industrial nurseries.' These 'industrial nurseries', according to Marx, were set up either at sea-ports or at points inland removed from 'the control of the old municipalities'.[56]

If the capitalist work-place presupposes the commodification of time, capitalist urbanism is based upon the commodification of space. The early industrial towns in Britain, which were quite often 'planted colonies' of workers, in urban environments built and controlled by industrialists, are not typical in this respect of capitalist urbanism – for the most distinctive feature of the latter is the alienability of building land, which consequently becomes drawn into housing markets, that intersect with labour and product markets. Capitalist space is what Harvey calls 'created space', contrasting this to the 'interrelationships between social activities and organic nature' which characterised the city in non-capitalist societies.[57] As Mumford emphasises strongly in *The City in History*, cities in class-divided societies were created in conjunction with the natural contours of the land.[58] The typical distribution of areas in the city described earlier frequently took advantage of such contours: the 'ceremonial centre', for example, would often be built upon a hill or hills naturally dominating the surrounding landscape. The city sustained a close ecological integration with nature that almost completely disappears in much capitalist urbanism, especially where streets are organised in a grid-block pattern, as in many North American cities.[59]

Castells is one of those who has emphasised the disjunction between non-capitalist cities and capitalistic urban space. Accepting the redirection in modern urban analysis that Castells has played a major part in fostering does not mean necessarily adopting his view that 'the essential problems regarded as urban are in fact bound up with processes of "collective consumption" ' or with 'the organisation of the collective means of reproduction of labour power'.[60] A more accurate characterisation, at any rate, would seem to be that the 'created space' of capitalist urbanism is the outcome of the integration of the three sets of market relations mentioned above – housing, labour and product markets – within both localised and national economic systems. (Of course, the role of urban planning cannot be ignored, but I should argue that this has to be connected with more general problems of state 'intervention' in the economic order of capitalist societies.) I do not intend in the present context to seek to analyse the connections between these commodity markets in any depth. They mean that the factors influencing settlement patterns, and patterns of urban regionalisation, are quite different from those of traditional cities.

Many of these factors are well enough known, though they have frequently been presented in a positivistic fashion as universal tendencies – most notoriously so in the case of concentric-zone theories. The massive extension of rapid transport and communications has of course played a part in integrating cities within both a national and international division of labour. Internally, together with the influence of housing markets, the larger capitalist cities are marked by a fluid dispersion of neighbourhoods along class lines. As I have argued elsewhere,[61] neighbourhood regionalisation, dominated chiefly (in Britain) by the availability of mortgages and the situation of local labour markets, is a fundamental element in class structuration.

## The Production of Everyday Life

In the theory of structuration, social life is taken to consist in regularised social practices. Life is not experienced as 'structures', but as the *durée* of day-to-day existence, in the context of conventions ordered above all on the level of practical consciousness. The continuity of daily life is not a 'directly motivated' phenomenon, but assured in the routinisation of practices.[62] In tribal and class-divided societies the routinisation of daily life is governed above all by tradition. There is no doubt that the significance of tradition in purely oral cultures is different from those in which some form of writing exists. Besides expanding the level of time-space distanciation, writing also opens the way for those divergences of interpretation which in modern historiography have come to be called 'hermeneutics'. Writing gives rise to texts that enjoy an 'objectified' existence independent of the sustaining of oral traditions in daily social practices. The 'conflict of interpretations' engendered by texts is very closely related to ideology, and illustrations of this can be seen very early in the history of the Near Eastern civilisations: in, for instance, the struggles of priestly groups in Sumer to protect one version of the scriptural past against that favoured by an increasingly independent and powerful monarchy.

But in all class-divided societies literacy was the monopoly of the few, and inevitably for the majority of the population the routinisation of daily life was carried in orally based tradition. Tradition, it is important to reaffirm, in tribal and class-divided societies is a source of legitimacy: daily social practices, and the *durée* of experience itself, are moralised through their antiquity (although not through that alone; see p. 93 above). The 'meaningfulness' of the day-to-day organisation of social life is a taken-for-granted feature of human existence, and guaranteed by tradition. The routinisation of daily life, it should be pointed out, is immediately and necessarily connected with the succession of the generations. The temporality of the *durée* of daily existence appears only to the sociologist to be a separate phenomenon from the temporality of the life-cycle, of the replacement of one generation by another. The continuity of routinisation controlled by tradition extends to the practices which influence the life-passages conventionally labelled as 'socialisation'.

The dissolution of the pervading influence of tradition in post-medieval Europe was undoubtedly the result of a number of divergent factors, not all of which can in any specific way be explained as deriving from the rise of capitalism. Equally certainly, however, the transformations of labour and property that assume concrete (*sic*) form in the emergence of capitalist urbanism are the chief origin of a radical weakening of tradition as the main source of the routinisation of day-to-day life. The 'pulverising and macadamising tendency of modern history' of which Maitland once spoke can be derived in a direct manner from Marx's analysis of capitalism as a system of commodity production founded in the labour contract, such as I have described it in the previous chapter. In my opinion this is just as consequential for social theory, in respect of those conceptions of the modern world which focus upon the notion of 'mass society', as it is when juxtaposed to the 'theory of industrial society'. According to most theorists of 'mass society', in the contemporary industrialised societies human beings feel vulnerable, chronically anxious and often 'alone in the crowd'. This is supposed to be the result of the sheer scale of such societies, but is more generally traced to the eradication of 'community' by the growth of urbanism. In this respect there are considerable overlaps between accounts of 'mass society' and conceptions of urbanism such as that offered by Wirth.

If such accounts are correct, these circumstances are neutral in respect of class theory: they are not, in any significant way at least, dependent upon the constitution of capitalism as a class system. I have no quarrel with the descriptions of the 'rootless' way of life offered by the 'mass-society' theorists, but consider it highly important to take issue with their diagnoses of the origins of the phenomena thus referred to. Marx's analysis of the commodity, it should be emphasised, opens out in two directions, one more familiar than the other. The first, the most discussed by Marx himself and by the majority of his followers, is that the commodification of social relations leads to the loss of control by workers over the labour they carry out and over the products they make. The second, while by no means completely separable substantively from the social changes referred to by the first, leads precisely in the direction of the 'meaninglessness' of modern social life – to the themes that figure so prominently in the writings of the 'mass-society' theorists – for commodification, as I have stressed, depends upon the transformation of substance into form. Less provocatively expressed, commodities have a 'double existence' as objects or phenomena having definite qualities on the one hand, and on the other as pure transformation/mediation relations. Now tradition always has a content, and is geared into the qualities of definite activities characteristic of the temporality of tribal and class-divided societies; temporality itself directly reflects an 'ontological security' that invokes a normatively secured continuity between the *durée* of presence and the *longue durée* of established institutions.

The ontological security of tradition (which should not be construed as a purely positive phenomenon) is fundamentally undermined by three of the sets of transformations that I have discussed in this and the preceding chapter:

(a) *The commodification of labour via its transformation into labour-power* as the medium of the production of surplus value. It follows from Marx's analysis that this is a major point of connection between the two themes mentioned above: loss of control over the labour process and of the fruits of production, and the undermining of the 'meaningfulness' of labour. The latter phrase is not a precise one, and it would be foolish merely to contrast forms of labour in capitalist economies with craft skills that have now disappeared. Marx was not prone to romanticise peasant labour, and neither should we.[63] But, however hard and unrewarding it may be in many contexts, peasant labour, as Marx emphasises in the *Formen*, was always carried on as an inherent element of a broader series of communal practices, and of course maintained the worker in an intimate and knowledgeable interrelation with nature.

(b) *The transformation of the 'time-space paths' of the day*, through its centring upon a defined sphere of 'work' physically separate from the household and separated in objectified time from 'leisure' or 'private time'. The capitalistic labour contract is explicitly drained of the moralised rights and obligations which (in principle at least) typically accompanied the exploitation of labour in class-divided societies. This is attended by technological innovations affecting labour (often but by no means always leading to the 'deskilling' of labour) on a scale quite without precedent in world history. This does not imply that work in capitalist industry is devoid of 'meaning' for workers, a matter that in any case varies widely within the high diversification of the division of labour in capitalist production. But there are no longer any guaranteed normative connections between the distinct time-encapsulated sphere of work and the remainder of social life, which itself becomes substantially disembedded from traditionally established practices. The converse of the 'public time' introduced by the rule of the clock is the 'private time' that is freely disposable by the individual, but remains objectified time in the sense that it has been severed from an integral involvement with the situated practices of social life.

(c) *The commodification of urban land, resulting in the 'created space'* that is the day-to-day habitat of the majority of the population in the developed capitalist societies. 'Created space' is long distant from the associations with nature characteristic in substantial degree even of cities in class-divided civilisations. Capitalist cities are almost wholly manufactured environments, in which an architectural functionalism produces the prosaic physical surroundings that become the settings in which the bulk of urban life is carried on. As Lefebvre writes, with the Incas, the Aztecs, in Greece or in Rome, every detail (gestures, words, tools, utensils, costumes, etc.) bears the imprint of a *style;* nothing had as yet become prosaic, not even the quotidian; the prose and the poetry of life were still identical . . . [the capitalist city], anti-nature or non-nature yet second nature, heralds the future world, the world of the generalised urban.[64]

In the phrase 'the production of everyday life', 'everyday life' has to be understood as having something of a technical sense: as being distinct from the more generic terms 'day-to-day life', 'daily life', etc., that I have employed. Everyday life refers to routinised day-to-day activities in which the routinisation of those activities is not strongly embedded normatively in frameworks of tradition.

Routinisation in this context certainly embodies residual traditions, as all social life must do; but the moral bindingness of traditionally established practices is replaced by one geared extensively to habit against a background of economic constraint.[65] The pervasiveness of everyday life in capitalist-industrial urbanism has to be understood as a historical product, not as the 'given' or existential conditions under which social life is universally carried on. This is in specific contrast, however, to how these conditions are experienced by the mass of the population. Large areas of the time-space organisation of day-to-day social life tend to be stripped of both a *moral* and a *rational* content for those who participate in it. There seems little doubt that the psychological implications and consequences of this, which naturally vary widely between different societies, classes and regional and other social groupings, are potentially severe and important to the experience of authority. If the theory of the unconscious I have suggested elsewhere is correct, the maintenance of ontological security in the routinisation of daily life is inherently involved with the control by ego and super-ego of repressed anxieties. In the everyday life of capitalist society ontological security is relatively fragile as a result of the purely habitual character of the routinisation of many day-to-day activities. In such circumstances, particularly in times of severe social or economic dislocation, large segments of the population are potential recruits for demagogic leaders or authoritarian political movements.[66] In terms of its consequences, therefore, the analysis of capitalistic everyday life supports important elements of the views of those who have written of 'mass society'.

Most self-professedly Marxist authors, as I have mentioned previously, have taken up the implications of Marx's analysis of commodification only in the direction of the loss of control of the worker of the labour process and its products. This is even true, I think, though in a more attenuated sense, of those who have been most preoccupied with the discussion of commodification as a general concept, such as Lukács (although not Adorno).[67] For them, the commodification of social relations is a highly pervasive feature of capitalist societies. But they link commodification above all to reification. This is defined in somewhat different ways, but in the main the burden of their accounts is that social relations as a whole (rather than labour as such) escape the control of their creators, human beings in society. For the Lukács of *History and Class Consciousness,* reification is 'the central structural problem of capitalist society in all respects'.[68] Whatever the abiding importance and subtlety of aspects of Lukács's dissection of reification – and in spite of the hostile reception the book provoked from Communist orthodoxy – the theme of reification continues Marx's major preoccupation with control of the production of material life as the main thread of history. Reification, as presented by Lukács, is basically an elaboration of the conception of the fetishism of commodities introduced in *Capital*. It leaves unquestioned the principal constituents of historical materialism as an evolutionary theory of history, though Lukács does, however, lay considerable emphasis upon the distinctive features of capitalism as contrasted to preceding types of society.

In this book thus far I have rejected historical materialism, as an over-all theory of history, for two reasons: 'modes of the production of material life' are not, in tribal or class-divided societies, the chief motor of social change, neither is class struggle; and historical materialism rests upon an ambiguous and badly flawed mixture of an ethnocentrically biased evolutionary scheme and a philosophical conception of history in which 'mankind always sets itself only such tasks as it can solve'. To this I would add a third, one with profound consequences for the critical theory of contemporary capitalism and for theories of socialism. Expressed bluntly, it is that Marx was wrong to regard human beings as above all tool-making and using animals, and to treat this as the single most important criterion distinguishing the 'species being' of humanity from that of the animals. Human social life neither begins nor ends in production. When Mumford calls man 'a mind-making, self-mastering, and self-designing animal', and when Frankel sees in human life a 'search for meaning', they are closer to supplying the basis for a philosophical anthropology of human culture than Marx was.[69] Such pronouncements are undeniably heretical to anyone close to orthodox Marxism, but I believe them to be compatible with acceptance of an important core of Marx's analysis of capitalism.

# 7

# Capitalism: Integration, Surveillance and Class Power

## Time-Space Edges and Societal Integration

In all types of society the media of time-space distanciation are simultaneously the means of societal integration (see Figure 7.1).

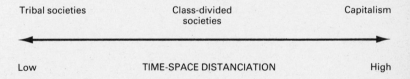

Tribal societies  Class-divided  Capitalism
societies

Low  TIME-SPACE DISTANCIATION  High

### FIGURE 7.1

Both tribal and class-divided societies are societies which rest primarily upon the immediacy of presence: in which the basic units of societal organisation are those of high presence-availability. As I have argued, this should not be equated with 'community' as that concept has appeared in the writings of large numbers of authors concerned with the origins and nature of industrial capitalism. I do not want to argue that the writings of such authors are without interest, or that certain of the themes of 'belongingness' versus 'rootlessness' are unimportant – on the contrary. However, as I have also claimed previously, for several reasons the twofold contrast between *Gemeinschaft* and *Gesellschaft,* or similar notions, must be placed in question. Durkheim's opposition between 'mechanical' and 'organic' solidarity is of the same order.[1]

Let me concentrate here on Durkheim. There are many objections that can be made against Durkheim's formulation of each of these types,[2] and I do not wish to discuss them here. But if we concentrate upon the division of labour, it follows from my analysis that there are three major modes in which the division of labour is organised in different societies, not two (and that these modes of socio-economic organisation should not be regarded as elements of an evolutionary scheme). Each of the three forms of society mentioned above, of course, subsumes a great range of variations. None the less, broadly speaking it is valid to agree with Durkheim that in tribal societies there is not a complex division of labour, with a sexual differentiation of labour task being virtually everywhere the most prominent axis.[3] In class-divided societies the principal axis of the division of labour is the differentiation between agrarian and urban occupations – with a more complex division of labour within the city than ever appears in the countryside. This unvarnished statement conceals once more a variety of different sorts of interpenetration between city and countryside, as Marx pointed out in a general way, and Weber concentrated upon in particular in comparing Occidental cities and those of traditional China.

It is interesting to note that some archaeologists have attempted to apply Durkheim's conception of 'organic solidarity' to the city in class-divided civilisations.[4] Whatever the usefulness of this, in this context I want to stress strongly that the over-all division of labour in class-divided societies is quite distinct in form (being founded upon the city–countryside relationship) from that ushered in by capitalism – and developed in capitalism upon such a massive scale. This conclusion follows from the discussion of the city in the preceding chapter. Dichotomous conceptions like that offered by Durkheim, or by Tönnies and many others, not only reflect a viewpoint derived primarily from European history, then stamped out as a theory of evolution, they also fail to pick up the crucial nature of the transformations of time and space, and thereby of allocative and authoritative resources, introduced by capitalism. In capitalism, 'labour' – and the driving-force of material change, spurred by the pressures of the accumulation process – acquire a quite novel significance. Correspondingly, the 'division of labour' also attains a new significance as an analytical concept, in a twofold sense. In a society in which a distinct sphere of the 'economic' has emerged, and in which the expansion of production acquires an entirely new importance, the divisions within production become of greater social consequence than they were before. But at the same time the basis of the division of labour is fundamentally altered. As the differentiation of city and countryside loses its cardinal organisational significance for the societal totality, so the division of labour takes on national and international dimensions. As I have pointed out elsewhere, the concept of the division of labour, as applied to modern capitalism at least, is a diffuse one that covers a series of distinguishable elements. The division of labour within the work-place ('paratechnical relations') can be distinguished from the division of labour between industrial or market sectors; and these are often distinct from regional (to some degree national) forms of specialisation.[5] Economic interdependence in the division of labour can be recognised as a major underpinning feature of the integration of capitalist societies – so long as one remembers that 'integration' here should not be read as 'solidarity'. That is to say, as Marx acknowledged so forcibly, the division of labour is simultaneously a socialising and a schismatic phenomenon.

The modes of societal integration of the three principal forms of society distinguished above may be represented schematically (see Figure 7.2).

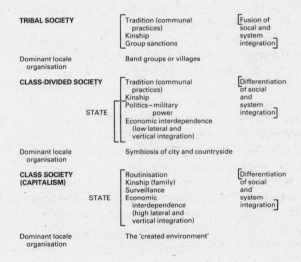

FIGURE 7.2   *Societal integration*

The scheme shown in the diagram both summarises the earlier chapters and introduces notions I shall develop in discussing the capitalist state in the rest of the book. The most distinctive feature of the integration of tribal societies is the fusion of social and system integration, i.e. societal integration depends over-whelmingly upon interaction of high presence-availability. It is again necessary to emphasise the range of variant forms of societal organisation included under the broad label 'tribal society' which, in terms of numbers of societies that have existed in the world, though certainly not in terms of over-all population numbers, far outweigh societies falling under the other types. Hunting and gathering societies depend upon different patterns of time-space organisation than settled agricultural communities; 'chiefdoms' probably represent a fairly distinct sub-type which have some affinities with, and perhaps have often been involved with, the origins of class-divided societies.[6] But in all kinds of tribal society tradition and kinship relations hold sway as the basic media of societal integration.

'Tradition', as I have stressed before, always involves definite contents: specific types of beliefs and specific types of practices embedded in the legitimacy of being 'time-honoured'. Tradition, understood in this way, does not necessarily imply 'mechanical solidarity' in the manner that Durkheim formulated that concept. Even among very small societies there may be considerable variations in the degree to which there are common practices shared by all; and the intersections between what count as distinct 'societies' may not be clearly marked. It may happen, for example, that small bands which operate largely in isolation from one another may meet with others in a periodic way for religious assemblies, trading contacts, or the formation of kin-based alliances. But these activities may exist in the context of quite a mosaic of 'primordial ties and sentiments'. Failure to recognise the significance of these possibilities derives usually in some part from the common tendency, to which Durkheim's style of thinking was particularly prey, to regard a 'society' as a necessarily clearly bounded and distinct entity.[7] In fact, only nation-states universally have this quality, and it will be an essential part of my argument later that the nation-state is a distinctively modern, and European, creation – which from the beginning, however, has itself never existed in isolation but as part of a network of other such states.

The locales that dominate the lives of those in tribal societies, of all types, including migratory bands, are pervaded by the immediacy of presence. To speak of high presence-availability here means more than to characterise formally the time-space range of most social interaction. As I have remarked previously (see p. 39), I use the term 'locale' in deliberate preference to the word 'place', favoured by most geographers, because it carries the connotation of the *settings* of interaction.[8] As the writings of Garfinkel in particular have made clear and, in somewhat different respects, those of Goffman, the settings of interaction cannot be regarded only as the 'backdrop' or the given physical 'environment' of interaction, but are actively organised by participants in the production and reproduction of that interaction. All 'face-to-face' interaction, in communities of high presence-availability, has textures and modalities that depend upon the constant utilisation of (largely taken-for-granted) cues of facial expression, bodily gesture and verbal styles. In tribal societies the primacy of face-to-face interaction in locales with only limited internal regionalisation means that individuals normally have a detailed awareness of their own 'time-demography'.[9] That is to say, they know the individual histories, and kin genealogies of each other, as well as many details about the physical milieux in which they move, utilising such knowledge as a chronic feature of the continuity of social interaction. 'Primordial attachments' are to the physical milieux as well as to other social beings, forming what Bourdieu calls 'practical taxonomies'[10] of locales.

In tribal societies there are no separate agencies of either political administration or of legal sanctioning. Whether or not 'political' and 'legal' institutions can be said to exist in such societies has been the subject of much anthropological debate. In terms of the institutional classification I introduced in Chapter 1, tribal societies do possess such institutions, but of course these are not within the separate administrative control of distinct regulative agencies. Matters of dispute are usually dealt with, when of a serious enough kind, within assemblies of the group; sanctions may none the less be backed by violence or threat of violence, as where vengeance is pursued by kin groups in the form of blood feuds.[11]

The distinction between social and system integration is not wholly without value in studying tribal societies, given the fact that such societies rarely if ever exist in isolation from others. Tribal societies, if looked at macroscopically over a given geographical area, normally form loosely organised inter-societal systems. Factors which influence one sector of such inter-societal systems may either regularly (in the case of, say, trade or forms of 'ceremonial exchange' – as in the famous Kula Ring), or sporadically, as in wars, famines, epidemics, impinge upon and influence sectors that are spatially quite distant from one another. But this does not affect the basic validity of the proposition that in tribal societies the mechanisms of social and system integration are largely one and the same.

Since the earliest origins of class-divided societies, the latter have existed in various sorts of more or less permanent relation with the 'barbarian' worlds of tribal societies. That history has been interpreted almost everywhere from the vantage-points of civilisations is indicated by the very fact that most civilisations seem to have had an equivalent term to 'barbarian', meaning beings who are less developed both technically and morally – although they have not infrequently succumbed to those self-same barbarians when the latter have managed to mobilise *en masse*.

In class-divided society tradition and kinship continue to play a fundamental role in societal integration. This is in some large part simply because of the low level of penetration of the local community by state institutions. Although there have been large variations in the degree to which both a distinct 'peasantry' has been created in agrarian states, and in the modes in which peasant production has been incorporated within markets, there have been no class-divided societies in which the vast majority of the population did not live in rural settings. In so far as the organisation of the local community was left relatively untransformed by the mechanisms of state administration and of surplus-product exploitation, the level of separation of social and system integration in class-divided societies remained for the most part relatively low – certainly as contrasted to the radical dislocations of virtually all elements of social life brought about with the rise of capitalism. In non-capitalist civilisations the city was the home of the institutions of the state. But, as I have indicated in the preceding chapter, there are fundamental discontinuities between non-capitalist cities and capitalist 'created urban space'. In the city in class-divided society the dominance of tradition and kinship, as of pervasive importance in the structuration of social relationships, is certainly not something confined to the rural hinterlands. Large cities in agrarian civilisations have frequently, though by no means universally, had a strongly 'cosmopolitan' flavour in several senses. They have been the meeting-points of individuals or groups drawn originally from differing cultural milieux; they have been centres for religious and courtly splendour; and they have formed the foci of sophisticated scientific and intellectual pursuits. But such cosmopolitanism has been generally confined to small elites, and even within these circles has remained strongly bonded to traditional symbols and practices. As Max Weber has perhaps done more than anyone else to illustrate (whatever reservations one might have about some of his formulations), the administrative apparatus of the state is generally only partly organised according to 'rational-legal' procedures. Among elite groups no less than among the bulk of the population, kinship ties constitute a basic focus of the organisation and continuity of power-holding.

The existence of a differentiated division of labour within the non-capitalist city, and the more deep-seated differentiation between city and countryside, foster modes of economic interdependence that are rare or unknown in tribal societies. Economic interdependence is not to be equated with 'organic solidarity', for reasons I have already mentioned. The division of labour within the city, between cities, and between the city and countryside, is simultaneously at the origin of both solidarities and class conflicts. Open class struggles in agrarian civilisations may take various forms, sometimes being concentrated upon divisions within predominantly urban classes, but more often setting peasant against local lord or against government officialdom. Notwithstanding the significance of 'peasant rebellions' at a variety of times and places in class-divided civilisations, open class struggle is normally sporadic and rare, as I have earlier explained: in contrast once more to capitalism, in which class struggle is an endemic feature of industrial production.

Military power has normally played a decisive role in the integration of class-divided societies, especially the larger imperial societies. While all class-divided societies have developed some regularised modes of government administration, again of widely varying degrees of effectiveness, the use or the threat of the use of violence in sustaining system integration is ever present in class-divided societies. This is of major importance to the conceptualisation of the state – for while the development of the state has everywhere (in both non-capitalist and capitalist societies) been associated with the consolidation of military power, and the presence of standing armies, prior to the emergence of the modern nation-state there have rarely been clear boundaries marking the administrative province of the state. The Great Wall of China does not give the lie to this. It was never wholly effective as an enclosure, and was not precisely co-ordinated with the administrative space of the state as is the case in modern nation-states. In any event, for long periods of its history, the Chinese state, in common with other class-divided civilisations, had what geographers call 'frontier zones' rather than 'boundaries': that is to say, areas of indefinite and fluctuating administrative control.[12]

The differentiation of social and system integration in class-divided societies, being so closely involved with the distinctions between city and countryside, is a spatial one in a very direct sense. The city is the locus of the mechanisms which produce system integration. What has been said about tribal societies also applies here, however. Class-divided societies have never been wholly isolated social forms, and have in various ways been involved in inter-societal systems of dependency and antagonism.

## Class-divided Society, Capitalism, 'World Time'

If the arguments of the preceding chapters are correct, the structural characteristics of capitalism are decisively different from those of class-divided societies. The history of human 'civilisation' stretches back some seven thousand years – so far as we know – while that of tribal societies dates back several hundred thousand years. Capitalism is at most some four or five hundred years old, yet it has introduced social and material transformations of quite staggering proportions, compared with the range of societal variations that existed previously. Not for nothing, and not without good reason, did Marx note in the *Communist Manifesto* that in the short period of its existence the bourgeoisie has created material achievements that far outweigh in their scale (if not in their beauty) the building of the Egyptian pyramids or the other 'wonders' of the pre-capitalist world.[13] But these material accomplishments, as Marx's analysis clarified in a fundamental and indispensable way, were made possible by massive alterations in the nature of society itself. Indeed, it has been part of my argument in this book that, profoundly important as they are to understanding the emergence and structuration of capitalism as a societal system, Marx's works in some respects underestimate the distinctiveness of capitalism as compared with pre-existing types of society. The world in which we live today certainly differs more from that in which human beings have lived for the vast bulk of their history than whatever differences have separated human societies at any previous period.

The separation of the 'state' from 'society' has been such a prominent theme of modern political theory, Marxist and non-Marxist, that in approaching the problem of the capitalist state it is essential to keep in mind the remarks I have made about this issue earlier. The state in class-divided societies was far more 'separate' from the rest of society – or, put negatively, the degree of penetration of the day-to-day life of the majority of the population was much lower – than in capitalism. What distinguishes capitalism as a society is the specific forms of 'insulation' that distinguish a sphere of the 'economic' from the sphere of the 'political'. But the 'state' is a much more intrusive and comprehensive set of institutions in capitalist than in class-divided societies, so far as those subject to its administration 'internally' are concerned. I shall seek to analyse the significance of this phenomenon by means of the concept of *surveillance*. Although surveillance is in certain forms characteristic of all states, non-capitalist and capitalist, I shall argue that it is a much more integral feature of capitalism than of any other form of society in history. I shall, however, defer discussion of the nature of surveillance until the following section of this chapter.

So far as the erosion of tradition is concerned, and its general replacement by the routinised practices of a constructed 'everyday life', there is no need to repeat the analysis provided in the last chapter. This is not the place to pursue a discussion of the significance of kinship relations in capitalist societies, and there is a good deal of controversy about how far the advance of the capitalist mode of production 'necessarily' destroys extended kin networks; but there is no doubt that in the heartlands of capitalism, in the West, the nuclear family is the chief focus of kin ties. Kinship is not a major medium of 'lateral' social integration – across space; and the dislocation between the generations associated with the correlation of the household and the nuclear family undermines the social importance of that 'embedding' of kinship in time so characteristic of non-capitalist societies. In capitalism, there is pronounced differentiation between mechanisms of social and system integration. At the same time, however, it is a form of society in which the interpenetration of the totality – increasingly a global system – with the minutiae of daily life takes on an entirely new character.

Since I shall be taking up the implications of this in what follows, I shall turn at this point to a consideration of certain problems that I have mentioned at various junctures previously but have not so far pulled together. These concern the significance of the fact that societies of all types normally exist in inter-societal systems, such that what happens 'internally' is influenced by what happens 'externally' (and, of course, vice versa). This phenomenon has been substantially ignored by many evolutionary theorists, whose work has been dominated by endogenous or 'unfolding' models of social change. In the literature of archaeology and anthropology, evolutionary theories have classically been challenged by 'diffusionists', who emphasise precisely the influence of 'external' connections between societies upon their development. To these one can add a third approach, 'comparative anthropology' or 'comparative sociology', which simply abstracts from time and space in the pursuit of universal sociological laws. The standpoint I wish to represent in this book differs from all of these. Disavowing evolutionism does not mean accepting diffusionism, at least as that approach has often been understood – for diffusionists have generally failed to acknowledge or analyse the importance of structural features of societies (contradictions, conflicts) that promote radical changes within them. The 'comparative' approach, on the other hand, when guided by the search for ineluctable laws, seeks for the impossible. In my view at any rate,[14] there are no universal sociological laws independent of time and place: all sociological generalisations hold within definable historical contexts.

The approach upon which this book is based recognises that there are both endogenous and exogenous sources of change in human societies (where what a 'society' *is* assumes widely differing forms), but that neither has a generalised primacy over the other. In some circumstances, influences emanating from 'outside' a society can entirely wreck or even eradicate that society; in other instances, there are strongly marked endogenous sources of societal transformation. There is no doubt that there are important differences between tribal societies and class-divided societies, and between class-divided and capitalist societies, in respect of the existence of endogenous pressures towards change. The 'cold' cultures of tribal societies, existing in the 'reversible time' of the saturation of tradition, undoubtedly contrast with the 'hot' cultures of class-divided societies, and with the 'white heat' of change generated by capitalism. But this does not affect the methodological stance I have indicated above. This portrayal, however, still lacks one vital element: a stress upon what Eberhard calls 'world time'.[15] By this he means that an apparently similar sequence of events, or formally similar social processes, may have quite dissimilar implications or consequences in different phases of world development. In our day a fundamental factor affecting 'world time' is the pervasive influence of what I have called *historicity*: an active and conscious understanding of history as open to human self-transformation.

We can represent the intersections of 'historical time' and 'world time' as shown in Figure 7.3. Tribal societies span a very much larger segment of 'historical time' than do class-divided societies, which in turn have existed for a much longer period of human history than has capitalism. But class-divided societies, once they have come into being, have existed along time-space edges with tribal societies and have decisively affected the fate of many of the

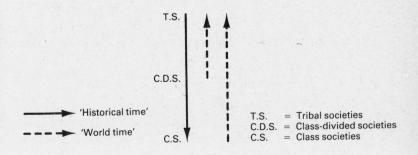

FIGURE 7.3

latter. The emergence of capitalism has injected a further set of time-space edges into 'world time'. But, crucially, capitalism for the first time in human history initiates the creation of an inter-societal system that is truly global in scope. I shall use Wallerstein's term 'world capitalist economy' to describe this, as in the few years since the publication of his book[16] it has already become something of a standard term. But I employ it with three reservations.

First, Wallerstein talks of the world capitalist economy as having succeeded other, prior types of 'world system', by which he means what I have earlier referred to as imperial societies. One must recognise that the term 'world system' is somewhat misleading in such a context, as Wallerstein is obviously well aware, since even the largest empires only managed to extend their sway over part of the globe. Second, the 'world capitalist economy' was not initiated only as an economic order, but as one in which the political and military ambitions of the European absolutist and nation-states were integrally involved. The 'balance of power' between military blocs that was a tenuous European creation of the eighteenth and nineteenth centuries has become today a horrifyingly fragile world 'balance of super-powers' – a balance upon whose symmetry all of our lives depend. Third, the contemporary world inter-societal system is not a wholly 'capitalist' one, even if it is true that capitalistic mechanisms operating on an international scale have a

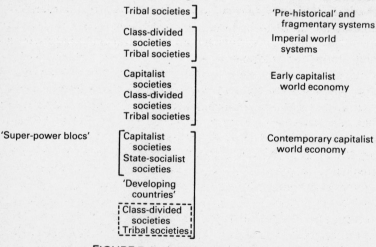

FIGURE 7.4   *Intersocietal systems*

dominant part to play – for the advanced capitalist societies exist along a whole series of time-space edges with other forms of societal organisation, including now the state-socialist societies.

In Figure 7.4 I map out a rudimentary portrait of different types of inter-societal system in the conjunctions of 'world time'. The dashed lines at the bottom of the diagram signify the impending demise of those two over-all types of society in which all human beings have lived until no more than 150 years ago.

## Surveillance and the Capitalist State

To introduce the topic of surveillance at this juncture may seem a diversion from the discussion immediately preceding, but such is not in fact the case – for I want to argue that the origins of surveillance, as a phenomenon of capitalism linked strongly, but not specifically, to the state, are directly bound up with the formation of the *nation-state*; and that, in turn, the European state system was the platform from which the world economy of capitalism was launched and sustained. I shall seek to analyse the nation-state and nationalism in the next chapter, however.

By 'surveillance' I refer to two connected phenomena. First, to the accumulation of 'information' – symbolic materials that can be stored by an agency or collectivity. Second, to the supervision of the activities of subordinates by their superiors within any collectivity. It is as important to distinguish these as it is to emphasise the potential connections between them. The garnering and storing of information is a prime source of time-space distanciation and therefore of the generation of power. Power is also generated by the supervisory activities of superordinates, since supervision is one medium of co-ordinating the activities of individuals to reach what Parsons would regard (but I would not) as inherently consensual 'collective goals'. But the two forms or aspects of surveillance are closely related in principle as well as frequently in practice in virtue of the fact that the collection, synthesis and analysis of information about the members of a society can either be an aid to, or constitute a direct mode of, surveillance over their activities and attitudes.[17]

The origins of writing, as I have pointed out earlier, have been historically closely related to the development of state power in class-divided societies. Writing seems to have originated in the tallying of information relevant to the activities of the state, or of the theocratic-monarchical elites at its head. If the gathering of tribute, or of taxation in developed monetary systems, has always been at the forefront of state activities, the gathering of information, and modes of reckoning and utilising information about the subject population, have always helped to further such activities. But the techniques available for garnering and for storing information were in all class-divided societies limited by the exclusiveness of literacy and by the slow channels of communication. Moreover, it follows from the whole weight of my argument previously that the availability of surveillance in the second sense was always low, and was mainly restricted to separate contexts which were not pulled together in the hands of the administrators of the state. Slavery, especially the slave plantation, is one example of an institution which made use of close surveillance in the second, supervisory sense. So, too, did the 'human machines' of *corvée* or slave labour that were utilised for major public projects, buildings and roads. But these have no organic connection to the bulk of agrarian productive activities, and even where centralised irrigation projects were involved the level of continuous administrative supervision of the mass of producers remained low (see pp. 135–6 above).

As an integral and pervasive element of societal integration, surveillance in each sense only becomes of major importance with the advent of capitalism. The contributions of Foucault to the analysis of surveillance are perhaps the most important writings relevant to the theory of administrative power since Max Weber's classic texts on bureaucracy. None the less, I shall not follow what I take to be some of the main themes of Foucault's work here, for several reasons. My objections are both of a theoretical and a substantive kind. I have no particular cavil against the following statement:

If the economic take-off of the West began with the techniques that made possible the accumulation of capital, it might perhaps be said that the methods for administering the accumulation of men made possible a political take-off in relation to the traditional, ritual, costly, violent forms of power, which soon fell into disuse and were superseded by a subtle, calculated technology of subjection.[18]

(These violent forms of power, however, continued to sustain the external existence of the nation-state in the European state system.) But although Foucault links the expansion of surveillance with the rise of capitalism and the modern state, he does so only in a very general way. Like the 'epistemic transformations' documented in his earlier works, the transmutation of power emanates from the mysterious and dark backdrop of a 'history without a subject'. I accept that 'history has no subject' in a Hegelian sense of the progressive overcoming of self-alienation by humanity, or in any sense that might be discerned in evolutionary theories, but I do not at all accept a 'subjectless history' – if that term means that the events that govern human social affairs are determined by forces of which those involved are wholly unaware. It is precisely to counter such a view of history or the social sciences that I elaborated some of the main tenets of the theory of structuration.

Human beings are always and everywhere knowledgeable agents, though acting within historically specific bounds of the unacknowledged conditions and unintended consequences of their acts. Foucault defines his 'genealogical method' as 'a form of history which accounts for the constitution of knowledges, discourses, domains of objects, etc., without having reference to a subject, whether it be transcendental in relation to the field of events or whether it chases its empty identity throughout history'.[19] This view exemplifies that confusion which structuralism helped to introduce into French thought, between history without a *transcendental subject* and history without *knowledgeable human subjects* (on the levels of practical and discursive consciousness). The disavowal of the first must be kept quite distinct from an acknowledgement of the cardinal significance of the second. History is not retrievable *as* a human project; but neither is it comprehensible except as the outcome of human projects.

This makes up my first objection to Foucault's discussion of surveillance. It has concrete implications for the analyses that Foucault has produced of the clinic and the prison. 'Punishment', 'the prison', etc., are spoken of by him as they were agents, forces of history with their own volition and needs – hence the functionalist tinge that can be observed in some of Foucault's analyses. But the development of modern clinics, hospitals and prisons was not a phenomenon that merely appeared 'behind the backs' of either those who designed them, helped to build them, or were their inmates. The reorganisation and expansion of the prison system in the eighteenth and nineteenth centuries were clearly connected with the perceived needs of state authorities to construct new modes of controlling miscreants in large urban spaces, where the more informal sanctioning procedures of the pre-capitalist village could no longer apply.[20]

The replacement of punishment as violent spectacle with the discipline of anonymous surveillance is regarded by Foucault as involved with the rise of capitalism. But Foucault draws too close an association between the prison and the factory. As I have mentioned previously, there is no doubt that prisons were in part consciously looked to as models by some employers in the early years of capitalism, in their search for the consolidation of labour discipline. Unfree labour was actually sometimes used. But there are two essential differences between the prison and the factory or capitalistic work-place. 'Work' only makes up one sector, albeit normally the most time-consuming one, of the daily life of individuals outside prisons; the capitalistic work-place is not, as prisons are, and as clinics and hospitals may be, 'total institutions' in Goffman's term. More important, the worker is not forcibly incarcerated in the factory, but enters the gates of the work-place as 'free wage-labour'. This gives rise to the historically peculiar problems of business 'management' already alluded to, and at the same time opens the way for forms of worker resistance (especially unionisation and the threat of withdrawal of labour) that are not part of the normal enactment of prison discipline. This point is of more general significance. Foucault's 'archaeology', in which human beings do not make their own history but are swept along by it, does not adequately acknowledge that those subject to the power of dominant groups themselves are knowledgeable agents, who resist, blunt or actively alter the conditions of life that others seek to thrust upon them. The 'docile bodies' which Foucault says discipline produces turn out very often to be not so docile after all.

By lumping together the surveillance of the prison with that involved in other contexts of capitalist society, and indeed in regarding the prison (in the form of Bentham's plan for the Panopticon) as the exemplar of power as discipline, Foucault produces too negative a view of 'bourgeois freedoms', and of the liberal-reformist zeal they helped to inspire. We are well aware of the tendency of certain Marxist traditions of thought to brand all 'bourgeois freedoms' as nothing more than an ideological cloak for coercion and exploitation. This does not seem to have been Marx's view, though he was certainly as ready as anyone to castigate the hypocritical character of much bourgeois political thought and practice. No one can plausibly deny that the freedom of 'free wage-labour' was largely a sham, a means to the capitalistic exploitation of labour-power in conditions not controlled by the worker. But the 'mere' bourgeois freedoms of freedom of movement, formal equality before the law, and the right to organise politically, have turned out to be very real freedoms in the light of the twentieth-century experience of totalitarian societies in which they are absent or radically curtailed. Foucault says of the prison that prison 'reform' is born almost together with the prison itself: 'it constitutes, as it were, its programme'.[21] But the same point could be made, and in less ironic vein, about various of the political and economic transformations introduced with the collapse of feudalism. Liberalism is not the same as despotism or absolutism, and the creation of universal principles of law, behind which lies an ethos of rational justice, has the same double-edged character as prisons and their reform. But with this major difference: prisoners are denied just those rights which the remainder of the population formally possess. Taken together, freedom of contract and freedom to organise politically have helped generate the rise of labour movements that have been both a challenge to, and a powerful force for change within, the political and economic orders of capitalism.

In the enforcement of discipline, Foucault makes great play with the notion of *sequestration*, the enclosure of those to be disciplined from the rest of the world. As a phenomenon of the rise of conceptions of 'deviance' and 'correction', Foucault has a lot to say of great interest here. But what he calls 'sequestration' opens the way to the analysis of features of capitalist society that he barely touches upon. In one aspect, sequestration returns us to the theme of the production of 'everyday life' in capitalism – in a manner that recalls some of the ideas of Elias.[22] The everyday life of capitalism, organised via commodified time, is smoothed of those interruptions that once provided the very marrow of the experience of temporality in the relations between human beings and nature. Not only the 'deviant' or the 'mad' are kept sequestered from view of the mass of the population, so also are the sick and the dying. In this way one more element severing the 'created environment' of capitalist space from pre-existing relations between human beings and nature is established. From another aspect sequestration is only a rather pronounced version of the time-space *regionalisation* of activities distinctive of life in capitalist society. The destruction of the 'public space' of urban life of which Sennett writes[23] is evidently part and parcel of the sequestration of intimacy (and sexuality) from public view in the enclosure of the 'private household'. For the public activities of *presence* in traditional urban life is substituted the 'absent' public of the mass media.

These reservations about Foucault's discussion of power and surveillance, I think, serve to distinguish my position very substantially from his; I do, however, want to emphasise the importance of the concept of surveillance to the analysis of the institutions of capitalism. I shall concentrate here upon the activities of the state, and especially upon the first sense of surveillance as information gathering and processing. Modern state-makers, as Tilly remarks, 'are papermongers'.[24] From about the turn of the sixteenth century onwards the documentation produced by the various branches of government becomes more and more abundant. The late eighteenth century in Western Europe, however, marks a distinctive burgeoning of the 'paper-mongering' of the state, being the time at which statistical information of a centralised kind on births, marriages, deaths and many other demographic and fiscal statistics began to be collected in a systematic way. Control of information, as I have mentioned, has always been a major medium of power of the state bureaucracy, but the modern state brings this to an altogether higher pitch. The significance of this was not adequately acknowledged by Marx, whose critique of political economy tended to operate within a framework in which the internal tasks of the state were regarded as above all bound up with the guaranteeing of contracts. Even the fiercest opponents of classical political economy picked up some of its most inherent presumptions. But the control and monopolisation of information permitting the surveillance of a population, with the disappearance of the more disaggregated class-divided societies, is a potent medium of power. 'Classical social theory' did not recognise the potentiality of what has become in our day a fundamental threat to human liberties, *totalitarian political control* maintained through a society-wide system of surveillance, linked to the 'policing' of day-to-day life. The expansion of surveillance in the hands of the state can support a class-based totalitarianism of the right (fascism); but it can also produce a strongly developed totalitarianism of the left (Stalinism). Indeed, as I shall try to show in the book to follow this one, liberal thinkers are quite right to suggest that there are strong tendencies to totalitarian control built into socialism, both as theory and practice. Anyone who believes, as I continue to do, in the possibility of forms of libertarian socialism must seek to deal with this problem directly, not plunge their heads complacently into soft sand.

One might suppose that the arrival of the computer, the most extraordinary extension of the storage capacity of the human mind yet devised, is the most recent important development in the expansion of surveillance as information control. Even as late as the 1950s, computers were rarely found outside universities and research establishments. Today, in the United States, and increasingly in the other advanced capitalist societies, large sectors of information control are computerised in both government and industry. The 'first generation' of computers of the 1950s has already largely ceded place to a second (transistorised) and third (microprocessing) 'generation' of computers, integrated into database systems.[25] But the computer is not as disjunctive from the early history of industrial capitalism as one might imagine; and to see computerisation alone as a new and quite distinct adjunct to surveillance is misleading.

These points are exceedingly important, because they run counter to a common view that a 'post-industrial society', based upon the coding of information, has replaced, or is in the course of replacing, the old 'industrial society' associated with the sweat of the factory.[26] But there is a much more integral and continuous connection between information control and processing and the rise of capitalist society than such a view would suggest. This is well illustrated by the example of the work of Charles Babbage in the middle of the nineteenth century. By 1843 Babbage had drawn up detailed plans for what has been described as 'a machine incorporating almost every major component and function of a modern computer'.[27] Babbage's computer was not built, not because of his failure to see its relevance to industrial production, but because the technology needed to construct it was not yet in existence.

It is of no small significance that Babbage's writings on the division of labour and profitability form an important feature of Braverman's analysis of management control within the business enterprise.[28] In the early days of capitalism, and in the small-firm sectors that persist today, the surveillance of workers was mainly the direct and personal overseeing of labour by bosses, foremen or other supervisors. Of course, there are very few occupational settings involving manual labour even now where such direct surveillance does not exist at all. But much more important as a resource generating managerial domination over the work-force today, in the large corporations, is the *merging* of the two forms of surveillance in what one writer has called 'technical control' of the labour force.[29] Braverman may have placed too much emphasis upon Taylorism in his discussion of this phenomenon, over-estimating the spread of what was a particular and especially oppressive version of management control. But there is no doubt that 'technical control' introduces a much more anonymous form of control than that allowed by the simple face-to-face supervision of workers, via the co-ordination of labour-power with technology, and through systems analysis of large segments of the labour process.

In the capitalist societies, through the mechanisms of the insulation of economic from political power, such systematic co-ordination of the two aspects of surveillance on the part of the business enterprise is still substantially separated from the organi-sation of the surveillance activities of the state. But the 'techno-cratisation' of the state, of which Habermas and others have written, increasingly tends to co-ordinate both aspects of surveil-lance in much the same way as occurs in the business firm. The factor of technology has proved a potentially obfuscating one here, since technology has a visible material form, and can be easily imagined – as proponents of the theory of industrial society have assumed –to have its own, autonomous 'logic'. But the 'logic' of the machine is not different in nature from the 'logic' of the technocratic control of politics, and in neither case can we rest happy with Weber's resigned conclusion that they embody inevitable processes of bureaucratisation, the 'steel-hard cage' against whose bars we can only scratch our fingers vainly.[30]

## The Labour Contract, Surveillance, Violence

In this section I want to begin to move towards a theory of organised violence in the context of the rise of capitalism. I have long contended that the neglect of what any casual survey of history shows to be an overwhelmingly obvious and chronic trait of human affairs – recourse to violence and war – is one of the most extraordinary blank spots in social theory in the twentieth century. While there have been thinkers in the late nineteenth and early twentieth centuries (Gumplowicz, Ratzenhofer) who have treated war as basic to their theories, their works can hardly be said to have made much impress upon modern social theory. All of this is especially true of Marxist writings, and indeed generally of those of authors of socialist persuasion. With certain partial exceptions, the works of Marxist authors, including those of Marx and Engels themselves, usually only touch upon violence as revolutionary violence, or as counter-insurgency, i.e. resistance to, or repression of, revolutionary movements. Those who have made violence, particularly war, more central to their ideas, such as Weber and Hintze, have not been radical thinkers in the left-political sense; moreover, although I shall draw in some part upon their conceptions, I do not think either author provides a fully satisfactory account of the questions I propose to seek to analyse.

What explains the extraordinary fact that, in a century that has witnessed two world wars of shattering ferocity, and where we all totter on the brink of a third such war that might destroy humanity altogether, sociological thought has given such little attention to the state as the purveyor of violence? The reasons, it seems apparent, lie in the very strong indebtedness that twentieth-century social theory owes to formulations worked out in the nineteenth century, the 'seven decades of European peace'. The leading liberal thinkers of classical political economy, writers such as Comte, Spencer and Marx, whatever their differences, generally assumed that the era of industrialism, or industrial capitalism, had replaced the militaristic society of the feudal period.[31] Whether founded upon class struggle or not, industrialism was seen as a fundamentally pacific force: a system of international production and exchange, which the state might help regulate, but which cuts across militarism. Bakunin's clarion call echoes down through the century:

No more wars of conquest, nothing but the last supreme war, the war of the revolution for the emancipation of all peoples! Away with the narrow frontiers forcibly imposed by the congress of despots, in accordance with the so-called historic, geographical, commercial, strategic necessities! There should be no other frontiers but those which respond simultaneously to nature and to justice, in accordance with the spirit of democracy – frontiers which the people themselves in their sovereign will shall trace, founded upon their national sympathies.[32]

If Marx had no elaborated theory of the capitalist state, as writers of all political persuasions today are prepared to admit, still less did he work out an analysis of the bases of the nation-state or of nationalism. Marx's attitude towards these phenomena was perhaps more complex than that of Bakunin, as most of his ideas were, but the main thrust of Marx's views is apparent enough. In the early phase of his career he inclined towards the blunt assessment that nationalism was a transitory 'bourgeois passion'.[33] Later he became more conscious of the deep-seated nationalistic feelings among some segments of the working class in Britain and in Germany. But he still seems to have regarded these only from a negative point of view, as both aberrant and abhorrent (e.g. rivalries between English and Irish workers). There seems little doubt that, whatever his differences with Bakunin, he regarded the disappearance of class struggle as the medium of the eventual disappearance of political rivalry and war. The views of the *Communist Manifesto* were not substantially revised:

National differences and antagonisms between peoples are already tending to disappear more and more, owing to the development of the bourgeoisie, the growth of free trade and a world market, and the increasing uniformity of industrial processes and of the corresponding conditions of life. The rule of the proletariat will efface these differences and antagonisms even more.[34]

Later Marxists were to write a great deal more than Marx ever did about nationalism, especially those involved in the fragmentation of cultural and linguistic groups in the period of the First World War and its aftermath; but for the most part their concerns were predominantly tactical. No great Marxist theoretical work on the nation-state or nationalism emerged of comparable status with, say, Hilferding's *Das Finanzkapital* in the realm of economic theory. Later, the question of nationalism was 'settled' for a longish period by one of the very few more abstract analyses of nationalism, penned by none other than Stalin.[35] It is difficult to resist the conclusion recently reached by Nairn, that 'The theory of nationalism represents Marxism's great historical failure.' None the less, as he goes on to add, other traditions of Western thought have for the most part not done very much better.[36]

I do not want to claim that there exists even the rudiments of a theory of the nation-state or of nationalism in Marx's texts. Nevertheless, I do think it possible to work out some of the elements of such a theory partly on the basis of analyses I have provided up to this point in this book. I shall defer a more extended discussion of the nation-state within the international state system until the following chapter. Here I shall concentrate upon the problem of the 'internal pacification' of the state that, in Western Europe at least, I want to claim was closely tied up with the growth of industrial capitalism in the late eighteenth and the nineteenth centuries. My thesis, broadly sketched, is this. I have earlier accentuated, following Marx, the essential significance of the labour contract for grasping the nature of capitalism, both as an economy and as a society structured around chronic class struggle. The capitalistic labour contract differs in a basic way from modes of exploitation of surplus production found in class-divided societies. In the latter, the exploiter is in some sense (variable in different systems) an agent of the state, and possesses access to the means of violence or its threat as one principal instrument of ensuring the compliance of the subordinate class or classes. The capitalistic labour contract, on the other hand, does not involve the appropriation of surplus products, but of surplus value, an exploitative relation that is hidden within the over-all system of economic production and distribution. In the capitalistic labour contract, as I have stressed previously, there is a purely economic connection of mutual dependency established between employer and worker. The capitalistic relations of production which the bourgeoisie fought to extend, and which eventually became the dominant economic order, were not brought about through military power or through a class monopoly of the means of violence. This is to my mind of quite crucial significance to understanding both the 'internal' workings of capitalism, and the co-ordination of the development of capitalism with the formation of the nation-state. There are many ways, as I have repeatedly stressed, in which post-feudal Europe differed from other class-divided civilisations (just as those differ widely among themselves). So there is no question of 'explaining' the emergence of capitalism, or of characterising its cardinal features, in terms of a single set of events or processes. But *one* historical conjunction of decisive significance was the centralisation of power in the hands of absolutist monarchs in a context of a class alliance with rising bourgeois elements. The monopolisation of the means of violence in the hands of the state went along with the *extrusion of control of violent sanctions from the exploitative class relations involved in emergent capitalism.* Commitment to freedom of contract, which was both part of a broader set of ideological claims to human liberties for which the bourgeoisie fought, and an actual reality which they sought to further in economic organisation, meant the expulsion of sanctions of violence from the newly expanding labour market.

The sphere of 'private' freedoms and the acknowledged need for labour discipline in co-ordinated production, rather than the licensed, forcible plunder of labour resources or of products, became institutionally distinguished from 'public' authority bolstered by monopoly of the means of violence. The view I wish to develop here has definite affinities with that recently presented by Hirsch. Hirsch's representation of it, however, has quite strong functionalist overtones that I want to repudiate. The following passage illustrates his style of argument:

In capitalist society the appropriation of surplus value and the preservation of the social structure and its cohesion do not depend upon direct relations of force or dependence, nor do they depend directly on the power and repressive force of ideology. Instead, they depend on the blind operation of the hidden laws of reproduction . . . The manner in which the social bond is established, in which social labour is distributed and the surplus product appropriated necessarily requires that the direct producers be deprived of control or physical force and that the latter be localised in a social instance raised above the

economic reproduction process: the creation of formal bourgeois freedom and equality and the establishment of a state
monopoly of force. Bourgeois class rule is essentially and
fundamentally characterised by the fact that its ruling class must
concede to the force which secures its domination an existence
formally separate from it.[37]

The functionalist ring to this passage is there in the use of the
terms 'depend upon', 'requires', etc., which are offered as if they
had explanatory power rather than being, as I suggested earlier,
counterfactual historial propositions. In spite of this, however,
Hirsch does stress that these matters have to be studied historically, even if he does not contribute much to this himself.[38]

# 8

# The Nation-State, Nationalism and Capitalist Development

## The European State System

The period of triumph of capitalism as a 'world capitalist economy', initiated at some time in the sixteenth century, and accelerating through to the present day, is also a period eventuating in the world-wide triumph of the nation-state as a focus of political and military organisation. Neither the rise to pre-eminence of capitalism on a world scale, nor the formation of nation-states as a world-wide phenomenon, are the outcome of any sort of evolutionary progression. Each, in their interconnection, represents the rise to domination of European power over the rest of the world. The Europeans have not created a world empire, though their ways of life, shaped by commodity production and the pre-eminence of the 'created environment', have corruscated traditional cultures the world over. Far from creating a world empire, the expansion of European power destroyed empires, at least of the traditional type – the class-divided civilisations some of which had existed for millenia.

All 'capitalist states' have been nation-states (although the reverse, of course, does not apply). In the previous chapter I claimed that the association between capitalism and the nation-state is not a fortuitous one, and in what follows I shall try to substantiate that claim. Any analysis of the relation between capitalism and the nation-state presupposes the two methodological prescriptions I outlined in the last chapter: an awareness of the significance of 'world time' in the formation and expansion of capitalism, and an avoidance of functionalism as an explanatory form. In explicating the relation between capitalism and the nation-state it is not necessary (nor is it legitimate) to suppose that one has to unearth how it came to be that capitalism 'needed' the nation-state for its development, or in which, *per contra,* the nation-state 'needed' capitalism.

However much one might distrust the nature of the contrasts drawn between Europe and the 'despotic' East by Montesquieu and his contempories, there is no question that the character of Europe, as a series of socio-political formations, differed over the long term from the imperial societies of Meso-America, the Near and the Far East. During the sixteen hundred years or so which succeeded the disintegration of 'its' empire, Rome, Europe did not experience the rise of another imperial society in its midst – although it was constantly menaced by others, most especially the Caliphates, from the outside. Europe was a 'state system' for the whole of this period, which can be divided very crudely into two over-all phases. The first was stamped by the influence of the Papacy, the Holy Roman Empire, balanced off by the localised powers of regional warlords and independent or semi-autonomous city-states. The second opens with the ascendancy of absolutism, succeeded by the consolidation of a system of nation-states. In neither period could any single state power re-establish the Roman Empire in the West, or create a new empire that would dominate the Continent. This was not because no one made the attempt but because those who did – for whatever reasons – failed.[1] Among such aspirant empire-builders, or rebuilders, one might list Charlemagne, who met with some brief success, Gregory the Great, Charles V, Louis XIV, Napoleon (and, one is tempted to add, Hitler, but this was already in a new era).[2]

We are today so accustomed to the dominant role which European capitalism has played in transforming the world that it is difficult to appreciate that for hundreds of years the independence of Europe was often only tenuously maintained in the face of the threat of outside powers. From the eleventh or twelfth centuries onwards, sectors of Europe showed an aggressive tendency to commercial expansion and aggrandisement. Medieval Europe, although founded internally upon a militaristic culture, was weak militarily (especially on land) when confronted by external intrusions. As Cipolla points out, the Europeans were not numerically strong (probably never numbering more than 100 million people), and chronically engaged in warfare amongst one another. The disastrous confrontation with the Mongols at Wahlstatt in 1241 showed that Europe was militarily unable to block the Mongol advance. Two factors inhibited the looming Mongol invasion of Europe: the death of the Mongol chief Ögödäi in that year, and the greater interest of the Khans in holding sway over the East rather than the West.[3] More dangerously, Europe was under threat from successive Ottoman empires. If Toynbee is right, the dominance of the West dates only from 1683, the time of the failure of the second Ottoman siege of Vienna, and the beginning of a Western counter-offensive.[4] A crucial backdrop to this, as Cipolla also stresses, was the earlier-established Western superiority in sea-power. This may have had more far-reaching consequences for the later development and world hegemony of the nation-state/capitalism combination than even Cipolla indicates – for the naval supremacy of the Europeans, which proved able to overcome not only Ottoman sea-power in the Mediterranean but was able to master the fleets it encountered further East, enabled the enforcing of various sorts of commercial or trading relations that might otherwise have been resisted. However, the West was unable to expand in any significant way overland beyond the Balkans.

In analysing the European state system, it is essential to make some preliminary conceptual distinctions. We should distinguish the *absolutist state,* which coincided only with the very early formation of capitalism in Europe, from the *nation-state,* which has some of its origins in absolutism but which is associated much more directly with the consolidation of capitalism as a mode of production; and it is important to distinguish the nation-state from *nationalism*, with which it is frequently confused, but which is in its essential aspects a rather recent development in history. I have already commented briefly upon absolutism, and do not want to enter more than marginally upon such contested intellectual terrain.[5] Absolutism, to repeat, was not a replica in miniature of Asiatic 'despotism' – even given the reservations one must have about the implications of the latter term. Various sorts of diffuse inheritance from Classical civilisation and from the Roman Empire were never lost in Europe, and substantially influenced both the rise of the absolutist princes and their fate; and the strength of certain residues of feudal society also made their contribution. Among the former one must mention, as Max Weber emphasised so strongly, the persisting influence of Roman Law, a legal framework which in turn was related to institutions of republicanism that seem to have found no parallel in any other class-divided civilisations (although some have looked for similarities in the early Sumerian city-states). The judgement of two recent authors writing about the Classical world appears accurate:

> It is generally agreed . . . that the polis represents a new concept of social organisation, different from that of any other contemporary civilisation in the known world [at that time]. More particularly, it is not the kind of social structure characteristic of the other advanced and stratified civilisations of the Mediterranean world and the East . . . Palace and King are replaced by a community of free men as citizens; it is not the king but the citizen-body – whatever portion of the population it constitutes – which represents and embodies the state.[6]

Both the idea and in some degree the reality of citizenship as a universal set of rights and obligations constantly resurfaced in Europe, finding their base in the urban communes. They stand alongside the early and tenacious persistence of deliberative assemblies, which the absolutist rulers tried with varying degrees of success to eradicate, but which were nowhere (in Western Europe) eliminated completely. Such assemblies, ranging from village councils to Parliament, Cortès and Estates, of course represented entrenched liberties only of privileged segments of the population. However, as Tilly argues, the common people of Europe 'for all their reputed docility' actively fought the consolidating power of absolutism over a long period. In England, as he points out, the Tudors had to cope with major rebellions in 1489 (Yorkshire), 1497 (Cornwall), 1536 (the Pilgrimage of Grace), 1547 (the West), 1549 (Kett's rebellion) and 1553 (Wyatt's rebellion), each of which was in some aspect a response to the centralising activities of the monarchy. The specific importance of this is that, as compared with the imperial societies founded in other times and places, the European states had no basis for expanding outwards from a strongly established centre into a weak periphery.[7]

The period of European absolutism thus formed a state system in which the power of rulers was blunted in shifting 'balances of power' externally, and by other influences internally. The absolutist state was not a nation-state, and in spite of the views of some authors it is generally agreed that sentiments of nationalism were scarcely developed at all. Huizinga claimed that elements of nationalism can be discerned in different areas of Europe throughout the middle ages; Hauser dates its origins at the conclusion of the Hundred Years' War, while Chabod finds it developing in France near the end of the sixteenth century.[8] But these views either do not withstand scrutiny, or else employ such a loose definition of 'nationalism' that the phenomena they describe have little similarity to the forms of nationalism which appear in later centuries, and today have swept through most of the world. This is true both of the mass of the population and of the major political writers who helped shape early modern ideas of sovereignty. As D'Entrèves points out, nowhere in the writings of Machiavelli, Hobbes or Bodin do we find any expression of ideas of nationality or nationalism in a significant political context. In the famous peroration in the last chapter of *The Prince,* Machiavelli argues the case for the establishing of a strong political unit in central Italy, but this is defended wholly in terms of sovereignty, and does not invoke any idea of an Italian nation.[9]

### Capitalism and the Nation-State

Perhaps at this point it would be useful to discuss the definitions of the three concepts, 'absolutist state', 'nation-state' and 'nationalism'. I regard each as, in origin, European phenomena, however much the latter two have now become integral to the world capitalist economy. By the absolutist state, a formation limited to the sixteenth, seventeenth and early eighteenth centuries in Europe, I refer to a political order dominated by a sovereign ruler, monarch or prince, in whose person are vested ultimate political authority and sanctions, including control of the means of violence. The absolutist state, in the terminology I have employed earlier, is still part of a class-divided society. Its locus of power, conventional wisdom to the contrary, is not the countryside but the city. We should not be misled by the importance of the partial political autonomy of 'bourgeois' cities (never of course a general phenomenon, as even Weber admits) into supposing that either the aristocracy or the monarchy were located in the countryside. Both late medieval and post-medieval Europe conform to the time-space organisation of class-divided societies generally in respect of the basing of the dominant class in the cities. The class struggles between aristocracy and bourgeoisie, unlike the peasant rebellions, were essentially urban struggles.[10]

The configuration of states elaborated in the period of absolutism was certainly the proximate source of the European system of nation-states, and many observers appear to acknowledge no distinction between the absolutist and nation-state for this reason. The wars conducted by the absolutist monarchs shaped the map of Europe with lasting effect. We should not forget that the 'long-enduring' European powers, England, France, Spain, etc., are the survivors of protracted periods of bitter warfare, in which most of the protagonists failed to survive. There were some five hundred more or less autonomous political units in Europe in 1500: a number which by 1900 had shrunk to about twenty-five.[11] The transition from the absolutist state to 'bourgeois rule' has characteristically been thought of in terms of dramatic political revolutions. But a concentration upon immediate processes of revolutionary strife actually hinders a grasp of how closely connected the ascendancy to power of the bourgeoisie was with the more gradual transformation of the absolutist state into the nation-state – and therefore of the fact that the nation-state and capitalism have close structural connections in eighteenth- and nineteenth-century Europe. Three factors have militated against the perception of those connections: (a) concentration upon the drama of revolution, already mentioned, which tends to conceal how far the Europe of absolutism provided favourable conditions for the development of the capitalist state; (b) concentration upon capitalism as an economic process, as the universalisation of exchange of labour and commodities, forgetting that the emerging bourgeois class could only further their economic ends through grasping the reins of power of already constituted state institutions; and (c) failure to observe a distinction between the nation-state and nationalism as a set of symbols, beliefs and sentiments.

So far as point (b) goes, we should remember that the creation of a capitalist *society* is not just a matter of the extension of commodity production writ large. Tilly seems to make this mistake when he writes that we cannot suppose that the connection between capitalism and the nation-state was 'intimate and eluctable', because early capitalistic enterprises – like the Hanse – were quite foreign to state formation, while on the other hand strong states that were formed early on (Spain, France) were not principal centres of capitalist development.[12] This is true of the period of the absolutist state, but not of that of the transition to the nation-state. In the eighteenth century, while certain notable and strongly formed state centres stood out, Europe can still be accurately described as a 'political patchwork', in which there were 'delicate and subtle shadings'. Such diversity was in substantial result the outcome of phenomena already noted specifically by, among others, Tilly, i.e. the persistence of localised rights and the continuing tensions between proprietorial rights and the absolutist princes. It has been remarked of these circumstances

> that they 'explain why it is still convenient to think of [seventeenth- and] eighteenth-century diplomacy in terms of relations between persons rather than relations between states. If Louis XIV actually *did* say 'L'Etat c'est moi', he was from a legal point of view expressing a truism, for legally he was the only tie between millions of men whom we now call French, but who might have thought of themselves as Languedociens, Bérnais, Bretons, or Strasbourgeois.[13]

The connection between capitalism and the nation-state is not to be looked for in the relation between the nature of capitalistic enterprise, as such, and the centralisation of state power – but in the transformations wrought by capitalism which I have described earlier in the book. That is to say, the state system of Europe from the sixteenth to the early nineteenth centuries was one, which for reasons I have touched upon, proved accommodatory to capitalistic accumulation. But until at least the late eighteenth century, and at that date only in Britain, the European countries continued to display most of the characteristics of class-divided societies in terms of their time-space organisation. The wholesale transformation of labour into wage-labour, the concomitant commodification of time and transformation of the city–countryside relation into one of 'created urban space', are all largely phenomena of the nineteenth and early twentieth centuries in Western Europe. They were only possible given the dramatic contractions in time-space convergence (cf.p. 38 above) that the railways began, and which have continued on down to our day. The earlier expansion of European power into the rest of the world, as I have mentioned, was mainly the result of 'action at a distance' made possible by (relatively) rapid movement by sea, and by superiority of naval force.

At the opening of the nineteenth century, the development of both communication and transportation overland was almost as rudimentary as it had ever been. The British had more or less firmly established themselves in India, but Napoleon took almost as long as Caesar to get from Rome to Paris.[14] As Pred says, when Morse's electromagnetic telegraph transmitted the message 'What hath God wrought?' between Baltimore and Washington in 1844, he initiated a new set of relations between presence and absence (as writing had done millenia before). Before that date the movement of information over long distances was identical with human spatial mobility – always very limited. This is perhaps not the place to labour the point, but sociologists (unlike modern geographers) have been prone to ignore the fundamental interpenetration of spatial presence and absence that has been as driving a medium of capitalistic expansion as the accumulation process. According to one estimate, nearly 70 per cent of the population of the United States knew that John F. Kennedy had been assassinated within a half-hour of the event. In contrast to such immediacy, the news of George Washington's death on 14 December 1799, in Alexandria, was only published seven days later in New York City.[15]

The nation-state replaced the city as the crucible of power only from the late eighteenth century onwards in Western Europe and the United States. The 'bourgeois revolutions' both expressed and furthered radical alterations in the nature of state institutions – that is, the institutions of governance and surveillance. In so doing, they consolidated the conditions for the full-blooded expansion of capitalism through industrialisation and the transformation of urban space. It is crucial in this that the bourgeois classes were 'national bourgeoisies': in other words that the political revolutions of seventeenth- and eighteenth-century Europe were made within an already constituted state system. While an international proletarian revolution may have seemed to some a possible scenario at a later date, an international bourgeois revolution never was. Capitalism developed within a military 'cockpit' in which the expansion of industrial production very soon came to be seen by all ruling groups as the *sine qua non* of national survival.

Monopolising the means of violence has both an internal and external connotation, directly connected with the expansion of the surveillance activities of the state internally, and with the 'balance of power' in Europe externally. The monopoly of the means of violence internally is associated above all with the formation of police forces, a phenomenon that everywhere accompanies the extrusion of control of the means of violence from the labour contract. The differentiation between the police and the standing army (or armed forces) has remained a fairly clear, but never wholly unambiguous, one in most European countries since the middle of the nineteenth century, and can be said to express the 'inward' and 'outward' stance of the state in respect of violence and its control. Territoriality associated with the state is not of course a new phenomenon, and indeed the laying claim to a 'territory of occupation' seems to have been characteristic of all forms of society. What is specifically late-European is the fixing of very precise boundaries which mark off the realm of administration of the state. To the claimed monopoly of means of violence and the scope of administration pertaining to clear (and internationally acknowledged) frontiers we must of course add the monopoly of the means of the creation of law. I shall therefore define the nation-state as follows. The nation-state, which exists in a complex of other nation-states, is a set of institutional forms of governance maintaining[16] an administrative monopoly over a territory with demarcated boundaries, its rule being sanctioned by law and direct control of the means of internal and external violence.

What makes the 'nation' integral to the nation-state in this definition is not the existence of sentiments of nationalism, but the unification of an administrative apparatus over precisely specified territorial bounds (in a complex of other nation-states). Such a unification of administration is only possible once the old city–countryside relation has been shattered by the commodification of production that has overcome the 'segmental' regionalisation of time-space in class-divided society.[17]

I shall define 'nationalism' as the existence of symbols and beliefs which are either propagated by elite groups, or held by many of the members of regional, ethnic or linguistic categories of a population, and which imply a communality between them. By a 'communality' here I mean something like Geertz's 'primordial sentiments' writ large, and stripped of their association with communities of high presence-availability. Nationalistic sentiments do not necessarily converge with citizenship of a particular nation-state, but very often they *have* done so. A definition of nationalism has to be a generalised one, because studies of the phenomenon show fairly clearly that there is no single criterion which forms the focus of communality. On the basis of the European experience in the nineteenth and twentieth centuries, for example, one might suppose that speaking a common language is the prime feature of nationalism. But looked at in a world context, the factor of common language seems to be the exception rather than the rule.[18] As a phenomenon of the late eighteenth century to the present day, nationalism is closely associated in time and in fact with the convergent rise of capitalism and of the nation-state – but to confuse it with the nation-state as such has just as disastrous consequences as regarding the nation-state as a mere epiphenomenon of capitalism.

## Nationalism: an Interpretation

The literature of the 'theorists of industrial society' of the 1950s and 1960s, which was the basis of so-called 'modernisation theory', was particularly prone to assimilate the concepts of the nation-state and nationalism. This was the literature of 'nation-building', and besides making the confusion just mentioned it also (a) extrapolated directly from the European experience to other contexts, suggesting that this could and should be repeated elsewhere, but (b) at the same time largely ignored the more noxious characteristics of European nationalism – its association with fascism, and with the waging of wars. Nationalism was treated as pre-eminently a beneficent force, one closely involved with the achievement of citizenship rights in newly emerging states in the 'Third World' (socialist nationalism being largely ignored). There are certain features of these views that are correct, in my opinion, and they cannot be dismissed as easily and contemptuously as they have been by some Marxist authors. Nationalism, like the nation-state, is a phenomenon originally generated from within Europe, and I think Kohn is right to stress that it would not have emerged without the bourgeois idea of popular sovereignty that ushered in the modern phase of European liberalism.[19] But it does not follow from this – as fascism in Europe itself showed – that nationalism is in any way a guarantor of what Marshall, Bendix and others have called political 'citizenship rights' (not that these authors argued anything as crude as that).

However much they may have wished to play down what Deutsch calls the 'dreams and images of savagery' produced by nationalism along with its images of 'self-government, enlightenment, and social justice',[20] all commentators on nationalism have acknowledged its 'Janus-faced' character.[21] Just as many writers on 'nation-building' in the Third World have tended to accentuate its positive side, others have been much more inclined to the opposite view. Kedourie stands out as one of the most prominent of these, holding nationalism to be 'an antiquarian irrelevance, a baneful invention of some misguided German philosophers'.[22] Such a view is surely no more defensible than the one which connects nationalistic sentiment above all to the liberal-democratic state of 'political citizenship'. Quite regardless of the various interpretations of nationalism within European development in the nineteenth and twentieth centuries, it is hardly possible to deny that nationalism has been a major influence upon peoples fighting to liberate themselves from foreign oppression.

Why such confusion on the subject of nationalism? Why should it have this Janus-faced nature, and what explains its tremendous significance in modern world history? In order to attempt to reach even a provisional approach to such questions, I think, it is necessary to be rather swingeingly critical of most discussions and theories – in so far as there are any – of nationalism that currently exist. First, it is vital to insist again upon the importance of distinguishing the nation-state from nationalism. Second, we have to recognise that, however frequently nationalistic feelings have been fostered and invoked ideologically by dominant elites, nationalism is not merely a set of symbols and beliefs force-fed to an unwilling or indifferent population (although such circumstances have occurred frequently enough). Third, we must again acknowledge the methodological import of 'world time', in avoiding the supposition that the first emergence of nationalism in

Europe can be used as a general model of nationalism as a whole.

If nationalism is not distinguished from the nation-state, a range of phenomena that have been rooted in the *Realpolitik* of the 'interests of state' are easily misinterpreted as the direct outcome of a nationalistic spirit. This sort of merging was just that which was promulgated, for example, in the conceptions of the Germanic *Volksgeist* involved in the antecedent circumstances of both world wars. The fascist state might almost be defined as comprising a successful linkage between an aggressive and exclusivist nationalism and a generalised commitment to the state as the ultimate arbiter of the interests of the community. The development of nationalism of an aggressive and militaristic type may or may not be successfully engendered in such circumstances, however much elites may seek to encourage its spread through all sections of society. Whatever the explanation, which undoubtedly involves a number of complex and difficult historical problems, the nationalism that spread through France following the 1789 revolution evidently reflected a quite divergent form of state mobilisation from that observed a century later in Germany – and seems almost certainly to have been more widely spread through different classes in the population as a whole.[23]

Nationalism is in substantial part a psychological phenomenon, involving felt needs and dispositions, in contrast to the nation-state, which is an institutional one. I believe that one can formulate an approach to a theory of nationalism against the backdrop of the time-space transformations by means of which the 'created environment' of urban space becomes the habitat of individuals in capitalist societies, and the nation-state the dominant 'power container'. Nationalism, I have suggested, feeds upon, or represents, an attenuated form of those 'primordial sentiments' of which Geertz speaks in tribal societies or village communities. The dissolution of the foundation of society in relations of presence substantially replaces the grounding of those primordial sentiments in tradition and kinship by a more routinised, habitual round of 'everyday life'. This is one point of intersection, I have argued, between notions of 'mass society' and the theory of the commodification of time and space deriving from Marx. In the spheres of 'everyday life' created by the expansion of capitalism the areas of 'meaningful' existence retreat – to the intimacy of personal and sexual relations on the one side[24] – and to the arenas of 'mass ritual' on the other (as in spectator sports[25] and in political ceremonial). In such conditions of social life the ontological security of the individual in day-to-day life is more fragile than in societies dominated by tradition and the meshings of kinship across space and time.

The sustaining of ontological security, I have argued elsewhere,[26] is based upon the continual 'regrooving' of the cognitive beliefs of the individual (a process each individual helps continually to achieve in the skilful production and reproduction of social life) in the course of his or her 'time-space paths' through the contexts of daily activities. Breaches of ontological security threaten the stability of the ego through the upsurge of repressed anxieties founded upon primitive object-cathexes. In modes of social life suffused with 'primordial sentiments', while there may be no lack of conflicts, disputes and tensions, the sustaining framework of ontological security is well bolstered. But in conditions of day-to-day life in which routinisation has largely replaced tradition, and where 'meaning' has retreated to the margins of the private and the public, feelings of communality of language, 'belongingness' in a national community, etc., tend to form one strand contributing to the maintenance of ontological security. To speak the same language is normally to share a series of other cultural elements or styles of behaviour with others. Nationalistic sentiments both have an affinity with, and may directly express, cultural similarities within or between groups, and language is a major 'carrier' of such similarities. This is why, in the 'original' settings of the formation of nationalism, in Europe of the nineteenth and early twentieth centuries, language appears as a major medium of nationalism. The leading nation-states were already (with various important exceptions) fairly settled language-communities. In the post-European expansion of nationalism, which I shall argue is in some ways quite different from its first development in Europe, the criteria of a common language by no means readily converges with the boundaries of newly established nation-states.

In circumstances of radical social disruption, mobilisation for war, etc. – which in modern times affect whole populations, not just the specialist military forces who bear the brunt of the actual fighting – the relatively fragile fabric of ontological security may become broken. In such conditions regressive forms of object-identification tend to come to the fore. Following the outlines of the theory of leadership worked out by Le Bon and Freud,[27] we can infer that large segments of the 'masses' become particularly vulnerable to the influence of symbols that are propagated by leader-figures with whom there is a strong emotional identification. These are, if one likes, 'charismatic leaders' in Weber's term, but the Le Bon–Freud theory helps explain both from where they derive their emotional appeal and why they are able to mobilise mass followings or mass movements. Now the influence of such leadership is particularly prominent in the history of nationalism, and it is surprising how little attention has been given to this by most of those who have written on the subject – for I believe it is certainly one element that helps explain the messianic quality which often distinguishes upsurges of nationalistic sentiments (in wars, or in periods when war appears imminent) as well as nationalist movements. Regressive identification with a leader-figure, and the symbols represented by that figure or comprised in his or her doctrines, carries with it that essential feature of nationalism, whether benign or militant, a strong psychological affiliation with an 'in-group' coupled with a differentiation from, or rejection of, 'out-groups'. This theory helps us to understand the 'Janus-faced' nature of nationalism, in conjunction with what I have already said about the various possible connections between nationalism and different forms and trajectories of development of the nation-state. For if the Le Bon–Freud theory of leadership is valid, regressive object-identification with a leadership figure is connected psychologically with increased 'suggestibility' and emotional volatility. Individuals then become vulnerable to identification with figures who may exemplify 'populist' or 'democratic' values, or a range of 'heroic' virtues inspiring acts of either nobility or savagery.[28]

I shall not attempt to deal at any length with the third point I made above: the necessity of understanding nationalism in the context of different phases of 'world time'. Various typologies of nationalist movements have been drawn up by students of nationalism; these mostly recognise that European nationalism (itself a varied, and as regards separatist movements within European states, a pheno-menon of continuing friction) cannot be readily used as a model of nationalism as a whole.[29] Both the extension of the nation-state system and the spread of nationalist movements outside Europe to embrace the world are the results of the world-wide expansion of capitalism and the pre-eminenece of Western military power. Nationalist movements in the colonial world and in post-colonial states have been largely formed in opposition to the dominance of the West in general, and to the corrosive influence of capitalism upon traditional modes of life in particular.

### Capitalism as a World System

Hägerstrand's time-geography shows that it is useful to think of the daily lives of individuals in a social system as a series of 'time-space paths' conjoining at intersections that can be represented topographically. The same applies, I think, to the development of societies, however valuable Hägerstrand's particular techniques of representation of such paths or trajectories may or may not be when adapted to such a larger purpose. Certainly it is important to emphasise the 'geographical' aspects of social change, much neglected by sociologists. Most of the significant processes of social change that have affected the world since the origins of capitalism have involved major spatial movements of human beings and material resources. This was of course true 'internally' in the formation of capitalism in the European countries: most obviously in the case of migrations of agrarian workers to the cities (one must not forget either the massive migrations of populations between countries, especially the waves of European migration to the United States). The older-established theories of social development, such as the theory of industrial society, concentrating as they did on endogenous models of change, analysed these 'internal' patterns of movement almost exclusively.

But it has now become clear that, since its inception, capitalism initiated the creation of a world system quite distinct from other inter-societal systems that existed in previous phases of 'world time'. The time-space paths that chart the progressive ascendancy of the world capitalist economy take a very different form from those characteristic of preceding periods, when the largest societal entities were imperial societies. Wallerstein has made a notable contribution to opening out the study of these matters and, within the scope of the qualifications I indicated about his views in the previous chapter (pp. 168–9 above), I consider his general position to be an illuminating one – and one which conforms closely to several of the main arguments I have developed in this book. In imperial societies the scope of military sanctions basically determined the boundaries of economic relations both within and between those societies. With the development of capitalism, however, this situation is in a sense reversed. The capitalist state maintains a monopoly of political and military power within its own bounds, but the world system which it initiates is fundamentally influenced by capitalistic processes operating on a world scale. The world capitalist economy, according to Wallerstein, beginning in about the sixteenth century and continuing through to the present day, consists of three principal 'zones' or established 'time-space paths' (in the language of Hägerstrand rather than Wallerstein). These are the capitalist core (Europe, the United States and, more latterly, Japan); the semi-periphery, which is both exploiter and exploited; and the peripheral regions with their 'coerced cash-crop labour'.

What is correct about the over-all stance which Wallerstein adopts, I think, is: (a) his insistence upon the methodological necessity of studying inter-societal systems (although in his own work he has said nothing in any detail about pre-capitalistic 'world time'); and (b) the idea, which I infer from his writing even if he has not stated it directly, that the separation of polity and economy 'internally' within capitalist societies is, in a world context, directly related to such a separation 'externally'. That is to say, the capitalist state has internal political dominion but, outside of directly colonised areas, exists in an external environment in which economic mechanisms hold sway.

Wallerstein's work has already been subject to extensive critical debate. There are two major respects – of relevance to my discussion here at any rate – in which his views can, and have, been subject to quite basic attack.[30] Each, however, is illuminated I believe by the analyses I have offered in prior parts of this book. One is that, by concentrating upon international capitalist markets, Wallerstein neglects the driving-force of capitalism as the accumulation process founded in the capital/wage-labour relation. The other is that he fails to examine the emergence of capitalism within the European state system, and hence underplays the role of military power and warfare among states in shaping the world we live in today. As I have tried to emphasise, basing my argument upon Marx's analysis of the intersection of labour and commodity markets in the very process of production, capitalism for the first time in world history introduces a dynamically expanding economy. Only in capitalism (and this is, of course, also using Marx against himself) do the forces of production have an internal dynamic stimulating chronic technological innovation and economic transformation. But this new dynamism of the economic, as I have tried to show, was released in the context of a state system to which it was more than contingently related. Capitalism does not, as Marx tended to think, inevitably sweep away all significantly competing forms of socio-political and cultural organisation. On the contrary, the conjunction between the rise of capitalism and the absolutist state system produced a system of nation-states that, far from being ephemeral, is integral to the world capitalist economy – which is at one and the same time a world military order. Weber and Hintze perceived this, but both over-stretched the concept of the nation-state historically and did not satisfactorily analyse its relation to the 'created space' wrought by capitalistic production. For both writers, too, the nation-state is coterminous with nationalism, a matter which has far-reaching consequences for Weber's 'philosophy of history'.[31] In Weber the modern struggles between nation-states are a contemporary version of the eternal – and unresolvable – clash between cultures embodying divergent ultimate values. In case it is not obvious, I should perhaps say here that I have no sympathy with any such view in this book, as the concluding chapter will indicate.


**Contemporary Developments**

So far as the over-all charting of the international division of labour in the world capitalist economy is concerned, an important analysis has recently been made by Fröbel *et al*.[32] They distinguish several major phases in the economic relationships between the expansion of capitalism at the core, and the nature of production in semi-peripheral and peripheral regions. In the period from the sixteenth to the eighteenth centuries, independent crafts and domestic production in the putting-out system were the main foundation in Western Europe of manufacture in such industries as textile production, the production of metals, ship-building and armaments.[33] These were already complemented in the periphery by forced or slave labour involved in, for instance, the mining of precious metals in Peru and Mexico, and by the existence of sugar plantations in Brazil and the West Indies. At the same time, in Eastern Europe, the 'second serfdom' produced something of a reversal of the dissolution of feudal relations that had occurred in the West, helping to supply in a 'semi-peripheral' way demand for cereal goods from Western Europe. In the eighteenth and nineteenth centuries, wage-labour as capitalist-industrial labour-power, based in the capitalistic work-place, increasingly replaced other forms of labour, first of all in England, then spreading to the rest of Western Europe. This was also the period, though Fröbel *et al.* do not make much of it, of the 'communications revolution' producing the dramatic increase in time-space convergence that was an essential element of the mass circulation of commodities on a national and world scale. Of primary importance 'internally' was the growth of the railways, and the opening of the new era of communication across time-space made by Morse. At this period, slave labour was the foundation of the production of raw cotton in the West Indies and the Deep South of the United States. While indigenous cotton production was being undermined in India, China and Japan were forcibly prised open for trading relationships with the West. The 'barbarians' rapidly accomplished an 'opening up' of the East such as had seemed inconceivable to the Chinese Emperor Ch'ien Lung not many years before. Marx once commented on this, that it was 'an amusing circumstance that the oldest and most unshakeable empire on earth should within eight years have been brought by the cotton-bales of the English bourgeoisie to the eve of a social revolution which cannot fail to have the most important consequences for civilisation'.[34] How amusing the Chinese found it is open to some question, and the cotton bales did not roll in unaided but were backed by Western sea-power; but one cannot dispute the over-all exactitude of Marx's judgement.

The first half of the twentieth century saw the consolidation (through successive economic crises) of wage-labour as the basis of manufacture in Europe, the United States and Japan – to which one can add the further advancement of time-space convergence through the development of increasingly rapid mass transportation and communications media spanning virtually the whole globe. In semi-peripheral and peripheral areas, modes of capitalist penetration, and the role of the core, changed somewhat. The growth of wage-labour and of various 'secondary economic activities' in Latin America, Africa and Asia fed a partially indigenous capitalist-industrialisation process in certain sectors; but established or emergent nation-states in these continents continued to form the basis of the production of raw materials for world markets dominated by the Western core.

In the past few decades, Fröbel *et al.* argue, a new world division of labour is emerging, involving the partial 'deindustrialisation' of the West, and the siting of manufacturing production by transnational corporations in peripheral sectors. Largely as a result of the corrosive influence of capitalism upon traditional modes of agrarian production, a vast 'reservoir of disposable labour' has come into existence in semi-peripheral and peripheral areas that constitutes 'a real world industrial reserve army of workers, together with a world market for production sites'.[35] Thus contemporary valorisation and accumulation of capital on a world scale is probably undergoing major changes. These include possible large further increases in the relocation of manufacturing industries from core to periphery, a chronic tendency towards 'stagflation' at the core coupled with unemployment rates far above those typical previously, and a partial shifting of economic power from core states to certain semi-peripheral states that are able to cartelise supplies of raw materials (most significantly, of course, oil).

Two of the main limitations of this analysis are that it ignores the economic role of the state-socialist countries, and that it again seems to express the 'economic reductionism'[36] for which Wallerstein has been criticised – and which also applies to the writings of other Marxist authors (e.g. Amin, Emmanuel, Frank) writing on aspects of the contemporary world capitalist economy.

One must reiterate that the 'world capitalist economy' is a misnomer in two respects: that it deflects attention from the military power of nation-states, and especially of the influence of overt wars, upon the development of the modern world system; and that the 'world capitalist economy' never has been, and is not today, wholly capitalist. The Eastern European countries, China or Cuba do not fit readily into the differentiation of 'core', or 'semi-periphery' and 'periphery'. Several of the European state-socialist societies in particular are tied into the economy of the West on various levels of product markets and the production and exchange of raw materials, and (for example) are today experiencing 'secondary inflation' and other economic difficulties that derive from this. In other respects, of course, they stand outside the world capitalist economy because their capital valorisation involves different mechanisms from those of the West, and because they form a separate trading area among themselves. The fact of their existence can hardly be ignored (but it *is* in so much contemporary writing on economic issues on a world scale). Moreover, they also indicate the relative crudeness of the concepts of 'core', etc., when these are applied as general notions. That there is a metropolitan 'core' in the world capitalist economy, centred upon the three foci of the United States, Europe and Japan, is undeniable. Most of the seeds of the dynamism of modern economic life remain buried in that core, even if the apple now appears slightly rotten as compared with its seemingly rosy hue in the period of the 1950s and early 1960s.

But, as everyone in practice admits when getting down to details, the concepts of 'core' and 'periphery' are not of much value save as over-all orientating notions. The 'core' is clearly shifting, unstable and subject to major internal diversification. The instance of Britain's participation in the development of capitalism from the early nineteenth century to the present day illustrates this very well. For a certain time the world's leading capitalist power, the core of the core, the British economy has declined relatively to a position in which it is a weak partner even within Europe, let alone compared with the economic centrality of the United States. These differentiations within the gross concepts of core, semi-periphery and periphery can, I think, be regarded conceptually as the interweaving of time-space paths of development, in which the intertwining of trajectories can be understood as (shifting) relations of autonomy and dependence. So called 'dependency' theories have come in for a considerable amount of criticism on their 'home ground', Latin America,[37] but while such criticism is relevant to the content of some such theories, it does not compromise the usefulness of the notions of autonomy and dependence as such. Indeed, I would argue that from the point of view of the theory of structuration this indicates the universal applicability of the conceptualisation of power I elaborated previously, as ranging from the most trivial of everyday encounters right up to the processes influencing large-scale transformations in the world system.

The coexistence of Western capitalist countries, and the world economy in which they are pre-eminent, with the state-socialist societies is nowhere more evident – no phenomenon presses in upon us more urgently – than in the realm of military power. Marxism, now constituted as the official doctrine of 'actually existing' socialist societies, has proved no less resistant to the two-fold influence of the organisation of the nation-state and of nationalism than capitalism has been. Of course, the beneficent side of the 'Janus face' of nationalism has been of fundamental importance to the creation of the state-socialist societies and to liberation movements the world over. But it has not only shown one cheek, as the confrontations between the Soviet Union and China, the Soviet Union and its more recalcitrant partners among the Eastern European nations, and the horrific events involved between Kampuchea and Vietnam, demonstrate. If the most significant contemporary changes on the level of the international division of labour are those described by Fröbel *et al.*, the major politico-military changes of the past quarter of a century are those that have produced a triadic division of world power. The 'super-power blocs' tread the tightrope of mutual nuclear oblivion, and neither the other industrially mature nations nor the 'developing countries' can forge policies independently of forced, acquiescent or implicit alignments with the super-powers. None the less, it would be a mistake to suppose that the end of the era of the nation-state has at last arrived, or that we are anywhere near the formation of a world government system – for, after all, the super-powers are still nation-states, and there are no more embracing world organisations that even remotely threaten their power. While there may be systems linking certain sectors economically (the EEC, Comecon), and while they may incorporate aims such as broad European parliamentary sovereignty, they seem to exacerbate national divisions as much as curb them. As for the transnational corporations, while they are playing a major role in the relocational changes in the international division of labour, and heavily influence world product and monetary markets, they are for all that nationally based companies within 'parent' states.[38] The only seemingly genuine transnational organisation, the United Nations, like its pre-war forerunner, has for better or for worse chronically shown itself to be no more than an instrument for the power interests of its member states.

# 9

# The State: Class Conflict and Political Order

## The State in Social Theory

The past few years have seen an extraordinary efflorescence of writings on the state, especially among Marxists, following a long period during which the subject had been largely ignored. In Lenin and Gramsci, Marxism has two figures who can lay claim to having made highly important contributions to the theory of the state in capitalist society. But for a considerable while Lenin's *State and Revolution* achieved canonical status and was assumed, in orthodox Marxist circles at any rate, to have settled issues relating both to the state and power within capitalism and the 'smashing' of the state with the arrival of socialism. Gramsci, on the other hand, was revered but for various reasons not widely read – and certainly not well understood – outside Italy. In non-Marxist sociology, especially during the period of dominance by the reworked version of the theory of industrial society in the years of 'Keynesianism' and apparently firmly established Western economic growth, the state was barely discussed at all. The industrial-society theorists mostly took it for granted that the state was a benign instrument for the progressive achievement of goals of social reform: the redistribution of wealth, the spread of welfare programmes, the ever-increasing expansion of education, and so on. The changes which seemed to be occurring on these levels were made the focus of attention, with the state as the unanalysed medium of their realisation. The academic division between sociology, the study of 'society', and politics or political science, the theory of 'government', helped to reinforce this tendency to ignore the state as a direct object of study on the part of sociologists. For their part, the

non-Marxist political theorists fostered the image of the benevolent state via the pervasive emphasis upon 'pluralism', which,
although developed primarily in the context of the United States,
exerted a strong influence upon authors elsewhere too.[1]

Marxism and academic sociology – as represented especially by
Durkheim and modern functionalism – share certain common
roots that are certainly not irrelevant to the fact that the state has
not figured as a major focus of theoretical concern in either
tradition. Each was in some part influenced by Saint-Simon
(Durkheim much more than Marx, and then mainly by different
aspects of Saint-Simon's thought).[2] There is more than a hint in
Marx of the Saint-Simonian doctrine that, in the society of the
future, the administration of human beings by others will give way
to the administration of human beings over things. Durkheim was
less preoccupied with this theme of Saint-Simon than by the idea
that the state in an industrialised order will have a moral role to
play in relation to the societal community. That is, he was
explicitly, in contrast to Marx, more influenced by Saint-Simon's
later writings than by his earlier ones.[3] But in neither case do Saint-
Simon's ideas support the conceptions that the state in an
industrial society is integrally involved with military violence, or
that administrative control within definite territorial boundaries is
a significant feature of the state. The industrial state, in short, is
not a nation-state, the driving-force of nationalism is absent, and
the industrial order is portrayed as completely different from the
rule of absolutism which preceded it. I have already mentioned
that Marx apparently had little prescience of the role nationalism
was to play from the late nineteenth century onwards. Exactly the
same is true of Durkheim, who lived to witness the phenomenon,
and who struggled ineffectively to come to terms with it within the
framework of his social thought at a late stage of his career.[4]

In some respects, of course, the respective views of Marx and
Durkheim on the (capitalist) industrial state make an interesting
contrast – and one that is preserved in the literature of the 1950s
and early 1960s. According to Marx, who derived most of what
little he wrote on the state from the critique of Hegel, the capitalist
state is a sham because its claims to universality (as embodied in
declarations of the freedom, equality and dignity of all citizens) are
shown upon examination to protect the sectional interests of the
dominant capitalist class (not that Marx thought that 'bourgeois

rights and freedoms' were wholly without substance, a matter that is quite important to later Marxist attempts to analyse the capitalist state). The state is a sham in the narrow sense that the franchise and other forms of political participation were, in Marx's time, dependent upon property rights, subject to various more or less open forms of corruption, and hence the immediate preroga- tive of the bourgeoisie. The capitalist state, for Marx, is a sham in a much more profound sense, however, in so far as the 'universal' political rights accorded the whole community of citizens only embrace one restricted segment of their existence. The right to elect a government at fixed periods leaves untouched – and thereby underlies – the power of capital over the worker in the production process. Again, the capitalist labour contract is central to this thesis, and it is of course directly involved with the theme of the separation of the 'political' from the 'economic' in capitalism. The capitalistic labour contract establishes a purely economic relation between employer and worker, which in effect means that the worker formally sacrifices all control over that segment of his or her life spent within the walls of the workshop, factory or office. The transcendence of the state, in a socialist society, is thus very much bound up in Marx's thinking with the recovery by the worker of control over the production process. Just how this is to be achieved, of course, remains one of the most difficult issues confronting Marxist theory from Marx's day to the present.

Durkheim expressly rejected the thesis that, in an industrial society, the state could or should be transcended, tracing this thesis to Rousseau rather than to Marx.[5] His view is perfectly compatible with his notion that the state is a moral agency that is responsible for furthering the interests of society as a whole. It is both 'normal' and desirable, in an industrial order, for the state to be distinct from civil society. The state is in fact the major vehicle of the realisation of liberal values ('bourgeois rights and freedoms', in Marx's terminology), and is generally able to set the pace for the rest of society since it is the 'organ of social intelligence'. Here Durkheim anticipated both the theme of the beneficent welfare state and 'cybernetic' views of politics worked out in the post- Second World War period. Rather than being a 'class state', the state is precisely the means of overcoming class divisions through the redistributive and egalitarian policies which it is able to initiate and carry through. The transcendence of the state, which Durkheim equated with the resubmergence of the state in civil society, is for him a potential menace rather than offering the hope of emancipation from political repression. Here Durkheim sketched the outlines of a theory of state tyranny which became one of the sources of later liberal theories of totalitarianism associated with proponents of the conception of industrial society. The state and the individual must be kept apart if both are to prosper. If the state were reabsorbed into society, the result would either be that the state would be too weak to carry out its role as the overseer of social progress, or that it would dominate all aspects of the life of the citizen. Durkheim's famous *corporations* or occupational groups were, in his political theory, to provide the counterbalance between these two alternatives.

Since large sectors of academic sociology are as indebted to Weber as to Durkheim, it may seem surprising that the two features of the state mentioned above – monopoly of the means of violence, and territoriality – have not been widely adopted by many of those claiming intellectual descent from Weber. So far as sociology in the English-speaking world is concerned, at any rate, this is, however, not in fact particularly puzzling. The reception of Weber's writings has been strongly influenced by the refraction of his ideas through the work of Talcott Parsons. As is well known by now, Parsons accentuated certain aspects of Weber's writings to the exclusion of others. Neither Weber's sombre view of modern capitalism, nor his emphases upon the centrality of military power and of violence more generally in history, survive prominently either in Parsons's representations of Weber's work or in Parsons's own theories. Most of the advocates of the theory of industrial society have recognised that Weber's analysis of bureaucracy poses awkward problems for liberal political theory, but if they have sometimes paid lip-service to Weber's conceptualisation of the state, they have not pursued its implications very far. The single important exception to this, if he be counted as an advocate of the theory of industrial society, is Raymond Aron, who is one of the few influential sociological theorists of modern times to have been preoccupied with warfare as a persistently evident feature of human social life.[6]

A tenuously shared connection to Saint-Simon is not the main factor making for definite similarities between Marx, Durkheim and the traditions of thought they helped to inspire. Much more important is that they shared a common set of intellectual opponents: utilitarian political philosophy and classical political economy. *Capital* is subtitled 'a critique of political economy', and the formulation of such a critique occupied much of Marx's attention even in his earlier works (such as the *1844 Manuscripts*). Durkheim did not draw directly upon Marx's critical dissection of political economy, the most essential element of which – that the class division between capital and wage-labour is inherent in 'modern society' – he was in compete disagreement. The *Division of Labour in Society* is none the less substantially centred upon a critique of utilitarianism and political economy in its classical guise. Whereas Marx attacked these schools of thought on the basis of a class analysis, disclosing surplus value as the 'hidden' mechanism of class exploitation in capitalism, Durkheim attempted to reveal the 'non-contractual presuppositions of contract' – without, of course focusing his discussion upon the labour contract and 'free' wage-labour. As so commonly happens, each of the critics assimilated a considerable measure of the views against which they directed their polemics. One cannot fail to see that this was consequential for their respective conceptualisations of the state. Both Marx and Durkheim, in their divergent ways, looked at the state through the spectacles of utilitarian liberalism. As I have earlier pointed out (pp. 177–81), the notion that industrialism is basically a pacific force, cutting through the militarism of former times, was deeply entrenched in nineteenth-century thought, and apparent in both Marx and Durkheim. But each picked up more from classical political economy than that. One cannot pretend that Marx's various references to the state are always internally consistent; to say this is not to express an adverse judgement on Marx, but rather to indicate the sheer range of intellectual insights that appear in different sections of his writings.[7] However, the principal line of Marx's reasoning on the state is not difficult to discern, and it does reflect important elements of the ideas he was arguing against.

For Marx, as for classical liberalism, the state is typically regarded, in the words of one recent author, as *'an arena* in which conflicts over basic social and economic interests are fought out'.[8] We can shelve for the moment recent arguments about whether the state is 'relatively autonomous' from such conflicts in Marx's view. There can be no doubt that he did discern circumstances, most especially in the now much-discussed case of Bonapartism, in which considerable power accrues to the state, and where that power cannot be 'reduced' to resources controlled by the dominant class. But both Marx and Engels (the latter, as usual, more bluntly and unequivocally in his *Origins of the Family, Private Property and the State*) made it plain enough that the state first arises in history when classes come into existence, and is the administrative agency that expresses the ascendancy of the ruling class over the rest of society. The transcendence of classes is hence the indispensable condition for the transcendence of the state in socialist society.

Durkheim, on the other hand, in concentrating his critique against utilitarian theories of contract in a general way, came to the view that the state has a guiding moral role to play in the industrial order. But while this view certainly gives more 'relative autonomy' (in relation to civil society as a whole rather than to classes) to the state than Marx allowed even in his more adventurous forays into political analysis, it is still quite closely linked to the ideas Durkheim set out to condemn. Marx's conception of the state as a substantially malevolent agency derives from similar sources to those whereby Durkheim conceived of the state as a benevolent agency of progress. In each case the state is seen primarily as *a co-ordinating framework within which economic relationships are carried on* – in the one case thus expressing mechanisms of class domination, in the other as injecting morality and justice into the occupational order.

These are the origins of the two views of the state which were prevalent in sociology until recently, the one connecting to Marxist analyses of 'capitalism', the other to the various versions of the theory of industrial society. These two traditions of thought have constantly collided with one another, but the terrain over which the battles were fought were concentrated much more upon issues of class conflict, industrial organisation, and the trajectories of development of the (capitalist) industrial societies, rather than upon problems of the state. If this is today no longer the case, if there is such a widespread revival of interest in the state, it is largely because of the socio-economic changes that have occurred in the West from the late 1960s to the present day. The contestations of the 1968–70 period, of which 'May 1968' is the symbol to both those who advocated revolutionary change in

Western capitalism, as well as to those who opposed it or derided the possibility, awoke sociology from at least some of its dogmatic slumbers. The turn from seemingly stable patterns of economic growth to much more parlous economic circumstances has also alerted everyone (it is hoped) to the dangers of overgeneralisation from a relatively limited period of Western economic prosperity. Since Marxists had claimed all along that capitalism is a far less stable social and economic order than the confident advocates of the theory of industrial society (with their pronouncement of the 'end of ideology') believed, it is not surprising that the result was a strong stimulus to, and revival of, Marxist theories.

## The State as 'Capitalist State'

Although there have been various important attempts to get to grips with issues of the state and political power from the side of academic sociology,[9] I shall concentrate my attention here upon recent Marxist accounts of the state. Even these, however, I shall not discuss in detail, but will elaborate a view both critical of certain of such accounts and drawing quite extensively upon others. Two of the main problems raised in recent Marxist literature on the state are these. First, what is the specific nature of the capitalist state: what makes it a *capitalist* state? While this question has usually been posed in terms of comparisons with socialism, 'actually existing' or hypothetical, I shall pose it here retrospectively. That is to say, I shall be interested in identifying what might be the main features distinguishing the state in capitalism from the state in class-divided societies. It is perhaps a sign of the embarrassment of Marxists with the legacy of the evolutionary scheme of history handed down to them by Marx and Engels that such an issue has barely appeared at all in contemporary Marxist discussions of the state. The second problem already has a depressingly dreary ring to it, having produced a number of remarkably leaden interchanges in the past decade: the problem of the 'relative autonomy' of the state. It is none the less a matter of considerable importance, that cannot be avoided simply because some of those who have written about it have advocated positions that are either frustratingly obscure or markedly implausible.

Since I think the question of the 'relative autonomy' of the state cannot be solved as an abstraction, but depends very directly upon how one answers the first question I outlined, let me begin with that. Most of the elements of an answer are already present in the ideas I have set out in the earlier parts of this book. The distinctiveness of the capitalist state is quite obviously bound up with the more encompassing matter of the distinctiveness of capitalism as a form of society. This, as I have stressed all along, has to be analysed as a combination of two issues: the specifically 'Western' character of capitalism; and the structural differences that distinguish capitalism generically from class-divided societies. The following considerations are those I consider of primary importance:

(1)  Capitalism emerged in immediate relation with a state system that seems to have had no close parallels elsewhere. The European state system both supplied some of the conditions for the emergence of capitalism as a distinct type of productive system, as a 'mode of production', and the interconnections between capitalism and the state system provided the means of securing a growing European domination over the rest of the world from the sixteenth century onwards. The maturity of industrial capitalism in the nineteenth century not only coincided with, but was again inherently involved with, the development of the European state system into a system of nation-states. Although difficult to avoid (and I shall continue to use the phrase), it is dangerously misleading to speak of 'the' capitalist state, rather than the more accurate designation 'capitalist states'.

(2)  In capitalism the power of the dominant class derives fundamentally from its control of allocative resources. This circumstance is the result of the transformations Marx describes, of labour into wage-labour, and property into capital, each being transformable into the other via their 'double existence' as commodities. The emergence of such phenomena marks a radical break with class-divided societies, in which the relation between allocative and authoritative resources was the other way round. In class-divided societies access to authoritative resources is the chief medium of achieving control over landed property (and often, but not so unequivocally, over commercial activity also). In class-divided societies, state and class power usually coincide quite closely, but the latter is largely derived from the former. While

Marx's analysis of the mechanics of capitalist production, as founded in the capital/wage-labour relation, where each exists in commodified form, is fundamental to the analysis of capitalism as a clan society, his treatment of what I have called class-divided societies underestimates the significance of the emergence of state power, which is *the* decisive break with tribal societies of all types. This is *one* aspect of 'class reductionism' in Marx, deriving from the polemical context of political economy I have already referred to, but it has to be clearly distinguished from the 'relative-autonomy' problem in capitalism precisely because capitalist societies are structured so differently from class-divided societies.

The fact that the power of the dominant class in capitalism is founded upon control of allocative resources has very important consequences for the nature of the capitalist state. Marx recognised these, but never developed a detailed analysis of them, and was hampered in doing so partly by insufficiently emphasising – at least in some of his writings – just how different capitalism is from class-divided societies. In capitalism, in Kautsky's famous phrase, 'the ruling class does not rule'.[10] What does this imply? To my mind, the following things. First, in a capitalist society, virtually everyone is dependent upon the activity of capitalist employers for their survival.[11] This only became the case when the mass of the population were wholly expropriated from control of the means of production. This signals, one should stress again, a fundamental break in history. Capital and wage-labour are economically mutually dependent (as well as being in conflict over interests) within a system of production that creates an unprecedented capability for the development of material wealth. Second, at the same time as all this applies, the capitalist class does not generally compose – as other ruling classes in history have done – the personnel of the state. The capitalist class's business *is* business. This is *one* factor opening up dislocations or divergences between state policies and the demands or interests of the capitalist class, or its subdivisions. None the less, the state, as everyone else, is dependent upon the activities of capitalist employers for its revenue, and hence the state operates in a context of various capitalistic 'imperatives'. This should not be rendered, although it often is, as a functionalist argument; the state officialdom, in an era in which economic theory has reached a high plane of development, in a climate of historicity, helps formulate what these 'imperatives' are, just as businessmen or women do. If Lindblom's comment which follows is divested of its explicit functionalism, I am in general agreement with it:

> Because public functions in the market system rest in the hands of businessmen, it follows that jobs, prices, production, growth, the standard of living and the economic security of everyone all rest in their hands. Consequently government officials cannot be indifferent to how well business performs its functions . . . A major function of government, therefore, is to see to it that businessmen perform their tasks.[12]

Lindblom's discussion is not based on a Marxist standpoint, and does not emphasise what I take to be a crucial element in the capitalist class–state relationship that is best illuminated by contrast to class-divided societies. I have constantly stressed, following Marx, the intrinsic significance of the capitalistic labour contract in distinguishing capitalist production from the production systems of other societies. Its relevance to the theory of the state is as follows. In class-divided societies, in which the state controllers were also the ruling class, the exploitation of surplus labour was usually backed by the direct threat of violence. This established a fundamental relation between the state and exploitation. In capitalism, however, the means of securing the compliance of labour – as labour-power – are economic, and depend upon the intersection of 'management' with the securing of 'labour discipline'. The state is not able to sanction directly the exploitation process, the extraction of surplus value, through its control of the means of violence. *The state's revenue is dependent upon the accumulation process, upon the valorisation process, but it does not control these directly.* This proposition holds true, though with somewhat different implications, even in industries that are nationalised or administered by the state.

(3) The capitalist state rests upon the institutional separation of polity and economy in the sense noted in Chapter 5. The recognition of a 'public sphere' in which a range of freedoms and rights are in principle universalised, as I have also remarked earlier in the book, rests historically upon a political inheritance that again seems unique to the West. One should not mistake the import of this. All emperors and princes in class-divided societies

have laid claim to the universality of their prerogatives of rule – nearly always by reference to a mixture of traditional and religious modes of legitimation. In the capitalist state, however, the overthrow of absolutism was simultaneous with the dissolution of sovereignty as embodied in a particular person, the stage having been set for this by the continuities in constitutional rights and assemblies that were not destroyed by the absolutist monarchs. There are no doubt long-term influences in Western culture of some importance here, as Weber has emphasised – including especially the residue of Classical republicanism as a model for political reform, and the inheritance of a corpus of Roman law. (I shall take up the question of the importance of 'bourgeois rights' of citizenship further below.)

I think there are elements of decisive importance in Marx's critique of the 'sham' character of citizenship. But I shall argue strongly against the implications that are often drawn from this – and for which some justification can be found in Marx's own dismissive comments upon bourgeois political pretensions – that 'bourgeois rights' are monopolised solely by the bourgeoisie. In my view, the emergence of the 'public sphere' in the American and French Revolutions, predicated in principle upon universal rights and liberties of the whole societal community, is as fundamental a disjunction in history as the commodification of labour and property to which Marx showed it to be intimately related. However asymmetrical they may have been in regard of the emergent capitalist class system, citizenship rights opened up new vistas of freedom and equality that Marxism itself seeks to radicalise. In view of the encyclopedic scope of his studies of world history, it is worth quoting Toynbee's judgement on this:

> For the first time since the dawn of civilisation, about five thousand years ago [Toynbee avers], the masses have now become alive to the possibility that their traditional way of life might be changed for the better and that this change might be brought about by their own action. This awakening of hope and purpose in the hearts and minds of the hitherto depressed three-quarters of the world's population will, I feel certain, stand in retrospect as the epoch-making element of our age.[13]

This, however, at the same time returns us to the existence of capitalist *states*, in a world system composed almost entirely of nation-states, and where similar principles of freedom, equality and the ubiquitous 'democracy' are invoked by governments of all complexions.

(4) The state in capitalism is a state in a *class society*, in which there is high degree of interdependence in the division of labour, inside the national economy and internationally. In contrast to class-divided societies, capitalist societies introduce a white heat of economic change and technological innovation that both resist and stimulate state 'management' of the economy as a whole. The accumulation process in capitalist societies, even in 'oligopoly' or 'monopoly capitalism', rests upon the mobilisation of privately owned capital, and (for reasons already mentioned) is not under the direct control of the state. At the same time, the state assumes responsibility for the provision of a range of community services derived from state revenues which depend upon the 'economic success' of the economic activities of employers and workers. Offe is certainly right in pointing to this as a major contradictory element of capitalism.[14] State 'intervention' has become the conventional term for referring to the managerial activities of the state, but it is obvious enough that the term is a misnomer, which again derives from a background of the premises of classical political economy. Although the experience of different capitalist societies has varied widely in this respect, in all such societies the state has from the beginnings of capitalism played a major part in economic activity. Since the late eighteenth century in particular, with the opening of the era of industrial capitalism, and the transformations of the time-space organisation of daily life that followed, the state's activities, within the economy and outside it, have continued to expand. The managerial tasks of the state include a spectrum of surveillance activities that are not purely economic. The modes of surveillance of the organisation of 'civil society', as I shall indicate later, are highly relevant to the 'relative autonomy' problem.

## The Autonomy of the State

To this I shall now turn, bearing in mind the points made above. The 'relative autonomy' issue has been approached from various angles in contemporary schools of Marxist state theories.[15] But Poulantzas and those involved in the so-called 'state-derivation' debate in Germany have been among the more prominent protagonists, together with Miliband.[16] Of these authors, those that have led the *Staatsableitung* debate are the most 'fundamentalist', in the sense that (partly in direct critical reaction to Offe)[17] their aim is to 'derive' the state from the 'form' of the capitalist mode of production. The approach sounds scholastic and unpromising on the face of it, though it has produced contributions of some interest, such as that of Hirsch (mentioned earlier). Like so much contemporary Marxist writing on the state, however, it contains a thinly veiled functionalism. The state is 'derived' from an analysis of the 'requirements' that capitalism has for its continued reproduction. Among these writers, as well as Poulantzas and those influenced by him, the word 'reproduction' is waved as a magic wand, as though it has an explanatory content. This is one strong line of connection with functionalism in non-Marxist sociology (which, after all, was always interested in 'system maintenance', a term that, as Poulantzas *et al.* use the concept, is more or less synonymous with 'reproduction'). It is important at this point to re-emphasise one of the main premises of the theory of structuration as I outlined it in Chapter 1. The concept 'reproduction' explains nothing at all in and of itself, but always refers to circumstances that have *to be* explained. To ask about the 'requirements' or 'exigencies' of a system is a perfectly proper and useful thing to do as long as it is understood that this is a counterfactual enquiry.[18] It is to ask: 'what would happen if . . .?' certain processes did not occur or events happen. The slide into functionalism occurs when an author supposes that to show *that* those processes or events are necessary for the reproduction of a social system explains *why* they occur.

The functionalist element, and even crudely functionalist language, are evident in Poulantzas's original formulation of the 'relative autonomy' of the state in *Political Power and Social Classes*.[19] In Poulantzas's conception the state's 'relative autonomy' from the interests of particular 'fractions of capital' is functionally necessary to protect the general interests of capital, which thus ensures the long-term perpetuation (reproduction) of capitalist society as a whole. It is only slightly uncharitable to Poulantzas to suggest that for him this *explains* the existence of the capitalist state.

Poulantzas has been so widely criticised in recent years,[20] often with good reason, that it is worth while remembering the positive elements of his attempt to break with 'state monopoly capitalism' ('Stamocap') orthodoxy.[21] If his adoption of Althusserian structuralism brought about major limitations that attach to any theory which has no way of coping with the reflexive character of human action, at the same time Althusser's critique of economism was applied in a fruitful way by Poulantzas to the analysis of classes and the state. Poulantzas was able to tackle the pluralists on their own terrain, arguing that a class is not a group or monolithic entity, but expresses structural relations constituting a social formation as a whole. Thereby he was able to acknowledge that certain elements of the pluralists' arguments are correct – for example, that there are diverse, and often conflicting, 'class fractions' in all capitalist societies – without compromising the significance of class analysis. The 'relative autonomy' of the state fitted neatly with this approach, albeit developed in a strongly functionalist vein, because the state is regarded by Poulantzas as cohering the system in the face of the various rivalries that might otherwise cause some sectors of capital to pursue their own interests to the detriment of the over-all framework of capitalism. Poulantzas's account of the state enabled him to allot a considerably greater role to the state as an independent source of power from class power than was allowed for in the 'Stamocap' view. By taking a somewhat improbable interpretation of Marx's discussion of Bonapartism in nineteenth-century France as typical of the role of the state in capitalism, rather than as an exceptional case, he tried to justify his view textually in Marx. In arguing that 'The state is not an instrumental entity existing for itself, it is not a thing, but the condensation of class forces',[22] Poulantzas also sought to continue to anchor his conception within the classical Marxian standpoint – hence the autonomy of the state can never be more than 'relative'. The state remains an 'arena' within which class struggles are fought out, but one in which there are influences at work that have a particular character of their own.

What are we to make of the idea of 'relative autonomy'? There are obviously two strands to be considered: In what sense is the state only 'relatively' autonomous? And what is it considered to be 'autonomous' from? Poulantzas's various formulations of the concept often seem vague and ambiguous in each of these respects, but if they cannot be pinned down then his attempt to rework the Marxist theory of the state cannot be accounted a success. A first comment upon the concept of 'relative autonomy' might be that the term 'relative' is redundant, since any social processes or institutions that were 'absolutely' autonomous from others by definition would have no connection with them anyway. All 'autonomy' is 'relative'. This is certainly my view, at any rate, and follows directly from the notion of power relations that I have made basic to the theory of structuration. Autonomy and dependence are the reciprocal defining criteria of power relations reproduced within social systems. It is enough, then, to enquire what autonomy the capitalist state might have (leaving aside for the moment the question of 'from what?') – which simply means the same as to enquire into the *sources of state power* and the *scope of the sanctions* which the state is capable of wielding. Behind this, of course, lurks the question of how the 'state' should be defined: whether it is accurate or adequate to persevere with the view that the state, in capitalism, is no more than an arena of the operation of class forces.

## Critical Observations

There are several respects in which Poulantzas's ideas on the autonomy of the state can be criticised, apart from the more general limitations of his views originating in his utilisation of segments of Althusserian theory.

We may first ask: how is the state *able to achieve* what Poulantzas would call its 'relative autonomy' from the particular interests of 'fractions' of the capitalist class? Poulantzas's formulation seems either to simply assert dogmatically that the state somehow manages to protect the over-all framework of the capitalist system, or leans on the functionalist argument I mentioned earlier. Given that neither of these tactics is defensible, can one formulate a plausible version of what Poulantzas is getting at? I believe that one can. It might be noted in passing that Poulantzas's idea of the far-seeing character of the state has a certain similarity to Durkheim's concept of the state as the 'organising intelligence' of society, save that of course for Poulantzas the state uses this ability to defend the institutions of a class society. Durkheim was not very explicit either upon how this special social 'intelligence' is achieved, using the organic analogy that the state is the 'brain' of the social organism. But there should be no particular mystery about it. All states, capitalist and non-capitalist, maintain surveillance activities in each of the senses I have distinguished. Capitalism introduces far-reaching changes in the time-space organisation of society, in the sense that the division of labour involves relationships that draw individuals and collectivities into connections across the space of national territories and across the whole globe. The surveillance activities of the state expand enormously once industrial capitalism becomes established, transforming urban space such that the localised forms of social and economic organisation which predominated in class-divided societies are largely dissolved. The collation of population statistics, statistics of births, marriages, deaths, etc., by centralised agencies of the state, as I have mentioned previously, developed from the late eighteenth century onwards in all the countries of Western Europe. Given that capitalism is a system in which the state depends upon a highly dynamic, but 'insulated', economic sector that it does not directly control, it is not surprising that the economic 'management' of the national economy has been a preoccupation of the state officialdom for the same period. How successful such management can be in a capitalist society is a problem that I shall put aside temporarily. But state officials normally have much greater opportunity to 'oversee' the system as a whole, in its national and international contexts, than do capitalist employers or industrial managers, even those in the giant international corporations. Neither is there anything particularly enigmatic about why state officials should be more concerned with the long-term protection and consolidation of capitalism than specific sectors of business may be. As I have tried to show earlier, the state depends, as the state officialdom is as aware of as anybody, upon the general continuity of capitalist production.

This does not so far deal with the question of how much *power* state officials have to implement particular sorts of policies that might be resisted by specific business interests. Such an issue forms one of the main bones of contention in the Poulantzas/Miliband debate. One of the reasons why the debate appears a little empty, or the protagonists tend to talk past one another, is that both have right on their side (and that their claims are not mutually exclusive). This controversy, in my opinion, reflects a division in respect of the concept and analysis of power that has to be reformulated in terms of the duality of structure. Poulantzas quite correctly regards power as embedded in the structural characteristics of capitalist society as a whole, and is dismissive of studies of elites and the capacity their members have to enact particular decisions. Miliband defends the importance of empirically examining the relations between what he (and I) prefer to call different elite groups (rather than 'class fractions')[23] to the analysis of the state. In this he is surely also right. It certainly does not seem possible to generalise about 'the' capitalist state, or even about certain types of capitalist states, without studying empirically what types of connection exist between those in positions of power in large corporations, parliament, the civil service, etc., and also without showing what kinds of policies they are capable of enacting. But, as in the theory of power more generally, the capability of actors to achieve particular ends must be connected to the resources that constitute modes of domination. In the case of the state officialdom, such resources have to be understood in the structural context of the state as 'capitalist state' that I have analysed earlier, at least so far as its 'internal' composition is concerned.

In a recent discussion Crouch mentions that, in liberal-democratic societies, the capitalist class frequently mistrusts the state.[24] I think this is very often true. Why should it be so, however, if the state 'functions to protect the over-all interests of capital'? It does not seem sufficient to say that this is because some groups of capitalists fear that state policies will unduly favour the interests of others, or because state officials try unsuccessfully to harmonise the various interests of business elites with one another. A much more compelling reason is the *power that the organised working class, in situations of industrial bargaining, and in the formation of labour or socialist parties, is able to mobilise vis-à-vis the state.* This means recognising the contradictory character of the capitalist state, which I have already mentioned with regard to the writings of Claus Offe. I do not agree with the whole substance of Offe's views on the capitalist state, and would particularly place in question the manner in which he (and Habermas) emphasise 'legitimation problems' in contemporary capitalism.[25] But I think Offe is right to accentuate that the state is directly enmeshed in the contradictions of capitalism. By undervaluing the power of the working class, functionalist Marxists curiously may tend to overestimate the 'relative autonomy' of the state in capitalist liberal democracy. But the important point in this is that the state, if it participates in the contradictions of capitalism, is not merely a defender of the status quo. The state can in some part be seen as an emancipatory force: neither a class-neutral agency of social reform (the theory of industrial society, social-democratic political theory), nor a mere functional vehicle of the 'needs' of the capitalist mode of production (functionalist Marxism).

There is one final set of factors relevant to the autonomy of the state: those that concern the capitalist state as a nation-state, as controlling the means of violence and as participating in a world military order and world capitalist economy. Although the interrelations between capitalist states on an economic level has been discussed by Poulantzas in respect of the rise and decline of fascism,[26] contemporary Marxist theories of the state have yet to come to terms with the significance of the capitalist state as nation-state (as Poulantzas has admitted: see note 36 to Chapter 7); the weakness of Marxism in coping with the ascendancy of nationalism I have also previously referred to. I have tried to show that these phenomena are not so distant from Marx's analysis of capitalism as a class society as some critics might imply. However, this also means at the same time making a substantial departure from any such view that the capitalist state can be exhaustively studied as 'a materialised concentration of class relations in a given society'.[27] We must also reject, I think, the definition of the state as a 'relation', to use Poulantzas's term – an obscure enough notion in his writings in any case. The state is best seen as a set of collectivities concerned with the institutionalised organisation of political power.

## Class Conflict and Liberal Democracy

A major claim that I make in this book is that – notwithstanding the comments I have just offered, leading to the rejection of the view that the state is only an 'arena' of class conflict, or a 'concentration of class relations' – capitalism is a *class society* distinct from 'class-divided societies'. Class relations enter into the

very constitution of the labour process in capitalism, the commodification of labour-power and property being the condition of the
processes of valorisation and accumulation that lie behind the
dynamism capitalism injects into the forces of production. Class
struggle is a chronic and everyday feature of capitalist industry,
and class conflict has been a major medium of the internal
transformation of capitalist societies – or, at least, so I wish to
argue. In this section I shall look at the implications of these
claims. I shall want to connect both to the concept of the *dialectic
of control* that I introduced previously as an inherent phenomenon
of the logical involvement of human agency with power relations.

I have often stressed the significance of the capitalist labour
contract as basic to understanding the source of some of the major
contrasts between capitalism and class-divided societies. In all
class-divided societies labour relations are entangled in a nexus of
ties characteristic of communities of high presence-availability,
even in the cities. For most of the population, who work in
agriculture, there is, moreover, an immediate involvement with
nature that is radically cut through by the creation of the
capitalistic work-place, and indeed more generally by the surrounding environment of 'created space'.

The worker who walked into the capitalistic work-place, in the
early period of the formation of capitalism, entered into an
economic contract which allowed him or her no acknowledged
control over either the process of production or the disposal of the
products of labour. As Marx pointed out so emphatically, the
'freedom' of wage-labour was an ideological sanction for the
authority of the capitalist and 'management' within the work-
place. However, it is also very important to see that even the
'freedom' of the labour contract has that double-edged character
which other bourgeois values have – for the employer can neither
draw upon the means of violence to coerce the labour force to
work in the manner he designates, nor can he invoke moral
obligations (although of course there has been no shortage of
thinkers, e.g. Durkheim, who have wished to see the labour
contract remoralised). In such circumstances the 'freedom' of
wage-labour turns out to involve more than mere formal freedom,
for it provides the means of mobilising sanctions against the
employer that were virtually unknown in class-divided societies.
The two principal factors involved here are the dependence of the

employer upon labour-power, and the concentration of workers in the capitalistic work-place. In class-divided societies the main locus of the dialectic of control is in the time-space separation of the localised agrarian community from the continuous presence of the exploiting class. But in the capitalist work-place the worker is subject to the direct surveillance of the employer or the managerial staff. The locus of the dialectic of control is thus quite different, and brings the work-force into a chronic relation of conflict/dependency with the employer, organised through the labour contract.

The main sanctions the employer possesses in order to control the labour-force are that the propertyless worker must have some sort of paid employment to survive, and the imposition of labour discipline within the work-place. *These form two major sites of chronic class struggle within capitalist societies.* The sheerly economic nature of the labour contract, combined with the employer's dependence upon the *regularised* organisation of labour-power within the production process, means that the threat of collective withdrawal of labour – epitomised by the strike or the threat to strike, but including also 'go-slows', 'working to rule' and similar modes of sanctioning the employer – becomes a major source in the hands of the workers. Acceptance of the right to the collective withdrawal of labour on the part of employers and the state was something which had to be fought for in virtually all of the now 'liberal-democratic' societies, often through bloody encounters. The sanction of collective withdrawal of labour, or its threat, on the part of the organised labour force may be regarded as beginning in the attempts of workers to achieve 'defensive control' of the conditions under which labour contracts are negotiated, in circumstances where such control was originally virtually nil. Out of such circumstances, one could say, the labour movement was born. Freedom to organise politically, also a bourgeois value whose implementation by the working class was fiercely resisted by its very originators in most capitalist countries, eventually culminated everywhere (with the notorious and debatable exception of the United States) in the formation of labour parties that have come to play a major part in the polity. I speak of attempts at 'defensive control'[28] because the sanctions available to workers are primarily negative, consisting of resources that can be drawn upon only to block or frustrate the aims of their employers.

In respect of the labour contract, both the formal rights of collective bargaining that have been won, and the actual conduct of negotiations in practice, have tended, like the contract itself, to concentrate upon economic issues: levels of wages first and foremost, conditions of contractual formulation, and conditions under which the labour process is carried on. I shall call this concentration of class conflict 'economism',[29] and I shall make the argument that the confinement of class conflict over the labour contract to economism is of central significance to the 'insulation' of economy and polity in capitalism, and hence to the conditions of societal reproduction.

There is a second site of chronic class struggle, overlapping in various ways, in different circumstances, with the first, but concentrated *in the labour process itself* rather than upon the contractual relations between workers and employers. From the beginnings of capitalism, paratechnical relations (the division of labour within the capitalistic work-place) have involved the direct co-ordination of labour-power with the technical organisation of production. Braverman's *Labour and Monopoly Capital*, as I have mentioned before, made a major contribution in showing how the systematic 'building in' of labour-power within industrial technology is of focal importance to the division of labour as an intrinsic medium of management control over the worker.[30] He places especial emphasis upon the introduction of Taylorism, or 'scientific management', as the culmination of this process, and as the continuing core of industrialism not only in capitalism but in the state-socialist societies also. But there are none the less very distinct limitations to Braverman's analysis, limitations that seem rather extraordinary in the light of the book's origin in a Marxist standpoint. The book charts a one-way process of the extension of control – control by management over the worker – not processes of the dialectic of control. In other words, Braverman barely touches at all upon workers' struggles, which were in the United States, and elsewhere, in substantial part successful, to resist Taylorism. Here again, as in the more abstract literature of functionalist Marxism, workers appear as mere dupes of the system. But, as several recent studies in economic history have made clear, workers understood the implications of 'scientific management' rather well, and effectively limited its application and success.[31] Worker resistance to Taylorism was undoubtedly one of the factors promoting the subsequent rise of the 'human relations' approach to management, which rediscovered that labour-power is a commodity which stubbornly refuses to be treated just like any other commodity.

Class struggle on the level of day-to-day practices in the capitalistic work-place, as Friedman points out, has been consistently ignored in a great deal of Marxist writing.[32] A whole range of phenomena can either be comprised under this category of struggle, or are in some respects expressions of worker disaffection with the circumstances of their labour. The most important of such phenomena concern modes in which workers seek to influence the nature, rate or type of labour process that they are involved in.

Struggle against being regarded as 'merely' labour-power, as a conforming 'part' in a broader technological system – and such struggle, to repeat, is endemic to the capitalistic organisation of the labour process – intimately relates the empirical behaviour of workers to the philosophical theme of human agency. And this connection, whatever Althusser may say to the contrary, exemplifies the continuing significance of Marx's early writings on alienation for a critical theory of modern capitalism – for to be a human agent is to have the capability (through either intervening in a course of events or refraining from doing so) of 'making a difference' in the world, which is the same as saying that the agent 'could have acted otherwise'.[33] To the degree to which an individual becomes reduced to being an 'automatic part' of a pre-given process, that person ceases to be an agent. If one were to use the Feuerbachian language of Marx's early works, the worker is alienated from his or her 'species being': from the human qualities of the reflexive self-monitoring of activity in which agency is anchored.[34] Fortunately, unless drugged or beaten – and usually not even then – human beings fight back, for part of being a human agent is to know that one is such, that one has the capability of exercising agency. Therefore, the dialectic of control operates in *all* circumstances where human individuals, however oppressed they might be, remain agents. In point of fact, for reasons I have pointed to earlier, the sanctions capitalist employers – in liberal-democratic regimes – are able to bring to bear upon the labour-force have definite limits. The scope of the influence that workers on the shop-floor or in the office are able to bring over what goes on in their day-to-day working lives is thus usually more than negligible, however little formal control they are supposed to have by the terms of the labour contract. Since commodified time underlies the valorisation process in capitalism, many struggles at the site of production are over time-allocation. As has been shown in a proliferation of studies, written both from managerial and from critical perspectives, workers are almost always able to operate 'informal norms' governing the speed at which production is carried on. In a more openly oppositional vein, 'go-slows' form the classic response to managerial demands for time more fully utilised in valorisation – for example, in reply to 'time-and-motion' plans that management may attempt to introduce to reorganise a pre-existing type of production process.

To these phenomena associated with modes in which workers exert direct control over the labour process, or over aspects of the organisation of the work-place itself, we have to add other types of behaviour relevant to day-to-day class struggle. These include actively destructive reactions to labour, the 'throwing of the spanner into the machine', which studies of particularly oppressive forms of work show to be remarkably common. Absenteeism is another factor worth adding. Not all absenteeism, of course, has any sort of oppositional character – but there is no doubt that a great deal does have such a character. Finally, one should mention high labour turnover, the refusal of workers to stick with particular kinds of work. All of these have more important consequences for the employer than might appear initially, for it is one of the features of capitalistic production to demand regularised conditions of the utilisation of labour-power, as I have previously stressed.

Day-to-day class struggle in the work-place does not ordinarily have much to do with the promise of the revolutionary overthrow of capitalism, which may be why it has been ignored by many Marxist theoreticians. The carving out of modes of influencing the immediate work environment is no doubt of quite crucial value to those involved; but power of this sort is mainly limited to the immediate milieux of presence. In capitalist societies, which are embroiled in forms of time-space distanciation of global dimensions, the span of most such power is very limited indeed; although considered as a whole the degree of recalcitrance or otherwise of the work-force to comply with disciplines of the work-place can of course substantially influence the over-all economic productivity of a society. This is not to say that class struggle on the level of day-to-day practices has no possible relevance at all to the generation of social change or even to revolutionary transformation. Under some circumstances, which I shall not attempt to spell out here, there certainly may be close ties between 'everyday resistance' in the work-place and major processes of social transformation.[35] There may also, of course, be various types of friction between the organisation of labour on the shop-floor, or in the office, and the activities of labour unions or parties.

## Class Struggle and Citizenship Rights

What part has the labour movement played in the internal transformation of the contemporary liberal-democratic societies over the past century or so? Has class conflict significantly altered the pre-existing nature of the capitalist state? These questions are obviously of quite essential importance, both for social analysis and in terms of the potential political implications they have for anyone interested in the practical achievement of future changes in capitalism.

One influential non-Marxist view of the transformative signifi-cance of class conflict in Western capitalism is that advanced by T. H. Marshall, and adopted in varying forms by other writers.[36] This standpoint has fairly close connections with the theory of industrial society, since it is an account of how the labour movement has become absorbed within the framework of Western capitalist societies, though by means of producing major changes in those societies. Hence it is also a theory of why class conflict is no longer a major threat to the stability of capitalism, even if such were the case in the nineteenth century. The theory looks to just those 'bourgeois rights and freedoms' which, as I have mentioned previously, many Marxists are prone to see as empty or purely formal. According to Marshall, the modern polity has been moulded by the successive development of three types of 'citizenship rights'. These are, in an overlapping sequence, legal, political and 'social' (or welfare) rights. The first of these three refers to rights of equality before the law, and the sorts of contractual freedoms that Marx diagnosed as ideological bolsters to the power of capital over wage-labour. Marshall sees these in a much more unequivocally positive sense as the necessary underpinning for a free citizenry in an industrial state. Political rights include above all the right to organise political parties and the extension of the franchise to the mass of the population. These in turn are further complemented, with the arrival of the 'welfare state', by rights to social welfare for the needy: the provision of 'social services', unemployment benefit and sickness pay. For Marshall, who based his analysis in some part upon ideas formulated by Hobhouse, the progressive expansion of the three types of citizenship rights takes the sting out of class conflict. Bendix's thesis is somewhat different, and in a way a much more radical attack upon Marx. According to Bendix, the class conflicts which Marx located in the capitalist mode of production, and therefore in the sphere of industry, are in fact the outcome of the exclusion of the working class from political citizenship rights in the nineteenth century. Once the universal franchise was secured, and the way lay open for the organised political participation of the working class in the state, the root source of class conflict was removed. This is offered as an explanation of a postulated general decline in the radicalism of labour movements since the turn of the century.

There are major criticisms that can be offered against these views. So far as the history of the labour movement is concerned, for example, Bendix's thesis seems to fit only certain cases (e.g. the German labour movement).[37] In other instances, such as the British labour movement, which began, and continues its career today, as strongly reformist in character, or the French or Italian, in which there is a continuity of radicalism, the pattern of development does not conform to that which Bendix specifies.[38]

More important for my concerns here, however, is T. H. Marshall's formulation. While I do not accept some of the main elements of his argument, I shall want to say that the significance of what he calls 'citizenship rights' has been very considerable in the fashioning of the contemporary liberal-democratic state. There are various related critical observations I want to offer about Marshall's account. First, the three types of citizenship right do not unfold in the kind of 'natural' sequence that he proposes. The legal rights of which Marshall speaks were above all fought for by the bourgeoisie against the residues of feudalism and in opposition to absolutism. These 'bourgeois freedoms', as I have said before, have introduced a fundamentally different plane of political possibilities into Western capitalism, as compared with all types of class-divided society. But these freedoms were none the less also strongly ideological, in the mode proposed by Marx. Just as 'legal rights' have their origin in class struggle – of bourgeoisie against aristocracy and gentry – so, too, do the second two types of right. But these were developed in the context of class conflict between capitalist ruling class and *the organised working class*. They were in some large part achieved by active struggle on the part of labour movements: first to make the bourgeois 'universal citizen' a reality by securing the universal franchise, and second by using the results of that achievement to construct systems of welfare. Both were in most Western countries substantially influenced by the imminent threat or actuality of military conflict: that is to say, by the two world wars.

That the new mass citizenry were also at the same time cannon fodder should alert us to the double-edged character of all the freedoms and rights which Marshall describes. All have been, and continue to be, caught up in the contradictory nature of the capitalist state. But I think there can be no doubt that (together with a variety of other changes, including the dominance of oligopoly or monopoly capital in the national and international economy) the struggles of the labour movement have played a leading part in an internal metamorphosis of the capitalist state. This is well characterised, in my opinion, by Macpherson's differentiation between the 'liberal' and the 'liberal-democratic' state.[39] The liberal state was the creation of the bourgeoisie, and was immediately involved with the massive economic changes on the level of the relations of production expressed in the rise of capitalistic enterprise: 'Everyone was swept into the free market, and all his relations with others were increasingly converted to market relations.' The advent of the capitalist market economy was complemented by the formation of the liberal state. The essence of the liberal state

> was a system of alternate or multiple parties whereby govern-
> ments could be held responsible to different sections of the class
> or classes that held a political voice . . . the job of the liberal
> state was to maintain and promote the liberal society, which was
> not essentially a democratic or an equal society.[40]

The translation of the liberal to the liberal-democratic state (and 'welfare state') was mainly secured through politically organised working-class pressure.

Marshall's conception of citizenship rights has been employed by Dahrendorf among other proponents of 'the theory of industrial society' to suggest that, in the capitalist – or, as he calls them, 'post-capitalist' – societies, class conflict has been broken down into two sealed-off institutional sectors. The achievement of political citizenship rights allows democratic class competition within the political order, while the emergence of forms of collective bargaining within the economic order creates a distinct sphere of 'industrial conflict'.[41] According to Dahrendorf, this cleavage between political and industrial conflict is a permanent feature of industrialism, and signals the transcendence of capitalist society itself – hence, of course, his introduction of the term 'post-capitalist' society.[42] But what else is this cleavage between political and industrial conflict but the separation of the 'political' and the 'economic' that, in my argument at any rate, is constitutive of capitalist state in general? Far from marking the disappearance of capitalist society, this has from the beginning been a distinguishing feature of that society – and has been implicated in the various transformations discussed above. And rather than being permanent and stable, the insulation of polity and economy is fragile, incorporating as it does a strong ideological element – for notwithstanding the real political progress that is inherent in the transition from the liberal to the liberal-democratic state, one principal element of Marx's critique of the capitalist state still applies. The capitalist labour contract, the sale of labour-power, and alienated labour, remain the 'other face' of the liberal-democratic state. Democratic organisation does not extend to the work-place, in which the power of those in subordinate positions remains largely negative, on the two sides of class struggle I have previously identified.

The fragile, shifting and ideological nature of the insulation of polity and economy in capitalist societies in my view provides the theoretical rationale for theorising other forms of capitalist state besides the liberal-democratic societies of the 'core', as well as for analysing the radical potential of worker protest and the labour movement today.[43] But once again it is important to insist that such analyses must be related to conjunctures in the world system of nation-states, and to the international capitalist economy, both of which I have discussed in foregoing chapters.

# 10

# Between Capitalism and Socialism: Contradiction and Exploitation

## The Concept of Contradiction

Pointing to the concept of contradiction, claiming that capitalism is 'inherently contradictory' – these are favourite tactics of Marxist authors when they try to emphasise what distinguishes Marxism from other varieties of social thought. In point of fact, the notion of 'contradiction' is often rather casually used in the Marxist literature, including Marx's own writings.[1] Perhaps not surprisingly, in virtue of the influence of manifest or surreptitious functionalism in recent Marxist thought, it is often not apparent in what way, if any, common uses of the term 'contradiction' on the part of Marxist writers differ from those current in functionalist throught – for in orthodox functionalism the idea of 'functional incompatibility' is often mentioned. To take one example, in Godelier's formulation of 'contradiction' in a well-known discussion, the term is applied in an explicitly Marxist context, but seems to mean exactly the same as 'functional incompatibility' does in the 'mainstream' literature of functionalism.[2] But at least Godelier does devote some attention to trying to make explicit what 'contradiction' is in Marxist thought. The same cannot be said of the literature of Marxism as a whole, in which 'contradiction' is frequently used as synonymous with 'conflict', but preferred to the second term perhaps because it has a more radical-sounding ring to it.

I shall claim here that the concept of contradiction, as applied to social analysis, can and should be defined in a non-functionalist way; that 'contradiction' can and should be clearly distinguished from 'conflict'; but that the substance of how Marx utilises 'contradiction' in his writings, as strongly implicated in his evolutionary scheme, has to be subjected to critique.

Marx picked up the concept of contradiction, of course, from Hegel, who had conjoined an interpretation of history to an epistemology that involved rejecting the traditional interpretation of negation in logic. History was to be understood in terms of the dialectical unity of opposites, overcoming self-alienation in the epistemological sense which Hegel gave to that term. Marx rejected this epistemology very early on his career.[3] As with so many other projects that he set himself in his youth, Marx never got round to completing an envisaged full-scale analysis of the role of dialectics in social theory. Since he disavowed Hegel's epistemology, the notion of contradiction in Marx cannot be anchored in the idealist connection between logic and history that was the basis of Hegel's position. This, however, leaves the logical status of the concept itself, where invoked for purposes of social analysis, rather ambiguous. It seems certain that Marx intended to preserve some version of the idea of a unity of opposites, whereby opposites are conjoined as driving-forces of historical change; and that such a dialectical interpretation of history was to be part and parcel of the theme that 'history is the history of class struggles'. This might be taken to indicate that Marx sought to use 'contradiction' as having the same sense as 'class conflict', and thereby to justify the indifferent assimilation of the two terms that Marxists often make. But I do not think this would be an accurate interpretation of Marx, in spite of his relatively free and easy manner with some of his terminology; and regardless of what Marx may or may not have intended, I say that it is important in social theory to distinguish contradiction and conflict.

I mean by 'contradiction' the existence of two structural principles within a societal system, whereby each depends upon the other but at the same time negates it.[4] Such a notion of contradiction, I think, sustains a close connection both with the idea of contradiction in logic and with dialectics. For its implication is that societal totalities are *structured in contradiction*, involving the fusion and exclusion of opposites. In other words, the operation of one structural principle in the reproduction of a societal system presumes that of another which tends to undermine it. This view supposes that, in any given type of societal system such as those I have distinguished in this book – tribal, class-divided, capitalist societies (and, I think, socialist societies also) – there is one principal axis of contradiction, which I shall call the *primary contradiction* of that type of society. In any particular juncture, however, and in different phases of 'world time', there may be various forms of secondary contradictions that overlap with primary contradictions. Such contradictions may be located along the time-space edges that connect societies of differing types.

According to this conception, 'contradiction' refers to structural properties of social systems. This is my main basis for distinguishing contradiction from conflict, whether class conflict or any other kind. There are two senses in which conflict can be understood, as I have mentioned earlier in the book, though I have not been particularly concerned with maintaining a clear terminological distinction between them. One is conflict in the sense of opposition of interest between individuals or collectivities; the other is conflict in the sense of active struggle between such individuals or collectivities. In some circumstances it is certainly important to separate these – for conflict of interest may remain latent, rather than being actualised as clashes between those involved, while on the other hand actors may mistake their interests and enter into struggle with others whose interests (in given circumstances of action) are the same as theirs.[5] But in neither sense is conflict the same as contradiction thus formulated. In saying this I do not in any way want to deny that contradiction and conflict, in both of these senses, may be empirically closely related. Conflicts of interest, short-term and long-term, and active struggle, tend to cluster around the intersection of contradictions in societal reproduction.

## Contradiction in the Context of Marx

Where Marx discusses contradiction in a general way, it is usually in the context of his evolutionary scheme. Thus in the 'Preface' to *A Contribution to the Critique of Political Economy* Marx writes of the contradiction between the forces and relations of production as the driving source of social change. Elsewhere, where he mentions contradiction, it is usually in relation specifically to capitalism – which is not especially surprising, given his overwhelming concern with the dynamics of capitalist production and the transcendence of capitalism by a socialist system. There has been some debate, as over almost everything else in Marx's writings, about where Marx thought the contradictory character of the capitalist mode of production is primarily to be located.[6] But it seems difficult to deny[7] that he regarded it as to be found in the contradiction between what, in short-hand terms, can be called 'private appropriation' and 'socialised production'. That is to say, the structural principle which is dominant in capitalism, the valorisation and accumulation of capital through its mobilisation as private property, can only operate in and through a contrary principle of societal reproduction: that of the control of resources by the societal community 'as a whole'. The potential for the construction of a socialist society, in other words, is from the beginning an immanent negative principle of the continued reproduction of capitalism itself. For Marxists, this has sometimes been regarded as posing something of a dilemma: does the dissolution of capitalism and the arrival of socialism occur through the operation of laws that inexorably destroy one system and establish the foundations of another? Certainly in a preface to *Capital* Marx writes in a way that suggests something of the sort.[8] Marxists prone to take a positivistic standpoint have often tried to 'objectivise' dialectics by looking for laws of the internal transformation of capitalism that would have the same logical character as those of the natural sciences.[9]

If one rejects a positivistic philosophy of social science, as I do, there is no problem about accepting that it is possible to formulate laws in social theory; and I consider that much of what Marx says about the 'laws governing capitalist development' is valid. But such laws are logically distinct from those of the natural sciences in one cardinal respect. In social theory laws involve causal connections that are capable of being modified in terms of what social actors know (believe) about the conditions of production and reproduction of the social systems they constitute in their action. The laws of capitalist production, as specified by Marx, presume certain parameters of knowledge of the conditions of reproduction of capitalism on the part of the social actors involved. That is to say, pursuing an interpretation of *Capital* that does not have the positivistic overtones of those just mentioned, one can say that for Marx the existence of capitalism is predicated upon the prevalence of reification, such that the laws of the valorisation and accumulation of capital *appear* to have the status of 'iron laws'. That is why political economy, which assumes that there are abstractly given, universal laws to which economic life is subject, is of major ideological importance in the capitalist economy itself. The penetration of the ideological blindspots of political economy consists in showing that the reified conceptions which it presents are only possible because of the concealment of a process of class exploitation, the appropriation of surplus value by capital, a major factor in the suppression of capitalism as *historical*. Capitalism is a system which, like others in history, will itself be transcended.

How are contradiction and class conflict presumed to combine in this process of the transmutation and supersession of capitalism? A charitable interpretation of Marx, but one which I believe accords with the main threads of his thought, would run as follows. Capitalism is a structurally contradictory form of society, the reproduction of which sets up tensions and pressures for those who live and work in it. So far as the capitalist class is concerned, these pressures are to do especially with problems of sustaining the accumulation process, in the light of the tendency of the over-all rate of profit generated by the system to decline, and because of the cyclical character of boom and depression to which capitalism is endemically subject. So far as the working class is concerned, the pressures are those associated with 'immiseration' – the economic constraints which restrain the income of the working class from rising relative to the profit accumulated by capital; and the existence of a 'reserve army' of unemployed or semi-employed, in which greater or lesser proportions of the working class find themselves.

The class relation in which capitalists and workers exist, Marx emphasises, is one of both dependency and conflict of interest. Because of factors I have mentioned in the previous chapter, workers begin to enter into active struggle with employers and management in order to achieve 'defensive control' of the workplace, struggle which broadens out into the formation of the labour movement. Class struggle, for Marx, leads to the expansion of revolutionary class consciousness[10] on the part of the working class. To become class-conscious is more than becoming aware of communality of class interest, or aware that the employers are a class enemy: it is to become aware *of some of the main mechanisms of capitalist production itself.* To expose capitalism as a system of class domination is to help tear apart the ideological premises of political economy – as Marx sought to do on an abstract level in *Capital.* But to begin to understand the system from its 'negative side' is also to begin to understand that it carries within it the possibility of the formation of a new type of social and economic order which can be actualised by the intervention of the working class itself. Consciousness of its 'mission in history' on the part of the proletariat is achieved through the very process of grasping the contradictory nature of capitalism, and recognising that the mobilisation of revolutionary activity is the medium of bringing about the new socialist order.

It is not my purpose in this analysis to examine once again what went wrong with this scenario – for however sympathetic one might be to Marx's writings it is plain enough by now that something *did* go wrong. Marx anticipated the occurrence of a socialist revolution in the relatively short term, and expected it to transform the whole of the capitalist world. Socialism was to put an end to human 'pre-history', marking the beginning of an era when human beings would become able to control their own destiny. Marx thus anticipated a felicitous conjunction of contradiction and class conflict, in which class struggle would be the very means of overcoming class divisions once and for all.

Now although Marx concentrated most of his attention upon the transformation of capitalism and the triumph of socialism, it is made evident in the 'Preface' and elsewhere that it is not only capitalism which is a contradictory social formation, for analysis of the contradictions between forces and relations of production is offered as a general key for understanding the mysteries of societal evolution. Moreover, in so far as Marx offers an account of the evolution of society, it preserves that character of 'universal history' about which Hegel wrote. What Marx describes in *The German Ideology* and the 'Preface' is not simply an empirical account of phases of development of specific human societies. It remains linked with a quite strongly affirmed, but only weakly elaborated, vision of humanity ascending through various stages of class society towards a new order that finally creates a 'truly human' society.[11] In spite of the firm disavowal of Hegel's epistemology, Marx's evolutionary scheme retains strong echoes of the Hegelian view of history as the progressive overcoming of human self-alienation through the clash of opposites, save that in Marx's case the contradictions are social, and their resolution occurs through class struggle.

## Contradiction and Social Transformation

If one rejects Marx's evolutionary scheme, and certain of the conjunctions between contradiction and class conflict associated with it, what role is left for the notion of contradiction in social theory? In this context I shall make no attempt to develop in full the implications of answering this question. I think that the concept of contradiction is fundamental to social theory in two related respects. One is the sense of *existential contradiction*, a phenomenon bearing directly upon the relations between human beings and nature. Human life is contradictory in the sense that the human being, as *Dasein*, originates and disappears into the world of Being, the world of nature, yet as a conscious, reflective agent is the negation of the inorganic. The mediator of the contradictory character of human existence is society itself, for only in and through membership of a society does the human being acquire 'second nature'. In all societies which remain closely involved with the modalities and rhythms of nature in day-to-day life, the institutions that both mediate and express such contradiction are centred upon religion, magic and myth. Such institutions are not normally (*pace* Durkheim) distinctly separated from the *durée* of daily existence but are chronically interpolated within it. This is most uniformly true of tribal societies, which do not experience the social schisms that arise with the creation of the state, and with the time-space differentiation of society into city and countryside. In tribal societies much of what Lévi-Strauss says about myth applies. Myths mediate the existential contradiction of humanity as originating in nature and yet not being of nature. Myths, as 'impersonal story-telling', relate time and Being, as constitutive of the world, to the finite temporality of *Dasein*, via the themes of incest, sexuality, and life and death.

Tribal societies are 'cold' societies, in Lévi-Strauss's sense. This is explicable in terms of the mediation of contradiction in the institutional basis of everyday life; it is not, as I have consistently accentuated, because such societies are only poorly 'adapted' to their environments. In cold societies contradiction expresses the intermingling of human beings with nature, accommodated in 'reversible time'. Existential contradiction, in virtue of its very character, remains fundamental in all types of society. But in class-divided societies it becomes partly 'externalised' rather than remaining directly incorporated within the sphere of day-to-day life. *This externalisation is the state.* I want to propose the following thesis: *in all except tribal societies the state is the focus of the contradictory character of human societal organisation.* In class-divided societies contradiction is located in the city–countryside relation. Agrarian states involve an antagonistic fusion of two modes of social organisation, the rural community on the one hand, and the city-based institutions on the other. Structural contradiction here is not distinctively 'economic', and sustains ties with the existential contradictions of tribal societies. The claim of the state to represent the society as a whole is also only partly posed as a 'political' claim, in an overt sense. State power still feeds upon existential contradiction, and is expressed in persistingly religious form. Princes, kings and emperors have virtually everywhere claimed either to be gods or to be the chosen instrument of the gods' will. This should not be seen simply as an ideological cloak of state power, though it always is this. It rests upon a real foundation: the expression of social power, 'appropriated' by the state.

In pre-capitalist phases of history the contradictory character of the state/society relation has to be understood against the background of a point I have insisted upon previously. Contradiction supplies 'fault-lines' along which conflicts are generated, but these are rarely if ever wholly 'internal'. Contradictions, in other words, take the form of time-space edges linking divergent types of society as well as entering into their 'internal' constitution. Various sorts of overlappings of contradictions may thereby exist. The structural contradictions that are signalled by the emergence of class-divided societies inject forms of dynamism that are much more muted in inter-societal systems composed solely of tribal societies.

Contradictions are structural fault-lines that tend to produce clusterings of conflicts. These may be class conflicts following along the principal fault-line, in the sense that they pit peasantry against either local lord or government official. But there is no inherent tendency for class-divided societies to generate the 'higher stage' of capitalism via class struggle. It is an entirely misleading approach (from which Max Weber was not entirely free, in spite of his strong anti-evolutionism) to begin from the question 'what stopped capitalist society from developing *here* (Rome, India, China, etc.)?' Other types of struggle relating to the contradictions of class-divided societies have been more perennial and historically important than class struggle. These include, above all, the frictions set up along time-space edges between class-divided and tribal societies, and the military confrontations between agrarian states.

Just as the advent of capitalism radically alters the relations between human beings and nature, through the commodification of time-space – and as a result of this phenomenon – so it severs contradiction from its foundation in existential contradiction. Or rather, existential contradiction is suppressed by structural contradiction, in which the state/society relation becomes detached from the intermingling of human social life and nature. The instrumental relation to nature that is promoted by the rise of capitalism, fuelled by the accumulation process, becomes one side of the fault-line of the contradictory character of the capitalist state. I have analysed this in some substantial part in the preceding chapter, and I do not think it unreasonable to represent it as constituting a contradiction between 'private appropriation' and 'socialised production'. Each of these terms, of course, as I have mentioned before, refers to a set of processes: on the one hand, the mobilisation of production through the processes of accumulation and valorisation; and on the other, the 'unified' or 'socialised' character of capitalism as involving much higher levels of societal integration than were ever characteristic of class-divided societies. The state stands at the centre of this contradiction, in the manner I have indicated in my previous discussion.

There is no difficulty in supposing that, according to such an analysis, socialism is 'immanent' in capitalism. But this can be said to be the case only in a purely historical manner: in the manner in which capitalism was at one point an immanent (contingent) 'possible future' in European post-feudal society – a possibility that became an actuality. If we abandon Marx's evolutionism, as linked to his version of 'universal history', there can be no question of adopting any such formula as 'humankind only sets itself such problems as it can solve'. A world tottering upon the edge of nuclear war is hardly one in which it is possible to have any faith in such evolutionary homilies.

The relation between capitalism and socialism in the modern world has a double implication, as an existing series of phenomena and as an (open) series of possibilities. One of the major fault-lines in the contemporary world economy is that between the capitalist and the 'actually existing' socialist societies. The other is the immanent (but probably not imminent) socialist transformation of the capitalist 'core' itself. Anyone who believes that, however flawed it may be, there remain substantial elements of validity in Marx's analysis of the tendential properties of capitalism, has to theorise socialism in each of these ways, and to seek to relate existing forms of socialism to 'possible worlds' of future socialist transformations. In the following section I shall indicate some of the consequences of this for contemporary political theory.

## Exploitation, Labour, Surplus Production

Marx's conception of exploitation is distinctively different from concepts of 'inequality', etc., as worked out in non-Marxist schools of social theory and politics. There are at least four respects in which this is so. First, Marx's treatment of exploitation is closely associated with his themes that production distinguishes man from the animals, and that the elaboration of the forces of production is the propelling impetus of societal advance.[12] In Marx, 'exploitation' is understood as the appropriation of the surplus product of subordinate classes by reference to production relations. Second, exploitation is therefore necessarily associated with classes, and is to be explicated in terms of the mechanisms of class domination. Third, the transcendence of exploitation is hence predicated upon the achievement of a society in which there are no longer any classes. Fourth, no ethical defence is offered, or thought necessary, by Marx as to the identification of exploitation and its transcendence. This is again because of the involvement of the concept with Marx's evolutionary scheme: the progressive ascendancy of humanity from the classlessness of tribal communities, via class conflict, to the classless society of the future finds no place for an ethics justifying practical action. To further the cause of the proletariat is to be on the 'progressive' side of history, since the working class represents the universal interests of human beings in creating a classless order. The reasoning behind this can be reconstructed as follows. Capitalism is the last form of class society; at the same time as it maximises the self-alienation of human beings in a class system, it prepares the way for the abolition of all class divisions because the proletariat is the 'universal class'. The proletariat bears within itself, as it were, the concentration of the evils inherent in the oppression of some human beings by others. In struggling to throw off its own chains, the proletariat thus fights for the universal interest of humankind as a whole.

There seems no point in beating about the bush. Much of this has today to be scrapped, and in any case loses its potency once Marx's evolutionary scheme is discarded. There are quite fundamental difficulties with Marx's writings on the transition from capitalism to a (fully matured) socialist society. We know that he was reluctant to say much about the projected society of the future, save for the 'transitional' stage of early socialist consolidation. The traditional defence of this reserved attitude is that Marx had no wish to produce just another version of utopian socialism, in which detailed blue-prints of the 'desirable' society would be drawn up; his distaste for such schemes sprang from the same sources as his distrust of ethics. But this paradoxically has the effect of leaving a strong *potential* utopianism in his own work, especially when one considers that, if he abandoned the more visionary statements of his youth, he never returned to correct them. It is not enough to say, I think, as proponents of Marxist orthodoxy have been prone to do, that Marx's early writings are the philosophical ramblings of an author who had not yet reached a mature view, and hence can be largely ignored. There is a real tension here, expressed in the distance between Marx's earlier and later writings when considered in the context of his intellectual career, and posed more concretely by the problem of what else can be expected to disappear in socialism when classes disappear.

Classes, the division of labour, the state, these are supposed to go – although no one thus far has managed to formulate particularly convincing versions of how such massive transformations are to be achieved while still preserving the fruits of industrial production. But what of political power, or, as Marx sometimes says, 'power' *tout court*? In linking these, as Marx does, to the state, one might presume that they will disappear in socialism. What of conflicts of interests, and struggles organised to further sectional interests? Marx connects division of interest in society so closely with class that once more it might appear that the dissolution of classes brings about the ending of all divisions of interest between different segments or collectivities in a society. Certainly one can find quotations that seem to imply this, if one cares to go quotation-mongering. What of ideology? Since again ideology seems to be intrinsically linked to class division, it might be presumed that it, too, will disappear in socialism – although Althusser has recently suggested to the contrary, at the cost of making ideology more or less convergent with the over-all symbol system of a society, and thus 'neutralising' it in respect of class domination.[13]

I shall concentrate for the moment upon the problem of exploitation, returning to the above issues in the concluding section of this book. In neither this section nor the next do I pretend to do any more than indicate some of the threads that might be tied together into a critical theory based on the analyses developed earlier in this book. I offered a broad conceptualisation of exploitation earlier (pp. 58–61 above), and what I attempt here is to list a few considerations which link that conceptualisation to Marx's analysis:

(1) If capitalism is not the 'high point' of a universal history of humankind (in a condition that maximises the exploitation of the 'universal class' of the proletariat), then the transformation of capitalism will not bring about the disappearance of exploitation. To suppose anything else is to fall for a dialectical conjuring trick, in which there is a leap from 'necessity into freedom'. As far as Marx's own beliefs are concerned, I do not think it would be fair to criticise him as a utopian thinker, nor on the contrary to suppose him to be a hard-nosed realist. In the mature part of his career, I should say, the latter trait predominated over the former. But equally there can be no doubt that Marx continued to accept some of his earlier ideas throughout his intellectual career. I have tried

to show that there are certain major inconsistencies and ambiguities that appear in Marx's attitude towards evolution and the emergence of capitalism. One must accept that the same is true of large sectors of Marx's writings, with the exception of the only area upon which he worked in great detail: the critique of political economy. In his critical dismemberment of political economy Marx identified the sources of surplus value, and was able to make a far-reaching contrast between the exploitation of labour-power in capitalism and the exploitation of labour in prior types of society. (I have argued that this contrast bites deeper than even Marx tended to acknowledge, because he wished to interpolate it within his evolutionary scheme.) But the exploitation of labour, analysed as surplus value, either in capitalism or in other types of society, however important it may be, cannot provide an exhaustive theory of exploitation in human society as a whole. In particular, it is inadequate as a basis for the critique of exploitation in socialist society, where surplus value supposedly disappears (although not surplus production).

(2) There are three axes of exploitative relationships – observable in societies at widely different times and places – which are not explained, though they may be significantly illuminated, either by the theory of the exploitation of labour in general or by the theory of surplus value in particular. These are: (a) exploitative relations between states, where these are strongly influenced by military domination; (b) exploitative relations between ethnic groups, which may or may not converge with the first; and (c) exploitative relations between the sexes, sexual exploitation. None of these can be reduced exhaustively to class exploitation, nor more particularly can they be derived from the theory of surplus value. None of them came into existence with capitalism, though they have taken particular forms with the development of capitalist society, and hence there can be no presumption that they will inevitably disappear if and when capitalism does. These are major 'absences' in Marxist theory, and notwithstanding a diversity of efforts to accommodate them to Marxism in a 'class-reductive' way they remain among its most obvious limitations. To say this is not, of course, to deny that Marx's analyses, especially his theory of the mechanics of capitalist production, do not illuminate each of these areas. Of course they do, or can be elaborated so as to do so. I have tried to show how Marx's analysis of capitalism, linked into

the commodification of time and space, and the prevalence of 'created space', connects closely to the theory of the nation-state as holding a monopoly of the means of violence. One could also offer analyses of the intersection of capitalistic mechanisms with the other two axes of exploitation. For example, on the level of international relations, the associations between capitalism, the nation-state and nationalism help to explain some of the most virulent forms of racism witnessed in our times. (Do not make the mistake of supposing that racism is an artefact of capitalism, however. There are clear evidences of its pervasiveness in ancient Sumer.) 'Internally', one can show how ethnic discrimination serves to create minority ethnic 'underclasses', whose economic circumstances are markedly inferior to those of the majority of the population.[14] The creation of 'everyday life' in capitalist time-space, with its characteristic separation of home and work-place, together with other aspects of the commodification of social relations, have decisively influenced the relations between the sexes, and at least in certain respects served to intensify the exploitation of women.[15] Feminism is, in my judgement, potentially more radical in its implications for a critical theory of contemporary society (capitalist and state-socialist) than Marxism is, however much each may help feed in to the other.

(3) 'Exploitation' is above all a concept that bears on the relations between power and *freedom*. This is an absolutely fundamental point, and hits at some of the most entrenched weaknesses of Marx's writings and those of subsequent Marxism. One way of grasping it within the nexus of Marx's own writings is by returning to the problem of the production of a surplus, and its part in Marx's interpretation of history. The origins of surplus production and the definition of 'surplus', although nowhere discussed with precision by Marx, are assumed by him to be economic – an assumption that conforms to the primacy which he accords to the expansion of the forces of production in stimulating social change. But I have sought to show that, until the arrival of capitalism and the transition from appropriation of surplus labour to the appropriation of surplus value, what is 'surplus' can only be specified in terms of asymmetrical distributions of power. What is 'surplus' is that which can be extracted, by whatever means, by the exploiting class. Now it might seem that surplus value in capitalism diverges from this, since it is calculated in units of exchange-value

(commodified time), and is therefore 'economic'. Indeed, I have constantly stressed the importance of this contrast. But the 'surplus' is still formed by power relations, even in this instance – for its extraction is only possible given the framework of class domination that can be traced out through the labour contract. In capitalism, control of allocative resources (capital) yields far more power than allocative control in any previous society.

(4) If the concept of exploitation is to do with the relations between power and freedom, no theory concerned only with the distribution of material wealth can suffice to explore more than certain aspects of the patterns of exploitation formed in a society. These assume particular importance in the context of capitalism, for the reason just noted: that control of allocative resources becomes of focal importance for the distribution of power. Criticising Marx's formulation of surplus production does not, I should hasten to add (although it should be clear enough already), mean dismissing the relevance of his work to the elucidation of power relations. For instance, in showing capital to presuppose wage-labour, the two being connected via the production of surplus value, Marx shows – *vis-à-vis* political economy – that the 'freedom' of wage-labour disguises coercive sanctions that employers are able to use to enhance their power. However, the lack of a satisfactory treatment of power, including the use of violence by individuals, collectivities and states, runs like a red thread (or perhaps one should say here, a blue thread) through the writings of Marx and of Marxists subsequently. The importance of this points both backwards and forwards: backwards in the direction of the inadequacies of historical materialism as an account of societal development; forwards to the anticipation of socialism. The influence of the Saint-Simonian strain of socialist thought on Marx is one reason, although only one, why Marx's thought supplies precious few clues indeed about the continuing significance of power in socialist society. But this is the century of Stalin and the Gulag. No socialist can afford to ignore this very basic 'absence' in Marxist thought.

Although the concept of totalitarianism has a fraught history, being part of the liberal apparatus of political thought of the Cold War period (and, on the left, being greatly over-extended by Marcuse), I think it to be an essential notion for examining exploitative aspects of state power. Certainly it cannot be applied as a concept *en bloc*; in the Cold War period liberal writers applied it to more or less all the industrialised societies that did not conform to their models of liberal democracy, to fascism and to the Eastern European societies. Instead of such a usage, I should want to distinguish between *right totalitarianism* (fascism), and *left totalitarianism* (Stalinism). I agree with Arendt that totalitarianism is a modern phenomenon, not to be equated with 'despotism' or its synonyms (see p. 104 above), though I would not accept all the elements of her standpoint. I think an approach to the theory of totalitarianism can be worked out via the concept of surveillance, against the backdrop of the time-space transformations I have documented in previous chapters. The expansion of the surveillance activities of the state, which is contradictory (not simply a one-way movement towards the 'steel-hard cage' of Weber's fears), has to be recognised as one of the basic issues to be tackled in social and political theory. The extension of surveillance, plus the secret co-ordination of information in the hands of dominant elites, used to further policies formed mainly by those elites, can together be taken to represent a provisional definition of totalitarian power. But this is not to say that right and left totalitarianism can be explained in identical ways, or that there are not major variations within these two types of totalitarian control.

(5) The concept of exploitation has to include the power of human beings over nature as well as over other human beings. Such a notion is evidently in some part elliptical, since it depends, like the direct exploitation of human beings by others, ultimately upon how relations with nature affect human interests. But it touches upon a very important theme in respect of Marx's writings and those of most subsequent Marxists. I have already pointed out that Marx adopted an instrumental attitude to nature, common enough in the nineteenth century to be sure, and assumed by virtually all of those who felt themselves in opposition to Romanticism. Nature is to be mastered and subordinated to human purposes. This makes it difficult, within the compass of Marx's thought, to cope with two sets of phenomena whose potential significance has emerged more and more sharply in the twentieth century. One is that nature does not contain an inexhaustible reservoir of resources available to be transmuted to human ends. Nature is not merely the medium whereby human beings 'make their history, and thereby make themselves'; nature

should rather be treated as an ally of humanity, in which human beings exist 'ecologically', depending upon natural phenomena which in principle or in practice they can destroy. There is more than a small theoretical hiatus between Marxism and 'ecological movements' of contemporary times, though it seems a matter of urgency that attempts at *rapprochement* should be set under way. This involves, in my opinion, drawing direct connections between modes in which capitalistic class exploitation intersects with the exploitation of nature. Some of these appear obvious: for example, the pressure towards accumulation may create a drive to the valorisation of capital in the short term regardless of the long-term consequences in respect of the exploitation of nature. But, in the contemporary world at least, it seems clear that the economic advantages of the exploitation of natural resources may equally well be sought after by those in the socialist societies. Scarcity of material resources is something else that does not disappear *ipso facto* with the dissolution of capitalism, if and when it should occur.

There are more subtle matters involved in human relations with nature than relatively straightforward questions of the damaging or exhaustion of resources which are of value to human beings. These bear in some part upon issues I have briefly touched upon in discussing contradiction. Nature, as the apparent infinity of time-space, is a 'mystery' to human beings; but nature as the intimate, aesthetically satisfying interchange between human beings and their immediate surrounds is a potential part of a 'meaningful' human existence. Certainly neither of these relations between human beings and nature can be grasped via the notion of labour, however broadly it is interpreted.[16] But some of the main ideas I have discussed in this book, especially those bearing upon the commodification of time and space, the dissolution of the differentiation between the city and the countryside, and the prevalence of 'created space', are relevant to these questions. And they have been addressed interestingly by various Marxist thinkers – although always those who have been strongly 'revisionist' in orientation, and critical of orthodox Marxism.

(6) The elaboration of a theory of exploitation in contemporary capitalism, as well as in contemporary socialism, seems likely to presuppose counterfactual conceptions of a normative kind. As I have pointed out previously, many difficulties are created for

Marxism by the paucity of Marx's comments on what socialism can be expected to be like, at least in its 'higher phase'. Since Marxism is predicated so strongly on the critique of capitalism, and more specifically upon the critique of class domination as the focus of exploitation, it is open to the utopian readings I have referred to above. When classes are transcended, then division of interest in general, and therefore exploitation in general, might be presumed to be superseded also. It needs no great perspicacity to see that Marxism then becomes highly vulnerable to itself being translated into ideology: 'in the workers' state there can be no division of interests between different sections of the community', etc., etc. As I have argued elsewhere, any theory which might be taken to imply that there can be an 'end of ideology' in an empirical society displays a vulnerability to itself becoming ideological[17] – in virtue of the fact that a regime guided by that theory may choose to declare that the time has arrived, that henceforth ideology exists no longer.

A counterfactual theory of exploitation would recognise that, notwithstanding revolutions and reforms that might take place, there is always room for further advancement. In the contemporary literature of social theory and philosophy, there are various normative counterfactual theories which command attention. One might instance especially, outside Marxism, Rawls's theory of justice and, more closely connected to Marxism, Habermas's conception of the 'ideal speech situation' as the basis for a critique of asymmetries of power. These have each been subject to considerable discussion, and each appears to have major weaknesses; but I do not intend to comment upon these debates here.[18]

## Between Capitalism and Socialism

Marx looked forward to the achievement of socialism as the overall transcendence of capitalism; there is no indication that he anticipated a world in which the capitalist 'core' would not experience a successful socialist revolution, and in which capitalism would coexist with societies governed by groups claiming affiliation to his doctrines. Socialism, as I have said, today must be confronted on two levels: as embodying ideals that still seem capable of much more profound development than has been achieved in any society to date, and as an 'actually existing' reality in the form of the state-socialist societies. The twentieth century is the century of two cataclysmic world wars, the century of Auschwitz on the one hand and of the Gulag on the other. Socialism today no longer has its hands clean, and whatever ways one may choose to criticise the state-socialist societies, including taking the easy option of declaring that they are not really 'socialist' at all, there is no way of plausibly attributing all the evils of the world in some diffuse way to 'capitalism'.

At the very real risk of inducing tedium in the reader, but in the hope of facilitating clarity of exposition, I shall end this book using the same style as I have employed previously in this chapter. That is to say, I shall emunerate some remarks in a fairly formal way – remarks that I propose to develop in detail in the volume to follow this one:

(1) Theorising socialism must continue on the two levels noted above, and must connect them. That is to say, instead of leaving aside problems of what the 'good society' might look like, it is today more necessary than ever to confront them directly. There is no need for such thought, however speculative it might seem, to relapse into utopianism if it is related to analyses of the 'actually existing' socialist societies, as well as to changes that may occur in the capitalist world and in Third World countries. Marxists today, at least those who write in the West looking East, are much more prone than they used to be to accept that the transition from capitalism to socialism is likely, or certain, to be a protracted one. Moreover, socialism is no longer seen as an unproblematic consolidation of a society which has eradicated classes by abolishing private control of the means of production. Rather, it is recognised to involve numerous difficulties, and to be open to various forms of 'regression'. Capitalism is not disposed of that easily.

(2) If the views I have sketched in at the beginning of this chapter are correct, socialism also has its contradictions. The principal contradiction of socialist societies, I would venture to suggest, is between the planned organisation of production, mediated through the state, and the mass participation of the population in decisions and policies that affect the course of their lives. As in capitalism, there is no reason to hold that the

contradictory character of socialism is a purely negative phenomenon, but, rather, it may well be an energising tension that stimulates progressive social change. One of the most basic themes of Marx, that virtually all Marxists have also adopted as a cardinal tenet of their political theory, is the notion of the transcendence of the state in socialism. In spite of the rise of 'Eurocommunism', and the various recent attempts to recast the doctrine in a plausible fashion, I have no doubt that this remains one of the least thought through conceptions in Marxist thought. Since Marxism has not generated convincing models of the capitalist state, and in addition has generally not adequately analysed the role of the state as the agent of surveillance and the purveyor of military violence in history, that such should be the case is not particularly surprising. The state is a much more formidable phenomenon that Marxism has traditionally allowed for, and the whole question of how its transcendence in a socialist society might be realistically contemplated, and carried through, has to be raised anew.[19] I do not mean to suggest, however, that this is just one more 'utopian strain' in Marxism, or that it is of no interest. I do not think this at all. On the contrary, that state power is an ineluctable feature of history thus far, including the current history of the state-socialist societies, makes the problems involved here all the more exigent.

(3) Let me repeat: this is the era of the Gulag, of confrontations of a warlike character between socialist states, of Pol Pot and something close to genocide in Kampuchea. Neither socialism more generally, nor Marxism in particular, walks innocently in the world. Marx saw socialism as the culmination of the 'pre-history' of humankind, as expressing the victory of the universal interests of the proletariat, and hence as needing no ethical justification apart from that supplied by the postulated future march of history itself. Who could be satisfied with this today? And yet many Marxists, including 'Western Marxists', appear to be. I think socialism does stand in need of ethical justification, and that a 'normative theory' of socialism, founded upon the critique of exploitation, is today of the first importance. Those in traditions of 'Marxist humanism' have always recognised this need, but all too often have formulated programmes of the utmost vagueness or generality; and they have rarely connected those programmes to any sort of analysis of 'actually existing' socialism.

(4) No socialist theory is adequate that does not attempt to

come to terms with some of the major 'absences' in Marxism: the role of violence and of military power in exploitation, and the significance of ethnic and sexual exploitation. Among these, by far the bulk of recent writing has been concerned with sexual exploitation, and I have already remarked upon its potential radical implications. Very little attention has been given by Marxist authors, or by those close to Marxism, to violence and ethnic exploitation and their various conjunctions. This is probably in large part because where such authors have written about these issues they have for the most part done so in relation to revolutionary activity. Ethnicity, like the nationalistic sentiments with which it may be linked, tends to appear in the Marxist literature showing only one side of its Janus-like face: as a phenomenon helping to inspire liberation movements. Similarly, violence has mostly either been discussed in terms of the 'internal' violence of the state (the police and the 'repressive apparatus' of power), or again as a positive factor, i.e. as defensible 'revolutionary violence'. But there is no matter that presses more heavily upon the contemporary world than that of international violence, and the threat of nuclear war. For reasons I have touched upon in various parts of this book, Marxism has no tradition of theorising violence either as an integral and chronic feature of repression, or as the 'world violence' of the contemporary system of power-blocs and nation-states. But a 'philosophy of violence' (i.e. ethical investigation of the conditions under which violence or war may be justified, if ever), and practical political programmes that have relevance to the nation-state as the propagator of violence, seem of the first priority for socialist thinkers as much as for anyone else. 'Actually existing' socialism has thus far certainly made no dent in pre-existing patterns of violence and its threat among nation-states. On the contrary, socialism has so far proved compatible with each of the three sets of phenomena mentioned above: violence, internally and externally, associated with the socialist nation-state; racism and ethnic exploitation; and the continued subjection of women.

(5) It would be a blinkered and bigoted theory indeed which failed to take account of the 'successes' of capitalism, however heavy the price the rest of the world may have had to pay for them in the shape of colonialism, 'old' and 'new'. Two achievements of the states of the capitalist 'core', for their own citizenry, have been

particularly important in the twentieth century – not least in so far as they are bound up with the non-occurrence of socialist revolutions in those countries. These are:

(a) Their 'internal' affluence. The 'affluent societies' of the West, as we know well, contain major pockets of poverty, and have achieved their wealth in some part by draining the resources of the 'periphery', and by the creation of 'underdevelopment'. These things being acknowledged, it is quite certain that never before in world history have large masses of the population been anywhere near as materially affluent as in the liberal-democratic capitalist societies of today.

(b) The political framework of liberal democracy comprises a range of citizenship rights, acquired in some substantial degree through class struggle, that are also unique in history – whatever their manifest and notable limitations. The modes in which the 'actually existing' socialist societies have managed to radicalise these rights are limited indeed, save in certain aspects of social welfare.

All these facts are relevant to those who declare themselves to be socialists. It is entirely possible to accept important elements of Marx's critique of bourgeois democracy (made in the context of the 'liberal' rather than the 'liberal-democratic' state), while still arguing that socialist theory should be more positively influenced by aspects of 'bourgeois liberalism' than hitherto.

(6) Capitalism has transformed, and continues to transform, the world in more profound ways than any other society has done before or – so far, at least – since. I do not have much sympathy with 'primitivism' as such – if that be regarded as the thesis that the small societies of hunters and gatherers, the 'original affluent societies', incorporate happier and more satisfying ways of life than anything to be found in 'civilisations'. But it seems to me very important to comprehend as much as possible of this 'world we have lost', or whose destruction is today finally being completed – for one does not have to be a primitivist to see that the commodified world that capitalism has created has stripped away a massive variety of institutions, skills and forms of human experience, many of which are now irretrievably lost. A philosophical anthropology relevant to socialism must attend closely to what we can retain of the human diversity that is being devoured by the voracious expansion of the 'created space' of capitalism – for in the

world that capitalism has originated, time is no longer understood as the medium of Being, and the gearing of daily life into comprehended tradition is replaced by the empty routines of everyday life. On the other hand, the whole of humanity now lies in the shadow of possible destruction. This unique conjunction of the banal and the apocalyptic, this is the world that capitalism has fashioned.

# Notes and References

## Introduction

1. Among the most prominent of recent works that belong to the second of these categories, see Leslek Kolakowski, *Main Currents of Marxism*, 3 vols (Oxford: Clarendon Press, 1978).
2. For a particularly important exposition, with which I have a great deal of sympathy, see Cornelius Castoriadis, 'Le Marxisme: bilan provisoire', in *L'institution imaginaire de la société* (Paris: Editions du Seuil, 1975).
3. Cf. my *Central Problems in Social Theory* (London: Macmillan, 1979) pp. 150–5 and *passim*.
4. Originally published in English as a separate booklet, under the heading of *Pre-Capitalist Economic Formations* (London: Lawrence & Wishart, 1964).
5. *Central Problems in Social Theory*, pp. 160–4.
6. Cf. my *New Rules of Sociological Method* (London: Hutchinson, 1976) pp. 110ff and *passim*.
7. Rudolf Bahro, *The Alternative in Eastern Europe* (London: New Left Books, 1978).
8. Cf. *New Rules of Sociological Method*, ch. 2.
9. 'Functionalism: Après la Lutte', in *Studies in Social and Political Theory* (London: Hutchinson, 1977).
10. Jürgen Habermas, 'Toward the Reconstruction of Historical Materialism', in *Communication and the Evolution of Society* (Boston: Beacon, 1979).
11. Karl Marx and Friedrich Engels, *The German Ideology* (London: Lawrence & Wishart, 1965) p. 39.
12. Stanley Diamond, *In Search of the Primitive* (New Brunswick: Transaction, 1974).

13. Marshall Sahlins, *Stone-Age Economics* (London: Tavistock, 1974) p. 2.
14. Pierre Clastres, *Society Against the State* (Oxford: Blackwell, 1977).
15. Cf. *Studies in Social and Political Theory,* 'Introduction' and *passim.*
16. Wolfram Eberhard, *Conquerors and Rulers* (Leiden: Brill, 1965) pp. 16ff.

**Chapter 1**

1. *Central Problems in Social Theory* (London: Macmillan, 1979).
2. I have analysed these in some of the papers in *Studies in Social and Political Theory* (London: Hutchinson, 1977) and in *Central Problems in Social Theory,* ch. 1.
3. See R. W. Connell, 'A Critique of the Althusserian Approach to Class', *Theory and Society,* vol. 8, 1979.
4. See *New Rules of Sociological Method* (London: Hutchinson, 1976) pp. 96–8.
5. Martin Heidegger, *Being and Time* (Oxford: Blackwell, 1978) pp. 41ff.
6. Ibid, p. 40.
7. See especially ibid, section 70.
8. 'Introduction' to Heidegger, *On Time and Being* (New York: Harper & Row, 1972).
9. Heidegger, *On Time and Being,* p. 14.
10. George Herbert Mead, *The Philosophy of the Present* (La Salle: Open Court, 1959).
11. Cf. David Harvey, *Explanation in Geography* (London: Arnold, 1969), and Tommy Carlstein *et al., Making Sense of Time* (London: Arnold, 1978).
12. Harvey, *Explanation in Geography,* p. 210.
13. M. Capek, 'The Fiction of Instants', in J. T. Fraser *et al., The Study of Time* (Berlin: Springer, 1972).
14. See Henri Bergson, *Durée et simultaneité* (Paris: Alcan, 1926) pp. 68–9.
15. Heidegger, *Being and Time,* p. 428.
16. Cf. Theodor Adorno, *The Jargon of Authenticity* (London: Routledge & Kegan Paul, 1973).

17. Maurice Halbwachs, *Les cadres sociaux de la mémoire* (Paris: Alcan, 1925).
18. Cf. *New Rules of Sociological Method*, pp. 82–3.
19. E. E. Evans-Pritchard, 'Nuer Time-Reckoning', *Africa*, vol. 12, 1939. For the most comprehensive available survey, see Martin P. Nilsson, *Primitive Time-Reckoning* (Lund: Gleerup, 1920). See also Helga Nowotny, 'Time Structuring and Time Measurement: on the Interrelation between Time-Keepers and Social Time', in J. T. Fraser and N. Lawrence, *The Study of Time II* (Berlin: Springer, 1975). One of the most penetrating discussions of these matters is that offered by Bourdieu, in an essay on Algerian peasants, called 'Simple Reproduction and Cyclical Time'. He says: 'It is true that nothing is more foreign to the pre-capitalist economy than representation of the future as a field of possibles to be explored and mastered by calculation. But it does not follow from this, as has often been supposed, that the Algerian peasant is incapable of fixing his sights on a distant future, since his distrust of any attempt to take possession of the future always coexists with the foresight needed to spread the yield from a good harvest over a period of time, sometimes several years.' But the peasant still 'lives in the very rhythm of the world with which he is bound up. He cannot discover himself as an historical agent.' See Pierre Bourdieu, *Algeria 1960* (Cambridge University Press, 1979). Also very instructive is E. R. Leach, 'Two Essays concerning the Symbolic Representation of Time', in *Rethinking Anthropology* (London: Athlone, 1966). Muratorio discusses time-reckoning among Quicha Indian communities living in Colta, in Ecuador. The peasants, who have become drawn into wage-labour, distinguish between 'Quicha time', which implies a 'leisurely social activity', or 'time in the community', and 'Mestizo time' – bosses' time, time calculation imposed from the outside, the latter relating to their participation in labour and commodity markets. See Blanca Muratorio, 'Capitalism and Protestantism Revisited in the Rural Highlands of Ecuador', *Journal of Peasant Studies*, October 1980.
20. *Central Problems in Social Theory*, pp. 120ff.
21. Alan Pred, 'The Choreography of Existence: Comments on Hägerstrand's Time-Geography and its Usefulness', *Economic Geography*, vol. 53, 1977. See also Carlstein *et al.*,

*Making Sense of Time,* vol. 2, for various papers by members of the so-called 'Lund School' of time-geography. Also relevant is the 'chroneographic approach' of Parkes and Thrift. See Don Parkes and Nigel Thrift, *Times, Spaces and Places* (New York: Wiley, 1980).

22. In *Central Problems in Social Theory,* pp. 123–8, I define as a 'critical situation' a set of circumstances which radically disrupts taken-for-granted routines (see Chapter 8).
23. Donald G. Janelle, 'Central Place Development in a Time-Space Framework', *Professional Geographer,* vol. 20, 1968.
24. *Central Problems in Social Theory,* ch. 1.
25. Paul Ricoeur, *The Conflict of Interpretations* (Evanston, Ill.: Northwestern University Press, 1974).
26. *Central Problems in Social Theory,* pp. 206–7.
27. *New Rules of Sociological Method,* pp. 106–7.
28. Erving Goffman, *The Presentation of Self in Everyday Life* (New York: Doubleday, 1959).
29. Cf. David Harvey, 'The Political Economy of Urbanisation in Advanced Capitalist Societies: the Case of the United States', in Gary Grappert and Harold M. Rose (eds), *The Social Economy of Cities* (Beverly Hills: Sage, 1975).
30. Cf. Rom Harré, 'Architechtronic Man: on the Structuring of Lived Experience', in Richard Harvey Brown and Stanford M. Lyman (eds), *Structure, Consciousness, and History* (Cambridge University Press, 1978); see also the same author's *Social Being* (Oxford: Blackwell, 1979).
31. Goffman, *Presentation of Self in Everyday Life.*
32. *Central Problems in Social Theory,* pp. 76–81.
33. R. K. Merton, *Social Theory and Social Structure* (New York: Free Press, 1963); cf. my 'Functionalism: Après la Lutte', in *Studies in Social and Political Theory.*
34. See, however, Piotr Sztompka, *System and Function* (New York: Academic Press, 1974).
35. Jean-Paul Sartre, *Critique of Dialectical Reason* (London: New Left Books, 1976) p. 45. It is important in the context of Sartre's ideas to emphasise that he complements this version of the totality with a stress upon 'totalisation'.
36. Louis Althusser, *For Marx* (Harmondsworth: Penguin, 1969) pp. 202–6.
37. Ibid, p. 204.

38. Louis Althusser and Etienne Balibar, *Reading 'Capital'* (London: New Left Books, 1970) p. 188.
39. *New Rules of Sociological Method,* pp. 104–13; and *Central Problems in Social Theory,* pp. 81–111.
40. *Central Problems in Social Theory,* ch. 5.
41. Cf. Georges Balandier, *Political Anthropology* (London: Allen Lane, 1970) pp. 23–5 and *passim*.

**Chapter 2**

1. *Central Problems in Social Theory* (London: Macmillan, 1979)
2. Ibid, ch. 2 and *passim*.
3. Michel Foucault, *Power, Truth, Strategy* (Sydney: Feral Publications, 1979). Cf. also Foucault, *The History of Sexuality* (London: Allen Lane, 1978) pp. 86ff.
4. See my 'Power in the Writings of Talcott Parsons', in *Studies in Social and Political Theory* (London: Hutchinson, 1977). A reworked Parsonian account of power appears in Niklas Luhmann, *Trust and Power* (New York: Wiley, 1979).
5. Daniel Bertaux, *Destins personnels et structure de classe* (Paris: Presses Universitaires, 1977).
6. *Central Problems in Social Theory,* pp. 150ff. Cf. the very important analysis in Roy Bhaskar, *The Possibility of Naturalism* (London: Harvester, 1979).
7. *The Class Structure of the Advanced Societies* (London: Hutchinson, 1973) pp. 108–9.
8. *Central Problems in Social Theory,* pp. 123ff, 215ff.
9. Marx, *Capital,* vol. I (London: Lawrence & Wishart, 1970) p. 185.
10. T. B. Bottomore, *Karl Marx: Early Writings* (New York: McGraw-Hill, 1964) pp. 126–7.
11. *Central Problems in Social Theory,* pp. 188ff.
12. *The Class Structure of the Advanced Societies,* pp. 156–76.
13. Cf. 'A Theory of Suicide', in *Studies in Social and Political Theory,* ch. 9.
14. See Nicholas Abercrombie and Bryan S. Turner, 'The Dominant Ideology Thesis', *British Journal of Sociology,* vol. 29, 1978, for a relevant, if relatively cursory, discussion. An

expanded version appears in Abercrombie and Turner, *The Dominant Ideology Thesis* (London: Allen & Unwin, 1980).
15. Gilbert Ryle, *The Concept of Mind* (London: Hutchinson, 1949) p. 27.

**Chapter 3**

1. Marx and Engels, *The German Ideology* (London: Lawrence & Wishart, 1965) p. 33. I have modified the translation here, which has 'ownership' for *Eigentum* rather than 'property'.
2. All the above quotations are from *The German Ideology*, pp. 32–78.
3. 'Preface' to *A Contribution to the Critique of Political Economy*, in Marx and Engels, *Selected Works in One Volume* (London: Lawrence and Wishart, 1968) p. 183.
4. Ibid, pp. 182–3.
5. Jürgen Habermas, 'Toward a Reconstruction of Historical Materialism', in *Communication and the Evolution of Society* (Boston: Beacon, 1979).
6. Hegel, *Reason in History* (New York: Doubleday, 1953) p. 28.
7. Marx and Engels, *The Holy Family* (Moscow: Progress Publishers, 1956) p. 125.
8. 'Preface' to *A Contribution to the Critique of Political Economy*, p. 183.
9. 'Afterward to the Second German Edition' of *Capital*, vol. I (London: Lawrence & Wishart, 1970) p. 20.
10. Letter to Engels, 14 January 1858, in *Selected Correspondence* (Moscow: Progress Publishers, 1975).
11. Claude Lefort, 'Marx: From One Vision of History to Another', *Social Research*, vol. 45, 1978. This essay appears as ch. XI in Lefort, *Les formes de l'histoire* (Paris: Gallimard, 1978). A second discussion, 'Société "sans histoire" et 'historicité', is also relevant to the present analysis.
12. Still perhaps the best summary of Marx's changing attitudes towards the Asiatic Mode of Production is George Lichtheim, 'Marx and the Asiatic Mode of Production', *St Anthony's Papers*, no. 14, 1963. See also Daniel Thorner, 'Marx on India and the Asiatic Mode of Production', *Contributions to Indian Sociology*, vol. 9, 1966.

13. 'Preface' to *A Contribution to the Critique of Political Economy,* p. 183.
14. Lefort, 'Marx: From One Vision of History to Another'.
15. Ibid, p. 618.
16. All the above quotations are from Marx, *Grundrisse* (Harmondsworth: Penguin, 1973) pp. 47–91.
17. Ibid, p. 489.
18. Ibid, p. 497.
19. Ibid, p. 506.
20. Cf. 'Marx, Weber, and the Development of Capitalism', in *Studies in Social and Political Theory* (London: Hutchinson, 1977).
21. See Roy A. Rappaport, 'Maladaptation in Social Systems', and the succeeding commentary by Anne Whyte, in J. Friedman and M. J. Rowlands (eds), *The Evolution of Social Systems* (London: Duckworth, 1977).
22. Ernest Gellner, *Thought and Change* (London: Weidenfeld & Nicolson, 1964) pp. 42ff.
23. Stanley Diamond, *In Search of the Primitive* (New Brunswick: Transaction, 1974).
24. Marshall Sahlins, *Stone-Age Economics* (London: Tavistock, 1974) p. 2.
25. Pierre Clastres, *Society Against the State* (Oxford: Blackwell, 1977) p. 165 and *passim.* A similar conclusion is reached in Marvin Harris, *Cannibals and Kings* (London: Fontana, 1978) ch. 2.
26. Clastres, *Society Against the State,* p. 171.
27. Thus, for example, Godelier, and Hindess and Hirst reject Wittfogel's theory of 'hydraulic society' as at best a crude version of some of Marx's comments on the Asiatic Mode of Production. Ernest Mandel, on the other hand, criticises Godelier's standpoint, and argues for a view similar to Wittfogel's, stripped of the latter's assumptions about 'bureaucratic classes'. See Maurice Godelier, 'The Concept of the "Asiatic Mode of Production" and Marxist Models of Social Evolution', in David Seddon (ed.), *Relations of Production* (London: Cass, 1978); Barry Hindess and Paul Hirst, *Pre-Capitalist Modes of Production* (London: Routledge & Kegan Paul, 1975); Karl W. Wittfogel, *Oriental Despotism* (Yale University Press, 1967); Ernest Mandel, *The Formation of the Economic Thought of Marx* (London: New Left Books,

1971). There is a massive literature on all this. See, for instance, F. Tokei, *Sur le mode de production asiatique* (Budapest: Kiado, 1966); M. Godelier, *Sur les sociétés précapitalistes* (Paris: Editions Sociales, 1970); Lawrence Krader, *The Ethnological Notebooks of Karl Marx* (Assen: Van Gorcum, 1972); Marian Sawyer, *Marx and the Question of the Asiatic Mode of Production* (The Hague: Mouton, 1977); U. Melotti, *Marx and the Third World* (London: Macmillan, 1977). The best critical discussion, in my opinion, is in Perry Anderson, *Lineages of the Absolutist State* (London: Verso, 1979) pp. 484ff.

28. V. G. Kiernan, 'Private Property in History', in Jack Goody *et al., Family and Inheritance* (Cambridge University Press, 1978) p. 381. 'Philosophical anthropology' is still often written in this vein. Consider Hannah Arendt, *The Human Condition* (University of Chicago Press, 1958), which in spite of its title concentrates wholly on the West.

29. Marx, *Capital,* vol. I, p. 479.

30. Ibid.

31. Edmund Leach, 'Hydraulic Society in Ceylon', *Past and Present,* vol. 15, 1959.

32. Godelier, 'The Concept of the "Asiatic Mode of Production"', p. 214.

33. For discussion of the various senses in which the 'materialist conception of history' might be understood, see *Central Problems in Social Theory* (London: Macmillan, 1979) pp. 150–5.

34. Marx, *Grundrisse,* p. 489.

35. Ibid.

## Chapter 4

1. No one has done more to illuminate this than Meyer Fortes in his various writings. See, for instance, his *Kinship and the Social Order* (London: Routledge & Kegan Paul, 1970). Cf. also Jack Goody, *The Character of Kinship* (Cambridge University Press, 1973).

2. Max Weber, *Economy and Society, vol. I* (University of California Press, 1978) p. 226.

3. Ruth Whitehouse, *The First Cities* (Oxford: Phaidon, 1977) p. 66.

4. Jack Goody, *The Domestication of the Savage Mind* (Cambridge University Press, 1977) ch. 5.

5. See I. J. Gelb, *A Study of Writing* (University of Chicago Press, 1963) and David Diringer, *Writing* (London: Thames & Hudson, 1962), which contains a useful bibliography.

6. Lewis Mumford, 'University City', in Carl H. Kraeling and Robert M. Adams (eds), *City Invincible* (University of Chicago Press, 1960) p. 7.

7. V. Gordon Childe, *Man Makes Himself*, 3rd edn (London: Watts, 1956). Cf. also Childe, 'The Urban Revolution', *Town Planning Review*, vol. 21, 1950; and Robert M. Adams, *The Evolution of Urban Society* (London: Weidenfeld & Nicolson, 1966) pp. 12ff and *passim*.

8. Childe, *Man Makes Himself*, p. 151.

9. Jane Jacobs, *The Economy of Cities* (London: Cape, 1970) pp. 42–3.

10. Mumford, 'Concluding Address' in Kraeling and Adams (eds), *City Invincible*, p. 236.

11. Samuel Noah Kramer, *The Sumerians* (University of Chicago Press, 1963) pp. 74ff.

12. There are many different attempts in the literature to classify imperial systems. One of the better known is that of Eisenstadt, who distinguishes the following overlapping types: 'patrimonial empires' (e.g. Carolingian, Ahmenid or Parthian), 'nomad or conquest empires' (e.g. Mongols, the Arab Kingdom under the first caliphs) and 'centralised historical bureaucratic empires'. See S. N. Eisenstadt, *The Political Systems of Empires* (New York: Free Press, 1963).

13. Wolfram Eberhard, *Conquerors and Rulers* (Leiden: Brill, 1965) p. 6 Cf. also H. A. Innis, *Empire and Communications* (Oxford: Clarendon Press, 1950).

14. This is, of course, an over-simplification. There may be several 'tiers' in the administration of imperial societies; but the most basic differentiation is between those belonging to the administrative apparatus and those forming localised agrarian communities.

15. See Weber's comments in *Economy and Society, vol. 1,* p. 232.

16. Cf. Michael Mann, 'States, Ancient and Modern', *Archives Européenes de sociologie,* vol. 18, 1977.
17. Marx and Engels, *The German Ideology* (London: Lawrence & Wishart, 1965) pp. 44–5.
18. Engels, *The Origin of the Family, Private Property and the State* (London: Lawrence & Wishart, 1972) p. 170.
19. Karl W. Wittfogel, *Oriental Despotism* (Yale University Press, 1967) pp. 302–3.
20. See my *Class Structure of the Advanced Societies* (London: Hutchinson, 1973) pp. 118ff.
21. Wittfogel, *Oriental Despotism,* p. 4.
22. See, for instance, Louis Baudin, *A Socialist Empire: the Incas of Peru* (Princeton: Van Nostrand, 1961).
23. Sally Falk Moore, *Power and Property in Inca Peru* (Columbia University Press, 1958).
24. This seems to me now a more accurate term than that of 'pre-class society', which I used in *The Class Structure of the Advanced Societies,* pp. 132–5.
25. I do not propose in this book to examine the very large literature on the 'origins of the state'. Although the question of the formation of 'primal states' is partly separable from that of the development of 'secondary states', it seems unquestionable that no 'single-factor' theory of the origins of the state can be sustained (e.g. the so-called 'conquest theory'). For a representative sample of available discussions, see R. H. Lowie, *Origin of the State* (New York: Harcourt, Brace, 1927); M. H. Fried, *The Evolution of Political Society* (New York: Random House, 1967); Henry T. Wright, 'Toward an Explanation of the Origin of the State', in James N. Hill (ed.), *Explanation of Prehistoric Change* (University of New Mexico Press, 1977); J. Cherry, 'Generalisation and the Archaeology of the State', in David Green *et al., Social Organisation and Settlement* (Oxford University Press, 1978); and H. J. M. Claessen and P. Skalnik, *The Early State* (The Hague: Mouton, 1978).

## Chapter 5

1. See *The Class Structure of the Advanced Societies* (London: Hutchinson, 1973) pp. 27ff.

2. For a relevant discussion, see Henry W. Pearson, 'The Economy has no Surplus: Critique of a Theory of Development', in Karl Polanyi *et al., Trade and Market in Early Empires* (New York: Free Press, 1957).
3. Max Weber distinguishes the following ways in which property can be 'owned' in non-capitalist societies: in (1) the household; (2) the clan or lineage group; (3) religious groupings; (4) village associations; (5) political associations of villages or of estates. All of these may operate under (6) the overlordship of land, where land belongs to the state, or (7) personal overlordship, 'when the individual is not free but in bondage to another' (slavery, feudalism). See Weber, *General Economic History* (New York: Collier-Macmillan, 1961).
4. Marx, *Grundrisse* (Harmondsworth: Penguin, 1973) p. 107.
5. Lewis Mumford, *The City in History* (New York: Harcourt, Brace, 1961). See also the massive recent survey in Leonardo Benevolo, *The History of the City* (Cambridge, Mass.: M.I.T. Press, 1980).
6. Cf. Lawrence Wright, *Clockwork Man* (London: Elek, 1968).
7. Georg Simmel, *The Philosophy of Money* (London: Routledge & Kegan Paul, 1978) p. 495.
8. Marx, *Grundrisse*, pp. 141, 145 and 166–7. For one of the few analyses of Marx's discussions of money, see Suzanne de Brunhoff, *Marx on Money* (New York: Urizen, 1976).
9. The notion of the arbitrariness of the sign, however, is one which has to be treated with some care. See my 'Structuralism and the Theory of the Subject', in *Central Problems in Social Theory* (London: Macmillan, 1979).
10. Marx, *Grundrisse*, p. 188.
11. Max Weber, *Economy and Society, vol. I* (University of California Press, 1978) pp. 80ff.
12. Weber, *General Economic History*.
13. Marx, *Grundrisse*, p. 140; *Capital*, vol. I (London: Lawrence & Wishart, 1970) pp. 39–40.
14. Marx, *Grundrisse*, p. 142.
15. Ibid, p. 143.
16. Ibid, p. 173.
17. *The Poverty of Philosophy* (New York: International Publishers, 1971) p. 54.
18. Cf. my 'Classical Social Theory and the Origins of Modern Sociology', *American Journal of Sociology*, vol. 81, 1976.

19. See especially Clark Kerr *et al.*, *Industrialism and Industrial Man* (Harmondsworth: Penguin, 1973).
20. Lewis Mumford, *The Myth of the Machine* (London: Secker & Warburg, 1967), and *The Pentagon of Power* (London: Secker & Warburg, 1971).
21. Harry Braverman, *Labour and Monopoly Capital* (New York: Monthly Review Press, 1974).
22. See this book, Chapter 6.
23. Mumford, *The Pentagon of Power*, pp. 132ff and *passim*. Cf. also Jean Gimpel, *The Medieval Machine* (London: Gollancz, 1977).
24. Mumford, *The Pentagon of Power*, p. 147.
25. Immanuel Wallerstein, *The Modern World-System* (New York: Academic Press, 1974).
26. I do not apply the term 'state system' anywhere near as broadly here as Wesson does, who seems to me to underestimate the distinctiveness of post-feudal Europe. See Robert G. Wesson, *State Systems: International Pluralism, Politics and Culture* (New York: Free Press, 1978).
27. Nicos Poulantzas, *Political Power and Social Classes* (London: New Left Books, 1973) pp. 151–2.
28. For a discussion, see *The Class Structure of the Advanced Societies,* ch. 11 and *passim*.

**Chapter 6**

1. Some later advocates of the theory of industrial society have, however, accepted that class divisions are structural components of the industrial order – as, for instance, in Lipset's account of the 'democratic class struggle'. See Seymour Martin Lipset, *Political Man* (London: Heinemann, 1969).
2. Cf. W. Eberhard, *Conquerors and Rulers* (Leiden: Brill, 1965); Barrington Moore, *Social Origins of Dictatorship and Democracy* (Harmondsworth: Penguin, 1967) ch. 9; E. J. Hobsbawm, 'Class Consciousness in History', in Istvan Meszaros (ed.), *Aspects of History and Class Consciousness* (London: Routledge & Kegan Paul, 1971).
3. Yi-Fu Tuan, 'Space, Time, Place: a Humanistic Frame', in Tommy Carlstein *et al.*, *Making Sense of Time* (London: Arnold, 1978) vol. I, p. 8.

4. E. E. Evans-Pritchard, 'Nuer Time-Reckoning', *Africa,* vol. 12, 1939.
5. Cf. also R. Zeutner, 'The Social Space-Time Relationship: a Theoretical Formulation', *Sociological Inquiry,* vol. 36, 1966. One should also, of course, note the extensive discussions stimulated by Benjamin Whorf's *Language, Thought and Reality* (Cambridge, Mass.: M.I.T. Press, 1956). Whorf comments: 'Whether a civilisation such as ours would be possible with a widely different linguistic handling of time is a large question – in our civilisation, our linguistic patterns and the fitting of our behaviour to the temporal order are what they are, and they are in accord' (p. 154).
6. Bernard S. Aaronson, 'Time, Time Stance and Existence', in J. T. Fraser *et al., The Study of Time* (Berlin: Springer, 1972) p. 293.
7. S. G. Morley, *The Ancient Maya* (Stanford University Press, 1947).
8. G. J. Whitrow, 'Reflections on the History of the Concept of Time', in Fraser *et al., The Study of Time*; Rudolf Wendorff, *Zeit und Kultur. Geschichte des Zeit Bewussteins in Europa* (Opladen: Westdeutscher Verlag, 1980).
9. Whitrow, 'Reflections on the History of the Concept of Time', p. 6.
10. Lewis Mumford, *Interpretations and Forecasts* (London: Secker & Warburg, 1973) p. 272.
11. Cf. Carlo M. Cipolla, *Clocks and Culture 1300–1700* (London: Collins, 1967).
12. Lawrence Wright, *Clockwork Man* (London: Elek, 1968) pp. 77ff. See also A. P. Usher, *A History of Mechanical Innovations* (Harvard University Press, 1962) ch. 7.
13. See especially E. P. Thompson, 'Time, Work-Discipline, and Industrial Capitalism', *Past and Present,* vol. 38, 1967. Cf. also Lukács's comments on time and labour discipline in *History and Class Consciousness* (London: Merlin, 1971) pp. 90ff.
14. Sidney Pollard, *The Genesis of Modern Management* (London: Arnold, 1965).
15. Ibid, p. 7.
16. This judgement is not radically altered by whatever may turn out to be the rights or wrongs of Macfarlane's arguments about the early origins of 'English individualism'. Cf. Alan

Macfarlane, *The Origins of English Individualism* (Oxford: Blackwell, 1978).

17. E. P. Thompson, *The Making of the English Working Class* (London: Gollancz, 1965) pp. 193ff; Malcolm I. Thomis, *The Town Labourer and the Industrial Revolution* (London: Batsford, 1974) p. 89. A detailed portrayal of early factory production is given in Jennifer Tann, *The Development of the Factory* (London: Cornmarket, 1970).

18. Thompson, 'Time, Work-Discipline and Industrial Capitalism', p. 73 and *passim*.

19. For a very suggestive discussion of this phenomenon in the terms of Hägerstrand's time-geography, cf. Allan Pred, 'Production, Family, and "Free Time" Projects: a Time-Geographic Perspective on Individual and Societal Change in Nineteenth-Century U.S. Cities', mimeo., Department of Geography, University of California, Berkeley, 1979. See also Patrick Joyce, *Work, Society and Politics: The Culture of the Factory in Later Victorian England* (London: Harvester, 1980).

20. M. Weber, *Economy and Society, vol. I* (University of California Press, 1978) p. 379.

21. From a now very large literature, see particularly Sheila Rowbotham, *Hidden from History* (London: Pluto, 1973); and Roberta Hamilton, *The Liberation of Women* (London: Allen & Unwin, 1975).

22. Hamilton, *The Liberation of Women*, p. 19.

23. R. J. Morris, *Class and Class Consciousness in the Industrial Revolution* (London: Macmillan, 1979) p. 52.

24. Quoted in Pollard, *The Genesis of Modern Management*, p. 184.

25. Ibid, p. 163. See also Edgar S. Furniss, *The Position of the Labourer in a System of Nationalism* (New York: Hart, 1920).

26. Morris, *Class and Class Consciousness in the Industrial Revolution*, pp. 57ff.

27. John Foster, *Class Struggle and the Industrial Revolution* (London: Weidenfeld & Nicolson, 1974) p. 34.

28. Cf., however, *The Class Structure of the Advanced Societies* (London: Hutchinson, 1973).

29. Stephen A. Marglin, 'What do Bosses do? The Origins and Functions of Hierarchy in Capitalist Production', in André

Gorz (ed.), *The Division of Labour* (London: Harvester, 1976).

30. One should note, as further support for this view, that there was no simple correlation between the creation of factories and advanced technology. The large factories of Benjamin Gott in the woollen industry in the West Riding of Yorkshire were widely accepted as exemplars of the new mode of industrial production. However in 1820, nearly thirty years after its construction, the majority of workers in the Bean Ing Works still used handwork processes (see Pollard, *The Genesis of Modern Management*, p. 8).

31. Marcel Granet, *La féodalité chinoise* (Oslo: Institute for Kulturforskning, 1952) pp. 112–13. In his book on the pre-industrial city, Sjoberg calls all non-capitalist agrarian civilisations 'feudal' (without attempting to defend this practice in any detail). See Gideon Sjoberg, *The Preindustrial City* (New York: Free Press, 1960). In his recent book *Classe et Nation* (Paris: Minuit, 1979), on the other hand, Amin proposes that all societies pass through three evolutionary stages: 'primitive communism', what he calls 'le mode de production tributaire', and capitalism. Feudalism in Europe is regarded as only a variant of 'le mode de production tributaire'. This approach seemingly owes a good deal to Godelier. Still an indispensable source on feudalism is Rushton Coulborn, *Feudalism in History* (Princeton University Press, 1956). Compare this, however, with Claude Cahen, 'Refléxions sur l'usage du mot "féodalité"', *Journal of Economic and Social History of the Orient*, vol. 3, 1960.

32. Louis Wirth, 'Urbanism as a Way of Life', *American Journal of Sociology*, vol. 44, 1938, p. 8.

33. Paul Wheatley, *The Pivot of the Four Quarters* (Edinburgh University Press, 1971) p. 388.

34. This has been remarked upon by a number of writers. See, for example, ibid, pp. 371ff.

35. Weber, *Economy and Society, vol. II,* p. 1220.

36. Ibid, pp. 1213, 1221–6.

37. Weber actually comments that if his definition 'were to be strictly applied, even the cities of the Occidental Middle Ages would qualify only in part' (ibid, p. 1226).

38. 'The Self-Regulating Market', in Karl Polanyi, *Primitive,*

*Archaic and Modern Economies* (New York: Anchor, 1968). It follows from my comments in the concluding section of Chapter 5, none the less, that I do not accept the equation suggested in the following sentence: 'A self-regulating market demands nothing less than the institutional separation of society into an economic and political sphere. Such a dichotomy is, in effect, merely the restatement, from the point of view of society as a whole, of the existence of a self-regulating market' (p. 30).

39. See, for example, Brian J. L. Berry, *Geography of Market Centres and Retail Distribution* (Englewood Cliffs, N. J.: Prentice-Hall, 1967); John U. Marshall, *The Location of Service Towns: an Approach to the Analysis of Central Place Systems* (University of Toronto Press, 1969); P. Haggett, *Locational Analysis in Human Geography* (London: Arnold, 1977).

40. These assumptions are that both suppliers and consumers have complete knowledge of product markets, and that suppliers rationally endeavour to maximise their profits and consumers to minimise their costs, all in circumstances of perfect competition.

41. Some authors none the less have tried to make use of the theory for non-capitalist cities. See, for instance, G. William Skinner, 'Cities and the Hierarchy of Local Systems', in his *The City in Late Imperial China* (Stanford University Press, 1977).

42. Some have doubted this, such as Eric Wolf, who wishes to recognise that there can be cityless states. See Eric R. Wolf, *Peasants* (Englewood Cliffs, N.J.: Prentice-Hall, 1966) pp. 11ff. There are those who have doubted that cities existed in ancient Egypt. See John A. Wilson, *The Culture of Ancient Egypt* (University of Chicago Press, 1954). See also the same author's contribution, 'Egypt through the New Kingdom', to Carl H. Kraeling and Robert M. Adams (eds), *City Invincible* (University of Chicago Press, 1960). Another contributor to the same symposium, however, points out that 'When the Assyrians came to Egypt, they spoke of hundreds of cities – for them the Egyptian towns were cities – and I remain unconvinced as to the extent to which Egypt was "a civilisation without cities"' (ibid, p. 140). There is also a particular

difficulty about archaeological evidence on Egypt, since there may well have existed cities in the Nile Delta the traces of which have disappeared.

43. Sjoberg, *The Preindustrial City*.
44. Oliver C. Cox, 'The Preindustrial City Reconsidered', *Sociological Quarterly,* vol. 5, 1964; see also G. Sjoberg, 'The Rise and Fall of Cities: a Theoretical Perspective', *International Journal of Comparative Sociology,* vol. 4, 1963.
45. Sjoberg, *The Preindustrial City,* pp. 76, 67.
46. Cf., however, David Harvey, *Social Justice and the City* (London: Arnold, 1973); see also Marx's brief comments in the *Grundrisse* (Harmondsworth: Penguin, 1973) pp. 483ff.
47. Wheatley, *The Pivot of the Four Quarters*. I differ from Wheatley, however, in not regarding 'dispersed ceremonial centres', but only what he labels 'compact cities', as cities proper.
48. Wolf Schneider, *Babylon is Everywhere* (London: Hodder & Stoughton, 1963) p. 32. As has often been pointed out, in Chinese the same character symbolised both the city and its wall (Wheatley, *The Pivot of the Four Quarters,* p. 182).
49. Sjoberg, *The Preindustrial City,* p. 104.
50. Arthur Birnie, *An Economic History of Europe 1760—1939* (London: Methuen, 1962) p. 33.
51. This is the figure quoted by Sjoberg, *The Preindustrial City,* p. 83, but it is not very clear how it is arrived at.
52. Thomas L. Blair, *International Urban Crisis* (London: Paladin, 1974) p. 25.
53. For contrasting surveys, see, for example, Robert A. Nisbet, *Community and Power* (New York: Oxford University Press, 1962); and Joseph R. Gusfield, *Community, a Critical Response* (Oxford: Blackwell, 1975). Cf. also the analysis in M. P. Smith, *The City and Social Theory* (Oxford: Blackwell, 1980).
54. Cf. Castells: 'The development of industrial capitalism, contrary to an all too widespread naive view, did not bring about a strengthening of the city, but its virtual disappearance as an institutional and relatively autonomous system ... Urban diffusion is precisely balanced by the loss of the city's economic and cultural particularism.' See Manuel Castells, *The Urban Question* (London: Arnold, 1977) p. 14. See also

Henri Lefebvre, *La révolution urbaine* (Paris: Collection idées, 1970); the latter author also offers an analysis of the theme of the city in Marx's writings in his *La pensée marxiste et la ville* (Paris: Casterman, 1972). Further relevant discussion is contained in Raymond Ledrut, *L'espace sociale de la ville* (Paris: Anthropos, 1968).

55. Marx, *Grundrisse*, p. 479.

56. Marx, *Capital*, vol. I (London: Lawrence & Wishart, 1970) p. 751.

57. David Harvey, *Social Justice and the City* (London: Arnold, 1973) p. 309.

58. Lewis Mumford, *The City in History* (London: Secker & Warburg, 1961) pp. 64ff and *passim*.

59. Cf. Ira Katznelson, 'Community, Capitalist Development and the Emergence of Class', *Politics and Society,* vol. 9, 1979, p. 230.

60. Castells, *The Urban Question,* p. 440.

61. *The Class Structure of the Advanced Societies.*

62. Cf. *Central Problems in Social Theory* (London: Macmillan, 1979) pp. 216–22. See also Pierre Bourdieu, *La Distinction, critique sociale du judgement* (Paris: Minuit, 1979) pp. 190ff.

63. For an imaginative discussion of this, see John Berger, *Pig Earth* (London: Writers and Readers Co-operative, 1979).

64. Henri Lefebvre, *Everyday Life in the Modern World* (London: Allen Lane, 1971) p. 29; and *The Survival of Capitalism* (London: Allison & Busby, 1976) pp. 14–15. My endorsement of this quotation does not, however, involve accepting Lefebvre's view that the 'urban society' is a phase beyond industrial capitalism. For a critique, see Castells, *The Urban Question,* pp. 86–95. For a partly convergent analysis of 'everyday life', see Agnes Heller, *Das Alltagsleben, Versuch einer Erklärung der individuellen Reproduktion* (Frankfurt: Suhrkamp, 1978). She, however, treats *Alltagsleben* as the basis of social life in every form of society, rather than giving the term a historically specific sense.

65. An important body of critical urban theory relevant to these matters has arisen over the past ten years, especially as represented by the writings of Richard Sennett. See his *The Uses of Disorder* (New York: Vintage, 1970) and *The Fall of Public Man* (Cambridge University Press, 1977).

66. *Central Problems in Social Theory,* pp. 120–30.

67. Cf. David Held, *Introduction to Critical Theory, Horkheimer to Habermas* (London: Hutchinson, 1980).
68. Georg Lukács, *History and Class Consciousness* (London: Merlin, 1971) p. 94.
69. Lewis Mumford, *The Myth of the Machine* (London: Secker & Warburg, 1967) p. 9; Viktor E. Frankel, *Man's Search for Meaning* (New York: Washington Square Press, 1963).

## Chapter 7

1. Emile Durkheim, *The Division of Labour in Society* (New York: Free Press, 1964).
2. See, for instance, John Barnes, 'Durkheim's *Division of Labour in Society*', *Man*, vol. 1, 1966.
3. Cf. Ernestine Friedl, *Women and Men* (New York: Holt, Rinehart & Winston, 1975).
4. Cf. Paul Wheatley, *The Pivot of the Four Quarters* (Edinburgh University Press, 1971).
5. *The Class Structure of the Advanced Societies* (London: Hutchinson, 1973) pp. 86ff and *passim*.
6. According to Webb, chiefdoms share with agrarian states 'a centralised apparatus of decision-making', but this is 'of far less consequence than the characteristic which they continue to share with the tribal, non-state "primitive" pattern, namely the lack of effective and reliable coercive force. Lacking this coercive force, chieftains cannot command, they must persuade, nag, beg, or obligate their following by making the latter's obedience clearly worth their while.' See Malcom C. Webb, 'The Flag Follows Trade: an Essay on the Necessary Interaction of Military and Commercial Factors in State Formation', in Jeremy A. Sabloff and C. C. Lamberg-Karlovsky (eds), *Ancient Civilisation and Trade* (University of New Mexico Press, 1975).
7. M. H. Fried shows that language and material culture often overlap between partially distinct tribal groups without clear dividing-lines. See Morton H. Fried, 'On the Concepts of "Tribe" and "Tribal Society"', *Proceedings of the American Ethnological Society,* Seattle, 1967; in the same volume, another author writes: 'like linguistic similarity, both economic and ceremonial interaction are very difficult to apply in

classifying groups because these also may grade from one society into another indefinitely in a series of neighbouring groups' (Gertrude E. Dole, 'Tribe as the Autonomous Unit', p. 86).

8. See *Central Problems in Social Theory* (London: Macmillan, 1979) pp. 206–10 and *passim;* Nigel Thrift and Allan Pred, 'Time-Geography: a New Beginning', mimeo., Department of Geography, University of California, Berkeley, 1980.

9. T. Hagerstrand, 'Survival and Arena', in Tommy Carlstein *et al., Making Sense of Time* (London: Arnold, 1978) vol. 2.

10. Pierre Bourdieu, *Outline of a Theory of Practice* (Cambridge University Press, 1977).

11. E. Adamson Hoebel, *The Law of Primitive Man* (Harvard University Press, 1954).

12. J. R. V. Prescott, *Boundaries and Frontiers* (London: Croom Helm, 1978).

13. K. Marx and F. Engels, *The Communist Manifesto,* in Marx and Engels, *Selected Works in One Volume* (London: Lawrence & Wishart, 1968) p. 38.

14. *Central Problems in Social Theory,* ch. 7.

15. W. Eberhard, *Conquerors and Rulers* (Leiden: Brill, 1965) pp. 13ff.

16. Immanuel Wallerstein, *The Modern World-System* (New York: Academic Press, 1974).

17. Which is *one* reason why, or one contributing element to, the position of social science as potentially an instrument of either domination or of emancipation. Cf. my *New Rules of Sociological Method* (London: Hutchinson, 1976).

18. Michel Foucault, *Discipline and Punish, the Birth of the Prison* (London: Allen Lane, 1977) pp. 220–1. Cf. also the important study of the family by Jacques Donzelot, *The Policing of Families* (London: Hutchinson, 1979).

19. M. Foucault, *Power, Truth, Strategy* (Sydney: Feral Publications, 1979) p. 35. Cf. Jean Baudrillard, *Oublier Foucault* (Paris: Galilée, 1977).

20. A useful counterbalance to Foucault on the prison can be found in Michael Ignatieff, *A Just Measure of Pain* (London: Macmillan, 1978). See especially ch. 3, on 'The Ideological Origins of the Penitentiary', and ch. 5, on prison reform.

21. Foucault, *Discipline and Punish,* p. 234.

22. Norbert Elias, *The Civilising Process* (Oxford: Blackwell, 1978) *passim.*

23. Richard Sennett, *The Fall of Public Man* (Cambridge University Press, 1977).

24. Charles Tilly, 'Reflections on the History of European State-making', in his *The Formation of National States in Europe* (Princeton University Press, 1975).

25. William S. Davis, *Information Processing Systems* (Reading, Mass.: Addison, 1978); C. J. Date, *An Introduction to Database Systems* (Reading, Mass.: Addison, 1975).

26. Two notable, but contrasting, versions of this appear in Daniel Bell, *The Coming of the Post-Industrial Society* (New York: Basic Books, 1973); and Alain Touraine, *The Post-Industrial Society* (New York: Random House, 1971).

27. J. M. Rosenberg, *The Computer Prophets* (New York: Macmillan, 1969) p. 65.

28. Harry Braverman, *Labour and Monopoly Capital* (New York: Monthly Review Press, 1974); see also the very interesting discussion in the more recent work by Richard Edwards, *Contested Terrain* (New York: Basic Books, 1979).

29. Edwards, *Contested Terrain,* pp. 112ff.

30. Edwards argues that 'technical control' is being supplanted by 'bureaucratic control'; this seems to me, however, misleading, and to miss the potential force of the analysis of technology as incorporating management control, which is important for the critique of Weber's bureaucratic theory.

31. Cf. the still illuminating work of Sheldon Wolin, *Politics and Vision* (Boston: Beacon, 1960).

32. 'Appeal to the Slavs', in Sam Dolgoff, *Bakunin on Anarchy* (London: Allen & Unwin, 1973) pp. 66–7.

33. Solomon F. Bloom, *The World of Nations: a Study of the National Implications in the Work of Karl Marx* (Columbia University Press, 1941) p. 80.

34. Marx and Engels, *The Communist Manifesto,* in *Selected Works,* p. 27.

35. See Horace B. Davis, *Toward a Marxist Theory of Nationalism* (New York: Monthly Review Press, 1978). This work provides a very useful survey of Marxism and nationalism, but hardly advances very far towards a 'theory'. A good example of an early-type Marxist discussion is Otto Bauer, *Die Nationalitätsfragen und die Sozialdemokratie* (Vienna, 1907).

36. Tom Nairn, 'The Modern Janus', in *The Break-Up of Britain* (London: New Left Books, 1977) p. 329. Cf. Nicos Poulantzas: 'we have to recognise that there is no Marxist theory of

the nation'. See *State Power and Socialism* (London: New Left Books, 1978) p. 93.

37. Joachim Hirsch, 'The State Apparatus and Social Reproduction: Elements of a Theory of the Bourgeois State', in John Holloway and Sol Picciotto (eds), *State and Capital, a Marxist Debate* (London: Arnold, 1978) pp. 61–2.

38. Cf. Gianfranco Poggi, *The Development of the Modern State* (London: Hutchinson, 1978) pp. 81ff.

## Chapter 8

1. Cf. Robert G. Wesson, *State Systems: International Pluralism, Politics and Culture* (New York: Free Press, 1978) pp. 21ff. I think in this book, however, Wesson uses the term 'state system' too widely, thereby downplaying the distinctiveness of the European experience. His thesis is that 'state systems' have existed at various periods and in various areas of the world (e. g. in Classical Greece or in Sumer). In his view, such 'pluralistic civilisations' have creative properties not shared by the more monolithic imperial societies.

2. Dorn's comment is an apt one: 'It is this very competitive character of the state system of modern Europe that distinguishes it from the political life of all previous and non-European civilisations of the world ... above all in the prevention of any single state power from reducing the others to a state of permanent subjection.' See Walter L. Dorn, *Competition for Empire 1740–63* (New York: Harper & Row, 1963) p. 1. On this point see also Felix Gilbert, *The Historical Essays of Otto Hintze* (New York: Oxford University Press, 1975) pp. 308ff; Terence K. Hopkins, 'The Study of the Capitalist World-Economy: Some Preliminary Considerations', in Walter L. Goldfrank (ed.), *The World-System of Capitalism* (Beverly Hills: Sage, 1979).

3. Carlo M. Cipolla, *Guns and Sails in the Early Phases of European Expansion 1400–1700* (London: Collins, 1965) pp. 16ff.

4. Arnold J. Toynbee, *The Present-Day Experiment in Western Civilisation* (Oxford University Press, 1962) p. 27.

5. Every sociological analysis of this phenomenon today must regard Perry Anderson's *Lineages of the Absolutist State*

(London: Verso, 1979) as a fundamental source. So also, for the development of early political theory, is Quentin Skinner, *The Foundations of Modern Political Thought* (Cambridge University Press, 1978) 2 vols.

6. Ellen Meiksius Wood and Neal Wood, *Class Ideology and Ancient Political Theory* (Oxford: Blackwell, 1978) p. 26. Cf. again Hintze's analysis, in Gilbert, *Historical Essays of Otto Hintze,* pp. 313ff. See also M. I. Finley, *Democracy, Ancient and Modern* (London: Chatto & Windus, 1973).

7. C. Tilly, 'Reflections on the History of European State-making', in his *The Formation of National States in Europe* (Princeton University Press, 1975) pp. 22–3. Cf. also Skocpol's comments on absolutism in France, in Theda Skocpol, *States and Social Revolutions* (Cambridge University Press, 1979) p. 52; and Helen Maud Cam, 'The Theory and Practice of Representation in Medieval England', in Frederic L. Cheyette (ed.), *Lordship and Community in Medieval Europe* (New York: Holt, Rinehart & Winston, 1968).

8. Orest Ranum, *National Consciousness, History, and Political Culture in Early-Modern Europe* (Baltimore: Johns Hopkins University Press, 1975); cf. also B. Guenée, 'The History of the State in France at the End of the Middle Ages as seen by French Historians', in P. S. Lewis (ed.), *The Recovery of France in the Fifteenth Century* (London: Stratum, 1971).

9. Alexander Passerin D'Entrèves, *The Notion of the State* (Oxford: Clarendon Press, 1967) pp. 171–2.

10. This point is made by Gideon Sjoberg, *The Preindustrial City* (New York: Free Press, 1960). On the fourteenth century, the age of 'popular rebellions', see Michel Mollat and Philippe Wolff, *The Popular Revolutions of the Late Middle Ages* (London: Allen & Unwin, 1973).

11. Tilly, 'Reflections on the History of European State-making', pp. 12ff.

12. Ibid, p. 72.

13. John Roberts, *Revolution and Improvement* (London: Weidenfeld & Nicolson, 1976) p. 47.

14. Raymond Aron, *Peace and War* (London: Weidenfeld & Nicolson, 1966) p. 96.

15. Allan R. Pred, *Urban Growth and the Circulation of Information* (Harvard University Press, 1973).

16. Contingently, of course. A major contribution to the growth

of state monopoly of territorial, financial and military power appears in Norbert Elias, *Über den Prozess der Zivilisation* (Bern, 1969) vol. 2, especially pp. 142–59.

17. My view therefore is quite distinct from that of Amin, whom it seems to me not only confuses the nation-state and nationalism, but hopelessly overgeneralises them. According to him, traditional China and Egypt were nations, and 'the nation is a social phenomenon that can appear at any stage of history, and is not necessarily associated with the capitalist mode of production'. It is basically an artefact of dominant classes, and 'can flourish or it can disappear, depending on whether the unifying class strengthens its power or loses it'. See Samir Amin, *Unequal Development* (London: Harvester, 1976) p. 28.

18. This point is accentuated strongly by Anthony D. Smith, *Theories of Nationalism* (London: Duckworth, 1971) pp. 18–21.

19. Hans Kohn, *World Order in Historical Perspective* (Harvard University Press, 1942). See also the very useful discussion of various related issues in Bertrand Badie and Pierre Birnbaum, *Sociologie de l'Etat* (Paris: Grasset, 1979).

20. Karl W. Deutsch, *Nationalism and its Alternatives* (New York: Knopf, 1969) p. 53.

21. Tom Nairn, 'The Modern Janus', in *The Break-Up of Britain* (London: New Left Books, 1977).

22. Smith, *Theories of Nationalism,* pp. 9–10; E. Kedourie, *Nationalism* (London: Hutchinson, 1961). Cf. also Harold J. Laski, *Nationalism and the Future of Civilisation* (London, Conway Memorial Lecture, 1932); and Louis L. Snyder, *The New Nationalism* (Cornell University Press, 1968), who states that 'Nationalism is repeatedly denounced as an anachronism in the contemporary world – as an outmoded, deep-seated disease which plagues mankind and which cannot be healed by incantation' (p. 2). Koppel S. Binson, *A Bibliographical Introduction to Nationalism* (New York: Knopf, 1935), provides a comprehensive bibliography to that date. More recently, see S. N. Eisenstadt and Stein Rokkan, *Building States and Nations* (Beverly Hills: Sage, 1973) 2 vols.

23. Smith, *Theories of Nationalism.*

24. Hence that helpless and hopeless endeavour in contemporary

Western culture to find salvation in sexuality of which Foucault writes. See Michel Foucault, *The History of Sexuality* (London: Allen Lane, 1978) vol. I.

25. Cf. Stuart Hall *et al., Resistance Through Rituals* (London: Hutchinson, 1976).
26. *Central Problems in Social Theory* (London: Macmillan, 1979) ch. 3.
27. See ibid. Also immediately relevant here, of course, are the writings of Adorno and Horkheimer on leadership and authoritarianism.
28. In making these points I do not want to suggest that the Le Bon–Freud theory of leadership is by any means wholly satisfactory. People may follow leaders in a much more reflective and critical fashion than Le Bon tends to presume, especially in the routine circumstances of social life (rather than under the pressure of extreme situations of tension). Le Bon's discussion was of course a directly political as well as a psychological tract, aimed at showing that democracy means rule by the 'baser instincts'. Cf. G. Le Bon, *The Crowd* (Dunwoody: Berg, N.D.). An important analysis of these issues appears in Richard Sennett, *Authority* (London: Secker & Warburg, 1980).
29. See, for example, Smith, *Theories of Nationalism*, ch. 9.
30. Among many discussions, see in particular Robert Brenner, 'The Origins of Capitalist Development: a Critique of Neo-Smithian Marxism', *New Left Review,* no. 104, 1977; and Theda Skocpol, 'Wallerstein's World Capitalist System: a Theoretical and Historical Critique', *American Journal of Sociology,* vol. 82, 1977.
31. Weber might have denied that he possessed a 'philosophy of history' in any sense; but Mommsen, among others, has made out a persuasive case to the contrary. Cf. Wolfgang Mommsen, *The Age of Bureaucracy* (Oxford: Blackwell, 1974).
32. Folker Fröbel *et al., The New International Division of Labour* (Cambridge University Press, 1980).
33. Ibid, p. 11.
34. Marx, *Marx on China* (Moscow: Foreign Languages Publishing House, 1958) p. 62.
35. Fröbel *et al., The New International Division of Labour,* p. 13.
36. Skocpol, *States and Social Revolutions,* p. 22.

37. See, for example, Harold Brookfield, *Interdependent Development* (London: Methuen, 1975) chs 5 and 6.
38. Cf. Amin: 'despite the name given to it, the transnational firm remains national in its origins and in its top management . . . It is usually American, and less frequently Japanese, British or German' (Amin, *Unequal Development*, p. 211).

**Chapter 9**

1. Pluralist theories form the major focus of critical dissection by Ralph Miliband in *The State in Capitalist Society* (London: Wiedenfeld & Nicolson, 1970).
2. As regards Marx, see the discussion of this in Georges Gurvitch, 'La sociologie du jeune Marx', in *La vocation actuelle de la sociologie* (Paris: Presses Universitaires, 1950).
3. Cf. Emile Durkheim, *Socialism* (New York: Collier, 1962) ch. 10.
4. Durkheim, *Qui a voulu la guerre?* (Paris: Colin, 1915); and *L'Allemagne au-dessus de tout* (Paris: Colin, 1915).
5. Durkheim, *Professional Ethics and Civic Morals* (London: Routledge & Kegan Paul, 1957) pp. 91ff. Cf. also 'Deux lois de l'évolution pénale', *Année Sociologique,* vol. 4, 1899–1900.
6. Cf. Raymond Aron, *Peace and War* (London: Weidenfeld & Nicolson, 1966); also his study of Clausewitz: *Penser la guerre, Clausewitz* (Paris: Sciences Humaines, 1976) 2 vols.
7. For an interesting discussion, see Victor M. Perez-Diaz, *State, Bureaucracy and Civil Society* (London: Macmillan, 1978). A valuable source-book is Hal Draper, *Karl Marx's Theory of Revolution, Part I: State and Bureaucracy* (New York: Monthly Review Press, 1977).
8. Theda Skocpol, *States and Social Revolutions* (Cambridge University Press, 1979) p. 25.
9. Especially Parsons's writings on politics, power and coercion. See Talcott Parsons, *Politics and Social Structure* (New York: Free Press, 1969); also very relevant are the works of Luhmann, which are strongly indebted to some of Parsons's ideas.
10. Cf. Fred Block, 'The Ruling Class does not Rule', *Socialist Revolution,* no. 33, May–June 1977, for an interesting recent

discussion of the implications of this phrase.

11. A useful analysis relevant to some of these matters appears in C. E. Lindblom, *Politics and Markets* (New York: Basic Books, 1977). Cf. also the comments of Colin Crouch, 'The State, Capital and Liberal Democracy', in his *State and Economy in Contemporary Capitalism* (New York: St. Martin's Press, 1979).

12. Lindblom, *Politics and Markets,* pp. 172–3.

13. Arnold J. Toynbee, *The Present-Day Experiment in Western Civilisation* (Oxford University Press, 1962) p. 40.

14. Claus Offe, *Strukturprobleme des Kapitalistischen Staates* (Frankfurt: Suhrkamp, 1972); various sections of this plus later articles by Offe exist in English. For an interesting account and critique of Offe's views, see John Keane, 'The Legacy of Political Economy: Thinking With and Against Claus Offe', *Canadian Journal of Political and Social Theory,* vol. 2, 1978.

15. See, among many recent discussions, the contrasting surveys in Bob Jessop, 'Recent Theories of the Capitalist State', *Cambridge Journal of Economics,* vol 1, 1977; and Boris Frankel, 'On the State of the State: Marxist Theories of the State after Leninism', *Theory and Society,* vol. 7, 1979.

16. The views of each of these two authors have been somewhat modified over the years. For their recent positions, see Ralph Miliband, *Marxism and Politics* (Oxford University Press, 1977); Nicos Poulantzas, *State, Power, Socialism* (London: New Left Books, 1978).

17. Selections appear in John Holloway and Sol Picciotto, *State and Capital, a Marxist Debate* (London: Arnold, 1978).

18. Cf. Jon Elster, *Logic and Society, Contradictions and Possible Worlds* (New York: Wiley, 1978).

19. N. Poulantzas, *Political Power and Social Classes* (London: New Left Books, 1973). G. A. Cohen, *Karl Marx's Theory of History* (Oxford: Clarendon Press, 1978) chs 9 and 10, defends a functionalist version of Marxism (one in other respects quite different from Poulantzas's).

20. Holloway and Picciotto, 'Introduction: Towards a Materialist Theory of the State', in their *State and Capital, a Marxist Debate.*

21. Especially in the light of Parkin's attack on 'the Marxist theory

of class', which he identifies mostly with Poulantzas. See Frank Parkin, *Marxism and Class Theory: a Bourgeois Critique* (London: Tavistock, 1979).

22. N. Poulantzas, *Classes in Contemporary Capitalism* (London: New Left Books, 1975) p. 26. (I have modified the translation.)

23. As Miliband points out, Poulantzas perhaps objects to the term 'elite' partly because it has rather different associations in the language of its origin to the more neutral sense it has acquired in English. However that may be, the terms 'elite' and 'elite group' are in my opinion superior to that of 'class fraction'. How can there be 'class fractions' if classes are not groups but expressions of the structural relations of the societal totality?

24. Crouch, *State and Economy in Contemporary Capitalism*, p. 27.

25. For an important critique, see David Held, 'Crisis Tendencies, Legitimation and the State', in John B. Thompson and David Held (eds), *Habermas: Critical Debates* (London: Macmillan, forthcoming).

26. N. Poulantzas, *Fascism and Dictatorship* (London: New Left Books, 1974); and *The Crisis of the Dictatorships* (London: New Left Books, 1976).

27. Göran Therborn, *What does the Ruling Class do when it Rules?* (London: New Left Books, 1978). Cf. also P. Corrigan *et al.*, 'The State as a Relation of Production', in Philip Corrigan (ed.), *Capitalism, State Formation and Marxist Theory* (London: Quartet, 1980).

28. Michael Mann, *Consciousness and Action Among the Western Working Class* (London: Macmillan, 1973).

29. Therefore using the term in quite a different context from that in which often appears, for example, in Althusser's critique of 'economism' as a version of historical materialism. See *The Class Structure of the Advanced Societies* (London: Hutchinson, 1973). However, in this case I can claim genealogical purity, since Lenin used 'economism' in the sense I adopt.

30. Harry Braverman, *Labour and Monopoly Capital* (New York: Monthly Review Press, 1974).

31. Bryan Palmer, 'Class, Conception and Conflict: the Thrust for Efficiency, Managerial Views of Labour and Working Class Rebellion, 1903–22', *Review of Radical Political Economy*, vol. 7, 1975.

32. Andrew L. Friedman, *Industry and Labour* (London: Macmillan, 1977). Cf. also Michael Burawoy, *Manufacturing Consent* (University of Chicago Press, 1979); and my 'Postscript' to the most recent edition of *The Class Structure of the Advanced Societies* (1981).

33. See *New Rules of Sociological Method* (London: Hutchinson, 1976) ch. 2 and *passim*.

34. Karl Marx, 'Alienated Labour', in T. B. Bottomore (ed.), *Karl Marx: Early Writings* (New York, McGraw-Hill, 1964).

35. Cf. *The Class Structure of the Advanced Societies,* ch. 11; and Mann, *Consciousness and Action Among the Western Working Class.*

36. T. H. Marshall, *Citizenship and Social Class* (Cambridge University Press, 1950). See also Reinhard Bendix, *Nation-Building and Citizenship* (New York: Wiley, 1964), and other books by the same author. Bendix's work has been synthesised in his recent *Kings or People* (Berkeley: University of California Press, 1980).

37. Cf. Günther Roth, *The Social Democrats in Imperial Germany* (Englewood Cliffs, N.J.: Prentice-Hall, 1963).

38. *The Class Structure of the Advanced Societies,* ch. 11.

39. See C. B. Macpherson, *The Real World of Democracy* (Oxford: Clarendon Press, 1966), and other publications by the same author.

40. Ibid, pp. 7, 9.

41. Ralph Dahrendorf, *Class and Class Conflict in Industrial Society* (Stanford University Press, 1959).

42. One of many 'post' thises and thats coined in sociology in the 1950s and 1960s – 'post-modern', 'post-industrial', etc., etc.

43. Cf. the interesting analysis in John D. Stephens, *The Transition from Feudalism to Capitalism* (London: Macmillan, 1979). Compare this with Ian Gough, *The Political Economy of the Welfare State* (London: Macmillan, 1979).

**Chapter 10**

1. Jon Elster, *Logic and Society, Contradictions and Possible Worlds* (New York: Wiley, 1978), has argued that Marx consistently distinguishes contradiction *(Widerspruch)* from other related terms such as 'antagonism', 'conflict', etc. I do

not think a textual perusal of Marx shows this to be the case. However, I am in full agreement with Elster's proposals that the term 'contradiction' should be precisely defined, and that it should be distinguished from 'conflict' and its synonyms. Cf. *Central Problems in Social Theory* (London: Macmillan, 1979) pp. 131–41.

2. Maurice Godelier, 'Structure and Contradiction in *Capital*', in Robin Blackburn (ed.), *Ideology in Social Science* (London: Fontana, 1972).

3. See Karl Marx, 'Critique of Hegel's Dialectic and General Philosophy', in T. B. Bottomore (ed.), *Karl Marx: Early Writings* (New York: McGraw-Hill, 1964).

4. *Central Problems in Social Theory,* ch. 4.

5. It is hardly necessary to point out that the concept of 'interest' (and especially regarding the conditions under which individuals may misconceive what their interests are) has received a great deal of discussion in social and political theory. I shall avoid any talk of 'true' or 'objective' interests, because those terms are open to various ambiguities; but I do hold that, in any given short- or long-term perspective, people may be ignorant of, or confuse, what their interests are. However, in my opinion, the idea of interest always involves the postulation of goals or needs that are attributed to the individuals in question by the social analyst. (See ibid, pp. 188–90.)

6. Gary Young, 'The Fundamental Contradiction of Capitalist Production', *Philosophy and Public Affairs,* vol. 5, 1976.

7. Although Elster, *Logic and Society,* p. 90, does deny it.

8. Karl Marx, 'Afterword' to the Second German Edition of *Capital,* vol. I.

9. Cf. Jürgen Habermas, 'Between Philosophy and Science: Marxism as Critique', in his *Theory and Practice* (London: Heinemann, 1974).

10. *The Class Structure of the Advanced Societies* (London: Hutchinson, 1973) pp. 112ff.

11. Some writers, not very plausibly, have seen this 'universal history' as having such a strongly chiliastic flavour that it forms a type of religious world-view. The best-known exposition of this kind is Robert Tucker, *Philosophy and Myth in Karl Marx* (Cambridge University Press, 1965).

12. Habermas has accentuated this very strongly in many of his publications. I have a strong sympathy with the over-all trend both of his critique of Marx and with some of his conceptions of what the 'good society' could and should look like. But I think he was led up a wrong alley in basing his criticisms of Marx on the distinction between 'labour' and 'interaction', accusing Marx of reducing the latter to the former. I have argued the case for this in my 'Labour and Interaction' in John B. Thompson and David Held (eds), *Habermas: Critical Debates* (London: Macmillan, forthcoming).

13. Louis Althusser, *Lenin and Philosophy* (London: New Left Books, 1971), and other works.

14. *The Class Structure of the Advanced Societies*, pp. 216–19.

15. Cf. Roberta Hamilton, *The Liberation of Women* (London: Allen & Unwin, 1975).

16. Cf. Jean Baudrillard, *Le miroir de la production* (Tournai: Casterman, 1973).

17. *Central Problems in Social Theory*, ch. 5.

18. On Habermas, see especially John Thompson, *Critical Hermeneutics* (Cambridge University Press, 1981), and various of the contributions in Thompson and Held (eds), *Habermas: Critical Debates*.

19. Whatever one may think of the 'new philosophers', they have brought this right out into the open. Cf. Bernard-Henri Lévy, *Barbarism with a Human Face* (New York: Harper & Row, 1979) pp. 4–5 and *passim*. Some trenchant observations on the dilemmas of current political theory are to be found in John Dunn, *Western Political Theory in the Face of the Future* (Cambridge University Press, 1979); cf. especially his comments on Marxism, pp. 100ff. One might contrast this with a view from Eastern Europe: Marc Rakovski (pseudonym for György Bence and János Kis), *Towards an East European Marxism* (London: Allison & Busby, 1978).

# Index